The Story of the Philadelphia
ELEVEN

DARLENE O'DELL
FOREWORD BY CARTER HEYWARD

D1500855

Seabury Books
NEW YORK

Unless otherwise noted, the Scripture quotations contained herein are from the New Revised Standard Version Bible, copyright © 1989 by the Division of Christian Education of the National Council of Churches of Christ in the U.S.A. Used by permission. All rights reserved.

Cover photo by Brad Hess
Cover design by Laurie Klein Westhafer
Typeset by Rose Design

Library of Congress Cataloging-in-Publication Data

A catalog record of this book is available from the Library of Congress.

ISBN-13: 978-1-59627-258-3 (pbk.)
ISBN-13: 978-1-59627-259-0 (ebook)

Seabury Books
19 East 34th Street
New York, New York 10016

www.churchpublishing.org

An imprint of Church Publishing Incorporated

Printed in the United States of America

In memory of Beverly Wildung Harrison

Dedicated to my mother, Nancy Crocker O'Dell

Contents

Acknowledgments

Looking back over the life of this project, I find myself overwhelmed by the level of generosity people displayed in helping me bring this book to fruition, beginning with the living members of The Philadelphia Eleven and The Washington Four. Alison Cheek, Alison Palmer, Merrill Bittner, and Lee McGee Street opened their homes, their collections, and, in some cases, their old wounds to help me come to some understanding of what it was like to have experienced—and to have helped create—a moment of radical change and transformation in our nation's history. Alla Renée Bozarth, Nancy Wittig, Betty Powell, Emily Hewitt, and Betty Bone Schiess all gave me fascinating interviews that illustrated in the most glorious ways why these women were ones who changed history. Interviews with others who participated in the ordinations, or helped keep their energy moving, were also illuminating and delightful. My admiration and gratitude go to Peter Thompson, Charles Willie, Barbara Schlachter, Linda Clark, Kathryn Piccard, Barbara Drebing, Midge Brittingham, Jean Hiatt Kramer, Webb Brown, and Carol Anderson. And thank you Bishop Tony Ramos for sending me your beautiful memoir *The Suffering Marias: Memories and Reflection* even before its release.

I thank Joan Gunderson, and other members of the Episcopal Women's History Project who provided travel monies, and all those who gave so generously to the Hiatt Legacy Fund created by Carter Heyward and set up by James Kowalski, Dean of the Cathedral Church of St. John the Divine in New York City. Also in New York, the faculty and staff at Union Theological Seminary made my visits to the city comfortable, enlightening, and joyful. A special thanks to Betty Bolden and to Ruth Cameron of the Burke Library at Union, who opened doors I did not know existed. And thank you to Joan Blocher of the Jessie Ball duPont Library of the University of the South and to Jennifer Brathovde of the Library of Congress who provided answers to questions that would have taken me days to uncover alone.

I owe a huge debt to many people within various dioceses of the Episcopal Church or within organizations and schools connected to it. Thank you to Brian Wilbert, Emily Horvat, and Grace Gamble from the Diocese of Ohio whose research into the Beebe trial went beyond the call of duty; to Mary Brinkman, Ellen Darnall, and Frances Barr from the Diocese of Lexington whose research shed light on their bishops; to Tobie Smith of the Diocese of Rochester who tracked down information that I would not have otherwise been able to access; to Angela Nedd of St. Mark's Episcopal Church in Washington, D.C.; to Wayne Kempton of the Diocese of New York; to Julia Randle of the Diocese of Virginia; to Isadora Wilkenfeld of the Cathedral Church of St. John the Divine; to Christopher Hartley of Episcopal Divinity School; to Mary Robison of the Episcopal Women's History Project, and to Matthew Price and Susan Erdey of the Church Pension Group.

Many people have helped throughout this project by providing housing, meals, transportation, directions, cell phones, or even a place to park my car for a week at a time. They made phone calls on my behalf or returned my calls at important moments within the research process. Thank you, Gerrie Kiley, Jennifer Rouse, Tanya Beck, Dan Carter, Anne Hurtt, Nancy Noppa, C. Parke Street, Jan Surrey and Steve Bergman, Jean and Robert Hiatt Kramer, and Luther and Marsha Carter.

As always, thanks to the dear friends and fellow members of the Mountain Mission of St. Clare, particularly Eleanor Mockridge, Jennifer and Ray Henley, LaVonda Blackwell, Ann Franklin, Elly Andujar, Bridget Rees—who has done much for women's ordination movement in England—and to Norene Carter—who published her own insightful overview of the story of the Philadelphia Eleven years ago. And thanks, also, to those who have worked so diligently to keep me healthy and well during this process: Anne Meijers, Drs. Nancy and Steve Cagen, and Kelley Toms. And my long-standing thanks to Priscilla Dooley for always being interested and to my teachers and friends John Idol and Jim Skinner and to friends Karen Schaffer and Pamela Blevins.

Throughout my life, my family has been a constant source of joy, wonder, and love. Thank you, Barry and Nancy O'Dell, Scott Keim and Nancy O'Dell-Keim, Bill and Kim Winslow, Judy Aman, Elizabeth and Alex Winslow, and Jake and Bryce Keim.

Nancy Bryan, my editor at Church Publishing, has been patient, professional, and knowledgeable in her response to my manuscript. Thank you. And thank you Ryan Masteller of Church Publishing.

I offer words of deep gratitude to Carter Heyward, Janine Lehane, and Alison Cheek. Without your efforts, this book would not have happened. The resources and talents you offered to this project and the hours you spent reading drafts and offering comments will not be forgotten. Carter and Alison gave me many spur-of-the-moment interviews and never gave me a sense that I was intruding on their time. Carter traveled with me to New York and Boston; Alison opened up her home for a month so that I could work my way through her extensive personal papers from the time period. Janine shared her exceptional editing skills throughout the project, including traveling with me to New York, Boston, and Maine to help me gather materials. Thank you all.

And thank you to the river that sustained and intrigued me—and never allowed me believe that I had undertaken this journey alone.

When one repeats a tale told by a man,

He must report, as nearly as he can,

Every least word, if he remember it,

However rude it be, or how unfit;

Or else he may be telling what's untrue.

Chaucer, Prologue to
The Canterbury Tales

Foreword

Darlene O'Dell heard about the Philadelphia ordinations when she was eleven years old, living with her parents and sisters in South Carolina. She recalls being fascinated. Almost four decades later, having completed graduate studies in English and American Studies and landing a job as a professor of Women's Studies at a major university, Dr. O'Dell had to leave her job in her early 40s, due to a debilitating struggle with multiple sclerosis. She moved to the North Carolina mountains in 2005 to spend time healing and to resume writing and teaching as her health would allow. She and I met soon after when we both attended a small mission church that had broken away from the local Episcopal church following a flap about the presence of openly lesbian and gay participation in church leadership.

Over the years, she has remained engaged with the story of the Philadelphia Eleven, with the histories of other women priests, and with other women reformers who pressed for social justice issues in spite of the costs to their personal and professional lives. She wrote about the first African-American woman priest Pauli Murray in her book *Sites of Southern Memory: The Autobiographies of Lillian Smith, Katharine Du Pre Lumpkin, and Pauli Murray*. When Darlene learned that no one had devoted a book to the Philadelphia ordinations, she and I began to explore whether she might take on this project. Though not an Episcopalian (she was a cradle Presbyterian), she is a writer by trade and a younger sister in spirit to the generations of feminist women who shaped the "irregular" ordinations in Philadelphia in 1974 and, the following year, in Washington. So, in the spring of 2012, Darlene O'Dell leapt in and began her research in private collections, in various diocese archives, and in the Archives of Women in Religion at Union Theological Seminary and Columbia University in New York, which houses the papers of several of the participants in the Philadelphia ordinations. She also interviewed seven of the eight "Philadelphia Eleven" (and the three "Washington Four") who are still alive, as well as others who were closely involved with the ordinations. Out of these interviews and Darlene O'Dell's archival work has come this book.

As one of the new and proudly "irregular" priests in the Episcopal Church in 1974, I have been stirred at my core by reading *The Story
of the Philadelphia Eleven*. What has moved me has been meeting my sister priests, through these pages, in ways and circumstances that I had not
known before. Through her interviews and other research, Darlene O'Dell
has come to learn things about each of us that we did not even know about
one another. And I must say, we were quite a lot! It is no small wonder so
many churchmen fled from us, often calling us nasty names as they tried to
barricade us out of meetings, refuse us honest dialogue, and do whatever
else they could think of, short of burning us at the stake, to keep us out of
the priesthood.

Forty years later, much has changed for the better. There are now thou-
sands of women priests and dozens of women bishops throughout the United
States and around the world. In 2006, the Episcopal Church elected Katharine
Jefferts Schori as its Presiding Bishop, something unimaginable to any Episcopalian in 1974, a bit like imagining a female Pope from where we stand in 2014!
Today, countless parishioners and other church people attest to the spiritual
gifts, intellectual strengths, and pastoral presence of their women priests as rec-
tors, pastors, preachers, teachers, chaplains, counselors, deacons, and bishops.
In most dioceses of the Episcopal Church and Anglican Communion where
women have been ordained priests and bishops, the ordination of women has
been a resounding success.

Yet, in an important way, much has not changed. Notwithstanding the positive presence of women priests and bishops, the Episcopal Church—through
its liturgy and, therefore, its basic theological assumptions—continues to
privilege patriarchy and sustain female subordination. There remains a major,
profoundly sexist disconnect between the presence of strong, loving women
in the church and the same church's fear-based refusal to celebrate liturgically
and teach theologically the presence of a strong, loving Sister Spirit in whom
women and girls can ground our self-respect.

Many of my colleagues in those still relatively few great Protestant churches
that routinely use "inclusive language" in worship and also welcome female and
LGBT ministers and leaders warn that, even in these remarkable congregations,
sexual and gender justice remains superficial, and that the roots of patriarchal
Christianity seem almost unshakable, which some readers may recall was feminist philosopher Mary Daly's point in *Beyond God the Father: Toward a Philosophy of Women's Liberation* (Beacon: 1973).

Still many of us continue to identify ourselves as Christian: feminist, womanist, liberationist, queer, progressive, postcolonial, or simply liberal. My argument with Mary Daly in the 1970s was that anything that humans have constructed can be deconstructed—and reconstructed—and that, when the problem is as deeply embedded among us as patriarchal assumptions about ourselves and God, its transformation will take generations, not simply decades, of intellectual, psychological, political, and theological struggle. The Philadelphia and Washington ordinations signaled a movement that neither began nor ended in the mid 1970s and has a long, long way to go.

Until we Christians can enthusiastically lift up our hearts to our Mother God as well as our Father, the presence of women priests will make little difference to the shape of patriarchal Christianity or to the Episcopal Church or to other churches in their efforts to empower women and girls to be ourselves in the world. Not until we are able to experience, and celebrate, Jesus' Christic power as truly the Sophia/Wisdom of God will we be fully awakened to who we are. Not until the Holy Spirit bursts us out of gender-role captivity and our collective sense of sexual shame—especially as women and girls—can the deepest meanings of the Philadelphia and Washington ordinations begin to be realized. Until then, the ordination of women remains, indeed, a gift to the church, but a muted one without much liberating power to spark our radical transformation into the fullness of who we are created to be.

Furthermore, not until we can see our ways beyond both androcentric (male centered) and anthropocentric (human centered) experiences of God can we begin to recognize the rest of creation as partners with us on a sacred journey that carries us into realms of earth-ethics in which we can begin to imagine all water as "holy," all bread that is shared as "the body of Christ," and all earth and space and time as "sacred." These are among the many radically transformative spiritual insights being shaped among feminist, womanist, queer, ecological, and other Christian liberation theologians in the twenty-first century.

No woman, ordained or lay, can be fully involved in these movements for a better world and church unless she breaks free of women's traditional place in patriarchal religion—breaks free in fact from patriarchal Christianity itself. This "breaking free" was at the heart of the Philadelphia and Washington ordinations, more I think than many of us realized at the time.

Darlene O'Dell is a gifted story teller. An author with published works in both history and fiction, she combines in *The Story of the Philadelphia Eleven* a careful attentiveness to detail with a narrative flair that grips the reader's attention in the first paragraph and holds it. O'Dell describes our experiences, and those of the Washington Four, as she loops back almost half a century to explore what was happening then—so that we may better understand what is happening now, and what is not. She has also written this book to help us realize that we share the work of making history from one generation to the next, in an unending process.

Carter Heyward

Chapter 1

JULY 29, 1974

A day or two before her ordination to the priesthood in the Episcopal Church, Carter Heyward received a letter from a priest in Texas, someone she had spoken with a few times. He was writing to plead with her to abandon her plans to be ordained that week, noting he respected her work as a minister of the Gospel, but that on this single point they were "sworn and bitter enemies." The letter filled four single-spaced, typewritten pages, concluding with a postscript squeezed into the left margin that read, in part: "When we next meet, I will truly be able to vent my anger with you by addressing you as 'The Rev *Mother* Fucker.' Love and Kisses, *Father* _____." This would obviously not be your run-of-the-mill ordination.

In fact, security for the event, which was held on July 29, 1974, at the Church of the Advocate in Philadelphia, a nineteenth-century Gothic structure modeled after the Cathedral of Amiens in France, included a busload of police officers stationed down the street, plain-clothed officers scattered through the congregation of two thousand, a large group of radical lesbians some of whom—according to the rector of the Advocate—were "trained in crowd control and karate," and buckets lined up along the church's walls in case of bombs or fire.

Episcopal churches haven't traditionally been feared as hotspots for unruly crowds and violent offenders, but this was the sort of day, as the priest from Texas had made clear, that created enemies. Eleven women, tired of waiting for the church to decide whether to allow the ordination of women priests, took the matter into their own hands and with the blessings of four bishops, became the first women priests in the Episcopal Church in the United States. Some in the Church would have preferred to have studied the issue further, but as supporters of women's ordination pointed out—and without a hint of exaggeration—the Church had been studying the issue for over fifty years and had never found theological reasons preventing the ordination of women; in fact, the Church was attempting to study the "women into submission." Others were much more direct in their opposition, declaring that one could no more ordain

1

a woman than he could ordain a rock, a piece of wood, a jackass, a cow, or even a monkey in a tree.

From the beginning, the media was captivated by the event. In the planning stages, the organizers had hoped and prepared for only a limited media presence, attempting to keep the ordinations quiet for as long as possible and notifying only those personally invited, the diocesan bishops of the eleven, and a few trusted media sources. In fact, the invitation Heyward sent to her family and friends asked for their confidentiality and warned them that the service would be "highly irregular and potentially dangerous." At one point, those involved discussed conducting the ordinations in a venue that would provide more privacy than an Episcopal church. A tennis court at the home of one of the ordaining bishops was mentioned, though that idea was quickly dismissed by those who wanted to hold the service in a church. Their efforts, however, to maintain a low profile were brought to a halt when the Bishop of Pennsylvania, Lyman Ogilby—who had attended one of the planning meetings to argue against the ordinations—wrote the members of the clergy in his diocese asking them to refrain from participating. The organizers realized that the news he had released would spread quickly and that it was only a matter of time before the press would begin asking questions. "For me, that was a red alert," wrote press agent Betty Medsger. Medsger had been a highly recognized and respected journalist from Philadelphia's *Evening Bulletin*, but was a freelancer when she was asked to be the event's press agent. Instead of waiting until a few days before the event as planned, she made a handful of phone calls to a few major media outlets and released the information in time for the July 20 editions of the newspapers. Then she sent out a news release of the event itself, two to three page biographies of each of the ordinands, plus plenty of quotes from the eleven women and the three bishops. "It was crucial," Medsger said, "that we be the first with the news. If anti-ordination forces preceded us to the press, the condemnation of the event would make the first and most memorable public impression. We had to announce the news so as not to be put in a defensive position." On the day of the ordinations, she set up thirty chairs for the press corps near the altar of the church, but would ultimately need two hundred. "I was pushed, shoved, even kicked by the reporters and photographers," Medsger said. "The jostling for position was unbelievable." Every major network was there, including the BBC. In the week leading up to the ordinations and in the months that followed, stories ran in *The New York Times*, the *Chicago Tribune*, the *Minneapolis Tribune*, *The Guardian*, *The Washington Post*, *The Philadelphia Inquirer*, the

Richmond Times-Dispatch, The Cleveland Plain Dealer, the *Miami Herald, The Boston Globe, The Newport News Daily Press, The Honolulu Advertiser, The San Diego Evening Tribune,* the *Los Angeles Times, The Times-Union, The Democrat and Chronicle, The Courier-Journal, The Kansas City Star, The Christian Science Monitor, The Charlotte Observer, The Sun, Time, Newsweek, Ms., Christianity and Crisis, Christianity Today, The Witness, The Christian Century, National Catholic Reporter, Commonweal, People,* among others at home and abroad. Heyward was on the cover of *Ms.* and one of the eleven, Alison Cheek, was named a *Time* magazine woman of the year. Heyward, Cheek, and fellow ordinand Nancy Wittig appeared on *The Phil Donahue Show.* The *Today* show covered the ordination, as did Walter Cronkite on the *CBS Evening News.* The story was recognized as the top religious story of 1976 by the Religious Newswriters Association, beating out the election of Southern Baptist Jimmy Carter as President of the United States and the Bicentennial Project of the Roman Catholic bishops. Bishop Robert DeWitt, one of the ordaining bishops of the eleven, wrote in humble understatement that they had "touched the nerve of institutional injustice."

The weather alone was the sort that would set a person's nerves on edge. It was "beastly hot and humid," ordinand Alla Bozarth-Campbell (referred to by her current name Bozarth throughout the book) remembered. "Blistering," another said. Unfortunately, the heat provided an apt—if not medieval—atmosphere for at least one of the prevalent metaphors that came to be associated with the event: the comparison of the eleven with witches. The editor of *The Witness* made note of the image years later, writing that the expressed fear was that when "you mix women and rituals . . . you get witches," adding, "and they burn witches, don't they?" Apparently the judge who was asked to issue a temporary injunction against the ordinations thought so. He refused to hear the case, telling the church to handle it in its usual manner, "at the stake." And one priest, protesting the ordinations, stood at the Advocate and told the congregation, "God here now as father and judge sees you trying to make stones into bread. You can only offer up the smell and sound and sight of perversion." He could, he warned, smell the sulfur in the air.

When the crowd began laughing at and booing this and other protests, the Advocate's rector Paul Washington asked the congregation to remain respectful. Washington was no stranger to handling situations where violent language and degrading characterizations were leveled against opponents. Some of Philadelphia's most powerful and vocal leaders had made such language infamous. A former police commissioner had once dubbed inner-city North

Philadelphia, where the Advocate was located, as "the Jungle." And the powerful and bombastic mayor at the time of the ordinations, Frank Rizzo—who had fostered a long, troubled, and violent history with the city's African-American community—was a constant source of controversial statements, boasting in a 1975 election campaign that he would be so tough as to "make Attila the Hun look like a faggot." But Paul Washington was not easily intimidated. An African-American born in Charleston, South Carolina, he had been promised to God even before his birth in a deal his mother had struck the Almighty: if God would give her a son, she would dedicate him to God's service. She named that son Paul after the apostle. "My course had already been carefully set," Washington wrote. He had come to the Advocate in 1962, after serving in the black parish of St. Cyprian in Philadelphia. While at St. Cyprian, the suffragan (assistant) bishop asked him to take on the additional duties of serving the all-white congregation of St. Titus. The official appointment, however, was never made. A delegation of lay people had sidestepped the suffragan bishop and approached the bishop directly, telling him that they liked Washington personally, but that they had daughters to consider. Washington never forgot it, writing in his memoir that he "lived with the feeling that whites whom I considered friends can come to a line of race that they cannot cross."

When he arrived at the Advocate, Washington was determined his new church would be an open and welcoming one, a place for people who, in the words of Barbara Harris, "had no place else to go." Harris was a member of the Advocate and a public relations officer for Sun Oil. She served as the crucifer at the ordinations of the eleven and would later be installed as the first woman bishop in the Episcopal Church—and in the worldwide eighty-million member Anglican Communion.

Washington's choices concerning who received refuge in the Advocate were not only controversial within the city of Philadelphia, but also within much of the nation at large, the ordination of the women being only one example. He also supported the Black Power Movement, hosting various Black Panther events and providing a place for Stokely Carmichael to hold a Black Panther rally in 1966. He opened the Advocate for a fund-raising defense rally for Angela Davis who, for a brief period, had been on the FBI's most wanted list and then imprisoned in California. Later acquitted of the charges against her and, continuing her activism, Davis became a renowned writer and scholar. As rector, Washington was adamant about his priorities: "If I have to offend *you* to please *God*," he once said, "I'll do it." And he did. On that hot day in

July, when the procession marched through the Advocate for the purpose of ordaining the eleven women, many within the Episcopal Church and from other denominations were more than offended. They were outraged.

The intense level of rage surrounding the event—the media firestorm that erupted, the amount of civil and uncivil discussion it evoked, the number of letters from other priests and bishops calling the women "childish," "selfish," or "arrogant," the ecclesiastical trials that ensued, the careers destroyed—has proved to be somewhat confounding in hindsight. The Episcopal Church was not even the first denomination to ordain women in the United States. The Presbyterians and Methodists had been ordaining women since 1956; the Universalist Unitarians, Congregationalists, and Disciples of Christ since the nineteenth century. In fact, the Episcopal Church was not even the first within the Anglican Communion to ordain women. In 1944, Li Tim-Oi was ordained in the Anglican diocese of Hong Kong, followed in 1971 by Jane Hwang and Joyce Bennett. Why, then, the media uproar?

Some argue that though the Episcopal Church is a relatively small denomination in the United States and not a leader in the women's ordination movement in the country, its historical influence and power is widespread in American politics and culture and its decisions carry great economic weight. To no small degree, then, these ordinations caught the attention of the dominant national culture because the women were white, predominantly middle-class, and from the United States. Additionally, those who were lesbian kept their sexual identities hidden. Others argue that the attention was the result of the ordinations occurring at an energetic moment in the women's liberation movement that included highly publicized debates around the Equal Rights Amendment, the decision in Roe v. Wade, the emergence of NOW, the coming of the International Women's Year, and even the defeat of Bobby Riggs by Billie Jean King in the tennis match *The London Sunday Times* called "the drop shot and volley heard around the world." Some have joked that the ordinations occurred on a slow news day, though in the context of Watergate, a global recession and spiraling inflation, and the continuing nuclear bomb tests spawned by the Cold War, it would seem that journalists had enough with which to occupy themselves.

The anger unleashed over the proposed ordinations also raised particular issues for Washington and many other African-Americans who placed themselves in the heart of the struggle. Historians and other critics have pointed to problems created by white liberals who assume that African-Americans and other disenfranchised groups will necessarily join their political battles out a sense of community. It can be a dangerous place for the vulnerable to occupy. "Whenever white liberals have been at odds with each other," wrote Mudflower—a collective of Black, Hispanic, and White Christian women that included Carter Heyward—"they've benefited from pulling in black folks to side with them, to bolster their positions. In this way black people have been used a great deal on behalf of white interests. In such a case the only sure loser is the black person." The morning after the ordinations, Washington believed his position within the larger church was the most tenuous of anyone involved: "At the time I knew only one thing: A black priest in an aided parish had disobeyed his bishop, the presiding bishop, and the General Convention in an action that was broadcast to the world. I was in trouble." It was, he wrote, "the lowest and perhaps the loneliest moment of my life."

Certainly, one of the reasons the debates about the ordinations became prominent is the relationship between the Episcopal Church and the Catholic Church and their shared tradition of Apostolic Succession. Simply stated, Apostolic Succession is a belief that the ordination of bishops has occurred in an unbroken line beginning with the original apostles, usually with the laying on of hands. Often connected to that argument is the idea that because Jesus and the apostles were men, women could not possibly be part of the succession, though scholars in the women's ordination movement pointed out that Jesus and the apostles were also first-century circumcised Jews (not twentieth century, English speaking Gentiles) and that to assume being a male was a necessary prerequisite for the priesthood was faulty theology.

Many of the supporters had hoped that the ceremony on July 29 would create a domino effect and influence the Catholic Church's own policy on ordaining women. Within the Episcopal Church, that minority who wished to reunite with the Catholic Church was terrified at the impact the ordinations would have on their chances for reconciliation. Their fears, of course, were not unfounded. The Reverend Richard Cornish Martin, curate at the time of St. Paul's Parish in Washington, D.C., warned that women's ordinations to the priesthood would be divisive to what he called an already vulnerable Episcopal Church:

> Schism is not a threat, it is inevitable, this is a promise! And this little Episcopal Church can ill afford further division. . . . within Catholic Christendom, Anglicanism is the weakest link, the most vulnerable church, and it will

be a push over. . . . For many such action will make Anglicanism incredible
and her claim to Catholicity a fraud.

At the 1976 General Convention (the governing body of the church that meets
every three years), the bishops opposed to the ordinations issued a statement,
emphasizing their most critical and crucial concern. They warned that "the
ordination and consecration of women priests and bishops will raise for us the
gravest of questions—that is, how far this Church can accept such ministrations
without fatally compromising its position as a Catholic and Apostolic Body."
In a statement indicative of how connected he believed the two churches to be,
Bishop Stanley Atkins wrote that "the General Convention of the Episcopal
Church has no more right to change the Catholic priesthood than it has to
change the Catholic creeds, or the Catholic canon of scripture."

In letters, sermons, press releases, and other statements, this fear of alien-
ating the Catholic Church was raised repeatedly by opponents of women's
ordination to the priesthood, prompting Sue Hiatt, who spearheaded the organization of the ordinations, to ask if these Episcopalians had remembered the
Protestant Reformation, when in the sixteenth-century Martin Luther nailed
his ninety-five theses to a church door in Germany and the then unnamed prot-
estants began a process of separating from the Catholic Church.

Roman Catholic theologian Frans Josef van Beeck wrote that the Episcopal Church should remember that it is a church in its own right and that the
Anglicans should see themselves as enlightening the Catholic Church on this
score. As Van Beeck's statement illustrates, Catholics themselves were not of
one mind on the issue of women's ordination. Roman Catholic Bishop Joseph
L. Hogan wrote in the Catholic *Courier-Journal*, "I am convinced we must
begin to think and pray about the issue. We must realize that St. Paul said nearly
twenty centuries ago that, in Christ, 'there is neither Jew nor Greek, male nor
female, slave nor freeman.' We must open our minds and hearts to the Holy
Spirit." And a group of eighty Roman Catholics, including some of the Catholic Church's most prominent theologians, signed a statement they forwarded
to the Vatican and to the Presiding Bishop of the Episcopal Church asking for
the Episcopal Church to "complete the approval of ordination" of the eleven.
On the other hand, twenty-six nuns from a convent in New York sent Heyward
a letter asking her to return to her role as a deacon. "We want you to know
that we do not agree with such disobedience, and are impelled to respond in
penitence for the injury done to the body of Christ." And just after the General

Convention of the Episcopal Church voted on the validity of the ordinations in the fall of 1976, the Vatican itself issued the Declaration on the Question of Admission of Women to the Ministerial Priesthood, approved by Pope Paul VI. "It is sometimes read and said in books," the writers of the declaration asserted, "that some women feel that they have a vocation to the priesthood."

> Such an attraction however noble and understandable, still does not suffice for a genuine vocation. In fact a vocation cannot be reduced to mere personal attraction.

The writers went on to say that Christ chose those he wanted and that the Church had received the charge and control of who would be ordained. And then in a statement that clarified their understanding of the nature of a woman's call to the priesthood, they wrote, "the priestly office cannot become the goal of social advancement."

The level of rage that erupted around women's ordination also raised the question of why some lay people, priests, and bishops in the Episcopal Church, many who had dedicated their personal and professional lives to eliminating racism, protesting the Vietnam War, and alleviating poverty, not only found it difficult to take a strong stand for a woman's right to be ordained to the priesthood, but adamantly opposed such a position. For instance, C. Kilmer Myers— Bishop of California—criticized the church for being guilty of the "heresy of racism" and attacked Cardinal Spellman of New York's support of the Vietnam War, but when asked two years before the Philadelphia ordinations if women should be ordained, he answered with a resounding *no*:

> The male image about God pertains to the divine initiative in creation. Initiative is, in itself, a male rather than a female attribute. . . . The priest acts as the commissioned agent of Christ. His priesthood partakes of Christ's priesthood, which is generative, initiating, giving. The generative function is plainly a masculine kind of imagery, making priesthood a masculine conception.

For Myers, the role model for a woman's ministry rested in the image of Mary as the mother of Jesus and as the mother of the church, as the one who "bore within her body that Word which enlightens the Cosmos." Motherhood, itself, was apparently neither generative, initiating, nor giving.

Though Myers argued that the conception of God as male was a false doctrine, he did believe the "analogy" to maleness had "meaning." His thoughts in *The Episcopalian* suggest that the meaning implicit in the analogy is that men are actors and thinkers while women, when responding to the will of God, are passive and obedient receptors, the use of their bodies determined by the needs and desires of men. Feminist theologian Mary Daly, whom many of the Philadelphia Eleven had read in their studies, critiqued positions such as Myers', writing famously and succinctly, "If God is male, then male is God." Other contemporary writers raised this issue with their readers, including *Newsweek* columnist Meg Greenfield who, after attending a service led by one of the eleven, wrote about the actual meaning of the ordinations, asserting that the eleven were not only asking for a "piece of the action or a right or a new measure of respect," but that they were "asking the faithful, in a particular way, to alter their whole image of God." When God is male or "is represented only as a father," as historian Mary Donovan points out, "and access to that God must be channeled through a male priest, then dominance of patriarchy is assured." Paul Moore, who was Bishop of New York at the time of the ordinations and head of the diocese in which three of the Philadelphia Eleven resided, wrote that "if God is thought of as simply and exclusively male, the very cosmos itself seems sexist."

More liberal on the issue of women's ordination than Myers, Moore still could not bring himself to ordain the three women who presented themselves in his diocese, though three years later, in 1977, he would ordain Ellen Barrett without the permission of the General Convention. Barrett was the first openly lesbian priest in the international Anglican Communion, and her ordination ignited another round of heated controversy within the church. Ironically, after her ordination in New York, Barrett left for California for a position in Myers' diocese. By this point, Myers' main concern had moved away from the issue of whether women should be allowed to assume priestly duties and to the question of whether homosexuals honest about their sexual identities should be punished. He asked a group of one hundred Episcopalians gathered in Sacramento their opinion on his re-licensing Barrett, saying that while he had never ordained an "avowed" homosexual, he had ordained those who had kept their sexual identities secret. "My quandary is this," he told the group, "should I consent to the ordination of out-of-the closet homosexuals? Or should I penalize them for honesty when I consent to the ordination of in-the-closet homosexuals?"

A problem, then, for the Philadelphia Eleven, and then later the Washington Four, was that even bishops liberal on most social issues could not necessarily be counted on to fight for women's ordination. Even those, like Moore, who supported them "in principle," made choices that alienated the women ordinands and left them often feeling betrayed, angry, or confused about where their bishops stood on the issue. Ultimately, most of the eleven made the decision to stop asking for permission to be priests and to simply begin exercising their priesthoods by presiding over the Eucharist. Even though they were roundly criticized, they also found plenty of support for this position among those in the Church. As one woman wrote to *The Episcopalian*, "All those remarks about patience, orderly perseverance, and debate—that's been tried. When in history did men ever change because women wrote a polite note?" Other women wrote directly to the leadership of the Church, not only expressing support for the eleven, but also voicing their concerns about their own position within the Church. "It is," Lucia Whisenand wrote to John Coburn, a leader in the House of Deputies, "incredibly painful to be sensitive, intelligent, highly educated, and an Episcopal woman."

In relation to the actual service that took place at the Advocate, it would be a mistake to imply that it was overwhelmed by threats, fears of violence, and the pushing and shoving that Medgser refers to in her dealings with the press. In fact, the service was joyful and life-changing for many. As Whisesnand wrote to Coburn about the day:

> I am not particularly knowledgeable about manifestations of the Holy Spirit. Something, however, was present in Philadelphia on July 29 that I have not experienced before. My bishop tells me it was just being part of the crowd. I have been part of many crowds in many places at many times for many causes. Something different happened in Philadelphia. If it was not the Holy Spirit, it was a religious phenomenon that I should like to find out more about and experience again. Perhaps it was because for once I was not left out.

The language later used to describe the event by those who were there often took on an epic, even apocalyptic, tone. It affectionately became known as "that great gittin' up morning," alluding to the African-American spiritual that celebrates the coming of Jesus, when Gabriel blew his trumpet like seven peals of thunder. Heyward called it the "most extraordinary and finest day" of her life, a day when she had been "privileged to participate in a holy moment of history." Barbara Schlachter, who was ordained in 1977, said that the ceremony was "loud, loud with singing," so loud that "you could almost hear the flapping of the Spirit's wings." Organist Linda Clark referred to the event as the "day the world cracked open," one of those moments that push us forward into the future. Harris said that she had heard "the rush of a mighty wind" and that she wanted to "stride forth like Joshua and lead that courageous band 'seven times around the wall.'"

The service lasted a hefty three hours, partly because it was interrupted by people stopping the procession to embrace the ordinands and by spontaneous applause and laughter during various high moments. The number of people who attended—estimates put the number at two thousand—caught many off guard. Alison Cheek said that she thought only a few people would show up and that the women and their bishops would be "rattling around" in a huge Gothic structure. "But it was packed full," she said. Describing those who filled the Advocate, John O'Connor in the *Philadelphia Daily News* wrote, "It was 'Joseph's coat' of celebrators: blacks and whites, stiff clerical garb and mini-skirts, Episcopal faces straight out of movies of the English countryside, gays and lesbians, nuns and Catholic priests." And Heyward tells of her surprise at being blinded by the television lights and the flashes from camera bulbs from the large number of media representatives in attendance.

One of the youngest ordinands, Merrill Bittner, drove down from Rochester with a large group of supporters who handed out orange ribbons to those in the congregation. Years later, Bittner said that she didn't know why those in the movement chose the color orange to represent themselves, but that she wore her purple high-topped tennis shoes, laced them with orange shoe strings, and reveled in the moment. "It was a joyous day," she said.

Bittner would need the memory of that day to help her through the coming months. Like the rest of the ordained women, she received her share of hate mail. One person sent her a piece of fish cord and told her to hang herself with it. A man from Rochester wrote a letter addressing her as "Big Merrill," and after quoting scripture, told her to try a "little humility and self denial . . . as for the latter, it would help your horribly rotund body." He continued, "Your self-indulgence is quite evident. Shape up in more ways than one." In case his point had not been taken, he added a P.S.: "You seem to be the classic, embittered—unattractive female. . . ." Another man from New York wrote her a letter in which he celebrated her work and discussed why he was for the ordination of women to the priesthood, but then turned her presence at the altar into another comment on her appearance: "I find you an attractive woman," he wrote, "and it would give me so much pleasure to sit in church looking at you giving a sermon, rather than to some ugly old duck we are so accustomed to seeing." Fortunately for the women, the letters of support that poured in outnumbered the letters of hate; nonetheless, the women endured an avalanche of criticism that included attacks on their morality, their motivations, their intelligence, their personalities, the sound of their voices, their appearances—even a run in their stockings didn't go unnoticed.

The story of the Philadelphia Eleven, and of the four who followed them a year later in Washington, includes the hate mail as well as the purple tennis shoes. It is a story about a group of women and their supporters who found themselves at the Advocate on that "great gittin' up morning" and how they stood up to the church to demand that it represent all of God's people. It is a story of Jeannette Piccard, the oldest of the group at the age of seventy-nine, who also happened to be the first woman ever to enter space, piloting herself and her husband (and a pet turtle named Fleur de Lys) 57,579 feet into the stratosphere in a balloon called The Century of Progress. It is about the youngest Alla Bozarth, age twenty-seven, who overcame a childhood of multiple surgeries and illnesses, only to lose her mother a few years before the ordination, a woman who gave Bozarth strength and identity by escaping Russia in the early part of the century in a hay-drawn wagon. It includes a woman who saved American journalists from execution in Africa and another who, in spite of her blindness, rode her horses across the landscape of Colorado. Finally, it describes a small band of women who, along with their bishops and supporters, faced a church bureaucracy that had managed to keep women subjugated for centuries in the name of a Christian God and how in their determination to overturn this tradition, they raised questions about the very identity of that God. And it is a story that continues to be written to this day.

One of the women, Sue Hiatt, has been credited for leading the movement for the ordination of women to the priesthood. Over the years, she was given various informal titles: "Our mother, our grandmother, our foremother, and saint." She's been referred to as a salty and at times ornery saint, an "agent provocateur," the bishop and shepherd and prophet and messenger to the women. Washington and DeWitt wrote that she was the Cassandra of the group. Others teased her that she was sometimes Eeyore-like in her despair.

All agree that the ordinations of 1974 would not have happened without her. We will begin with her story.

Chapter 2

THE DEACONS' TALE, PART I

Jean Hiatt Kramer thought back across the life of her younger sister Sue, or Suzy as the family called her. Jean was the eldest of the three children, Sue the youngest. It was during the Hurricane of '38 that Kramer came to believe that there was something distinctive about her sister. It was the sort of storm that, like Hiatt herself, had been given a litany of other names: the Great New England Hurricane, the Yankee Clipper, the Long Island Express. "We didn't think too much about it," Kramer said, referring to the intensity of the hurricane. Not until after the fact did they realize how powerful the storm had been. With the storm raging outside the house and Suzy in her highchair, the family had gathered around the dinner table to sing "Happy Birthday" to its youngest member. At the same instant that "Suzy blew out her two candles," Kramer recalled, "a tree went through the house next door and all the lights went out." The electricity had been blown. The moment wasn't lost on Kramer. "I knew then," she said, "that there was something special, something unusual, about my sister."

When Suzy was five or six, she saw an animal being mistreated. "She was inconsolable," Kramer said. "Mother tried to comfort her. 'Suzy, you can't change the world,' she told her. But Suzy stuck her lip out and said, 'Oh yes I can!' I think what she hated more than anything was cruelty. It would just make her sick." Around that same time, just after the family had moved to Minneapolis, she left the house to scour the new neighborhood in search of a girl to be a friend for her sister and a boy to be a friend for her brother. That she ended up at the home of the rector, who would later become her godfather, was only coincidence because the point here, of course, is that she was already working to ease lives through networking and knocking on a few doors.

Hiatt's search that day for friends for her siblings turned out to be a remarkably defining moment for her, and—for that matter—for her family, for the Episcopal Church, and one could argue, the world at large. But it wasn't an auspicious beginning, at least not for the adults. The rector, Bernard Hummel, had a little girl a year younger than Hiatt. The two of them struck up a friendship and Suzy was invited to dinner. She put on her best dress—struggled against the dress, as Kramer described it—and went out for the evening. Unfortunately, something went terribly wrong. First one person began throwing up, then another, and another, until, according to the children, it was nothing but one big "vomit party." Suzy wasn't the least bit fazed, telling her concerned mother, "Oh, it was great!" If nothing else, it was the beginning of a long friendship between families. Kramer remembered that her mother Frances and Mrs. Hummel became the closest of friends, laughing and smoking like chimneys. The Hiatts weren't a church-going family, but they began attending Hummel's St. Stephen's Episcopal Church. Alfred Hiatt (father of Jean, Sue, and brother John) sang in the choir. The children were baptized. For John, the baptism was an exercise in humiliation. He was a thirteen-year-old boy; most of the others, infants. But for Sue, the moment spoke to her: "I . . . remember feeling profoundly different after the experience and wondering if there might not be a commitment there that I would later be called to act on."

Both Hiatt sisters attended Northrop Collegiate School for Girls. Kramer remembered it as a place where the teachers were primarily single women who were intensely dedicated to their fields. "They loved their subjects," she said. She recalled their voices, captivating as they read Shelley and Keats. At Northrop, Sue was influenced by a teacher named Janet Gray. "They were soul mates" and spent a lot of time talking about things, about philosophy. "Janet Gray was a young liberal," Kramer said, "a feminist."

In her senior year, Sue Hiatt walked into Northrop and handed in a twenty page research paper she titled "The Domestic Animal," a seventeen-year-old's critique of domestic life in the United States. The year was 1953, a decade before Betty Friedan had published her groundbreaking work *The Feminine Mystique*, which would address the unhappiness of middle-class white women and help inspire the Second Wave of the feminist movement. In her paper, Hiatt argued that "although women in America gained political emancipation in 1920, they had not yet gained social and economic freedom, nor will they," she continued, "until social pressure, tradition, and upbringing stop forcing them to conform to outmoded patterns of life." She understood at that age the dangers of calling oneself a feminist, but even more so, the dangers of shrinking from the label:

Unfortunately, the word *feminist* connotes an ax-swinging old fanatic. Women do not like to be labeled feminist, and thus learn to keep quiet about the injustices of their lives for fear of ridicule.

She earned an *A* on the paper.

To please her mother, Hiatt spent a year at Wellesley, then transferred to Radcliffe, where she graduated cum laude with a degree in American History. She seldom attended church in her college years, but after graduation, while home visiting her family, she was paid a pastoral call by the Reverend Hummel. He had come to tell Hiatt that he believed she should be working in the church and that he was quite certain she was already aware of that fact. "Yes," she said, surprised by her answer, "I know that, but I can not and will not work for an organization that treats women as miserably as the Episcopal Church does." Though he dropped the issue, Hiatt continued to struggle with the implications of their talk.

Over the next few years, Hiatt became more convinced that she had been called to the priesthood. Then, in 1961, she came to a crossroads in her life. While she wanted to follow her calling to the church, she believed that door was closed to her and that she would be better off pursuing a degree in social work. She had applied to Episcopal Theological Seminary in Boston, but to be on the safe side, she had also applied to a school in Minnesota where she planned to study for a Masters degree in social work. On the Wednesday night before school was to begin at the seminary, she spent long, agonizing hours weighing her options, discussing possibilities over the kitchen table with Jean who had moved to Massachusetts. The school in Minnesota was scheduled to start on Monday. Jean suggested that she try the seminary the next day and if it didn't work out, she could always drive to Minnesota by Monday. On her 25th birthday, and once again in the midst of a hurricane, she walked though the doors of the seminary and never turned back. She received her Masters of Divinity Degree from ETS (now Episcopal Divinity School), but to cover all her bases, earned a Masters in Social Work from Boston University.

She returned to Minnesota to work in a Presbyterian church. When some of the faculty members at ETS learned about the position, they were relieved, thinking that she had been ordained as a Presbyterian minister and had been able to follow her calling. "I began to think for the first time that my ministry," she said, "might someday include insisting that the Episcopal church face up to its discrimination against women instead of cheerfully sending its promising women on to other denominations." In the meantime, she met Bob DeWitt, the Bishop of Pennsylvania, who discouraged her from trying to find work in the Episcopal Church because he believed the church would disappoint her over issues of gender. Hiatt took a job as a welfare rights organizer in Philadelphia and worked with a team to raise the level of welfare grants in Pennsylvania. They were involved in various high-profile projects to draw awareness to the needs of welfare recipients, including a Blood for Shoes drive in which mothers sold their own blood to pay for shoes for their children. Some of the mothers were not allowed to give blood; their inadequate diets had lowered their iron levels below acceptable norms.

Because Hiatt had developed an impressive set of community organizing skills, DeWitt decided to hire her as a missioner. Her job would be to help wealthy suburban Episcopalians find an outlet for working on problems faced by inner-city residents. She would have regular meetings with DeWitt, Paul Washington, and David Gracie—a young priest whose counseling of draft card burners had groups within the church calling for DeWitt's resignation. She met and worked with Barbara Harris, who was then a public relations officer with Sun Oil. And she met Ann Robb Smith, who would become intimately involved with the ordination movement and later become a priest herself. Smith was one of the wealthy white suburban women Hiatt helped to organize. Washington wrote that Smith had come to a point of near collapse by her frustration with the racism she found in the suburbs, so she moved her membership to the Advocate, where Hiatt had also become a member. In the early 60s, DeWitt had chosen the church as the site for his installation as the Bishop of Pennsylvania, sending the message that he was serious about prioritizing race issues in the diocese. His friend Paul Moore delivered the sermon. "When his people are oppressed," Moore told the congregation, "so is [the bishop] and their fight for freedom is his. Where necessary, he must cut away the barnacles of the past and move ahead to reshape the diocese." Ten years later, when DeWitt returned to the Advocate to fulfill the meaning of those words by being one of the ordaining bishops of the Philadelphia Eleven, Moore would feel deeply betrayed.

As bishop, DeWitt backed some of his diocese's most strident leaders, supporting Paul Washington and David Gracie. And he supported Sue Hiatt, telling a reporter from Philadelphia's *The Evening Bulletin*, "The margin of welfare fraud is less than two percent, and that is a far lower margin of fraud than is applicable to almost any other conceivable economic enterprise, not the least of which is income tax evasion." He added, "The crushing of people's pride through a welfare system that forces them to live at bare subsistence levels in an endless and vain struggle against dirt, disease, squalor, and implacable prejudice is not to be tolerated by Christian people."

DeWitt was born in the Jamaica Plain neighborhood of Boston in 1916. Somewhere around the age of sixteen, he was sitting alone in a small boat in the middle of a quiet lake in Canada when he became intensely aware of a presence. The presence didn't speak, but if it had, he recalled that it would have said something like, "I see you. I know you're there. I'm glad you're there." It was a gentle, though transformative, moment for him. Even as he told Heyward this story towards the end of his life, he remembered, "It's as clear to me as if it were yesterday."

DeWitt was a songwriter and played the saxophone, the guitar, and the accordion. He loved his pipe. He went to school in upstate New York and then attended Amherst College, making plans for law school at Harvard, but like Hiatt, found himself torn until the last moment over which school to attend—whether to study law or to study theology at Episcopal Theological Seminary. Like Hiatt, he decided that he could always change his mind if he found that theology was the wrong pursuit for him. It wasn't, and when he rose to the rank of bishop, he was the youngest ever elected in the Diocese of Pennsylvania.

One reporter called him a "flinty but gentle New Englander." Another said he was as "casual as a fellow fisherman sitting around discussing the heavyweight championship or the plight of the Philadelphia Eagles over a bottle of beer." He was a thin man who wore his hair in a near crew cut even in the longhaired days of the 60s. He was a masterful letter writer and often ended his letters with the closure "Keep your courage." He knew of what he wrote—a friend recalled that "he was a lightning rod for people who loved to hate."

Before he arrived in Pennsylvania, DeWitt served as a rector in several churches in Michigan where he began honing his skills of shared leadership, again not always with his parishioners' approval. He had one church with four thousand members, so he hired three assistants to help him, all sharing time in the pulpit. Some of the parishioners expressed frustration, thinking the rector should be the one primarily delivering the sermons. "Some people got quite upset about it," he said, adding this story:

> One day someone called up the rectory secretary and asked who was going to
> be preaching Sunday. She said, "I don't know, but God's being featured in all
> the services." That became a real joke to us. We didn't want to develop little
> followings, so we shared.

Besides a keen sense of team building, DeWitt credited his time in Michigan with teaching him about what he called the "bureaucratic mindset and the submission to a status quo." In Detroit, he had worked with middle management employees from General Motors and had been astounded by their acquiescence to the company:

> I was astonished by some of the men whom I knew who were working for General Motors for whom General Motors could do no wrong. Whatever General Motors said was fine with them and whatever General Motors didn't say was something on which they had no opinions.

By the time he had been installed as Bishop of Pennsylvania in 1964, DeWitt had committed himself to issues of social justice, but those issues did not include a commitment to women's ordination. This is where Hiatt would come in.

In the spring of 1970, the Episcopal Peace Fellowship—a justice group first organized during World War II—announced a conference to be held at the spiritual retreat center of Graymoor in New York for the purpose of discussing the church's discrimination against women. Hiatt described the meetings as difficult, bringing together "young, militant feminists," "seminary-educated women of all ages," nuns, clergy wives, and lay women. They all met head-to-head to discuss the issue raised by the EPF, and they released a resolution that called the church to action:

> We fought and talked and cried together for two days and finally came up with "the Graymoor Resolution" in which we branded the institutional Episcopal Church "racist, militaristic and sexist. Its basic influence on our own lives is negative." We resolved further "that women as well as men [must] be accepted and recognized as equals so that they may function in proportion to their numbers in all aspects of the Church's life and ministry, including but not limited to . . ." and here we listed every office in the church we could think of, from vestries to altar guilds and from bishops to thurifers.

Hiatt returned from Graymoor more convinced than ever to answer her call to the priesthood. "I decided that the time had come to face up to the fact that God had been steadily pushing me toward ordained ministry for many years and that, despite my resistance, here I was unaccountably still in the Episcopal Church." She went to DeWitt ready to argue her case, but found the arguments unnecessary. He had come to the same conclusion. She was accepted as a postulant for Holy Orders and in the normal course of events (had she been a man) would have been scheduled to be ordained by DeWitt in 1972. At this time, it came to her attention that the Church had established a commission to look into the matter of women's ministry. The members were to report to the 1970 Convention, scheduled to meet that fall. "But no one at church headquarters," Hiatt wrote, "had gotten around to convening it." The commission had planned to issue a no progress report. Hiatt and some of her colleagues from Graymoor talked the members into meeting before the convention. They agreed, and just weeks before the General Convention convened its October 1970 meeting in Houston, issued a report in favor of women's ordination.

The hopes of the women were running high in Houston. The first women deputies had been seated at this convention after decades of debate. Hiatt had been accepted as a postulant. Other women had declared their own calls to the priesthood. And still others had voiced their sorrow and anger over women being denied access to the priesthood. For them, the stance taken by the church presumed that they were "second-class" members.

Also in Houston, a proposal to eliminate a voting procedure used in the General Conventions (one that generally worked against the passing of progressive measures in the life of the church) had been given first passage and was expected to be fully implemented three years later at the next convention in Louisville. The procedure affected the way votes were counted in one of the two houses of the General Convention. The Episcopal Church is governed by the House of Bishops and the House of Deputies. A bishop is the head of a diocese (or geographical area) and, currently, there exist over one hundred dioceses in the Episcopal Church. The House of Bishops is made up of current, retired, and suffragan bishops, totaling around three hundred. The House of Deputies, however, is made up of clergy and lay persons. Each diocese can send four clergy and four lay persons to sit in the House of Deputies, giving that house a population of just over eight hundred. One of the voting procedures used in the House of Deputies is referred to as "vote by orders" and, in the 1970s, could be implemented at the request of either the clergy or the laity of any one diocese. When a vote by orders is taken, each diocese can enter only one clergy vote and one lay vote, rather than its usual eight votes. If either the clergy or lay vote is divided at 2–2, its four votes are entered as one vote of *no*. Divided votes, then, are not counted as neutral votes, but as negative ones. Theoretically, approximately eighty-eight percent of the House of Deputies could vote *yes* to a proposal and it could still be defeated. In Houston, the measure to approve the ordination of women to the priesthood was defeated not by a simple majority (which had voted in favor), but rather by the votes by order procedure. It cannot be overstated how important this voting procedure was in relation to what happened in Philadelphia on July 29, 1974.

After the vote in Houston, some fifty angry and disappointed women crowded into a small hotel room to discuss the defeat. "Women had just been seated as lay delegates after a twenty-five-year debate and the church was congratulating itself on that," Hiatt wrote, "when suddenly the women were no longer grateful but turned hostile." As a result of the women's protest, the convention approved, at the last moment, the removal of the distinctions between female deaconesses and male deacons. Before, there had been different rules governing the two, different educational standards, and different expectations. For the purposes of this book, references to the ordination of women generally refer to the ordination of women to the priesthood, even though in the Episcopal Church, deacons are one of three orders of ministry, the other two including priests and bishops. Deacons are referred to by the title *reverend* and often wear collars, but may not preside over the Eucharist, though they may assist in serving the elements. When the General Convention removed the distinctions between deacons and deaconesses, referring to both men and women as *deacons*, the church moved women one step closer to the priesthood, but Hiatt called the change in the status of deacons a booby prize. The pun, of course, wouldn't have been lost on her.

One other moment in the convention that created despair among some of the supporters of women's ordination was the contribution to the church of the United Thank Offering, which was begun by the women of the church in 1889, when members of the church were encouraged to save pennies in little blue boxes to be kept in the home. Over the years, millions upon millions of dollars have been raised by the offering and presented to the church at the General Convention. In Houston alone, the UTO contribution to the church was over four million dollars, almost a third of the church's proposed budget that year. But the contribution in Houston was laden with meaning for the supporters of women's ordination who had just been defeated in the vote. Betty Bone Schiess from Syracuse, New York—who would become one of the eleven—referred to the moment when the women delivered the money to the bishops as "a display of subservience," prompting action from one of her friends who had attended the convention. "So offensive was this to a friend from Rochester," Schiess wrote, "that she not only left the auditorium, she left the Episcopal Church."

Even with the convention's disappointments, Hiatt and many supporters of women's ordination left Houston energized and optimistic. Though Hiatt was set to be ordained by DeWitt in 1972, she decided to postpone her ordination until after the 1973 convention in Louisville, when she expected the General Convention to eliminate the vote by orders and to open the doors for women priests. In the meantime, she kept busy. She traveled the country conducting a study for the church, making contacts with those who supported women's ordination to the priesthood and creating networks among them. With the help of Betty Powell (who would become one of the Washington Four) and Nancy Wittig (who would become one of the eleven), she gathered a group of women in Alexandria, Virginia, in late October of 1971 and created the Episcopal Women's Caucus. Most of the eleven were there, along with approximately fifty other women, including the Washington Four (see Chapter 12). The caucus would work to establish networks, spread information, and influence deputies to the convention.

It was at this first meeting of the EWC that Hiatt met Carter Heyward. A simple red magic marker laid the groundwork for a relationship that saw them through the rest of Hiatt's life. In the thirty plus years they knew each other, they went about changing the church in relation to its deacons, its bishops, its Presiding Bishops, its seminaries, and its position on issues such as the rights of gays and lesbians. Though they did not become intimate partners themselves, they would come to share a home on Brattle Street in Cambridge, Massachusetts, where they grew to wield tremendous theological power throughout their professional lives. But on that fall weekend in Alexandria, Heyward was a young seminary student from Union Theological Seminary, age 26, and a recently ordained deacon who had found a red magic marker. And it came to her to draw a red fist on her clerical collar. Looking back on their initial meeting, Heyward recalled that Hiatt was taken back by the fist, but that she believed "she secretly liked it." Hiatt later told her that when saw the fist, she knew that her new friend would be a "key player" in the movement. Her instincts were correct.

Just before the EWC meeting in Alexandria, the bishops had met in Pocono Manor, Pennsylvania, and had discussed women's ordination. Sort of. The main theme of the weeklong meeting was missions, and the conference was packed full of presentations, commendations, and reports concerning the issue. But time was also allotted for other activities. On Tuesday, four male seminarians asked the bishops to "take the initiative in establishing closer relationships" with students of theology. According to reports, the seminarians came bringing gifts:

> As a thanksgiving offering, the young men brought along a bottle of Scotch. They opened the Episcopal Church Annual, at random, and the bottle fell to the Bishop of Chicago (retired). (Since it was Johnny Walker, somebody suggested it really should go to Washington's new Suffragan of the same name!)

The next afternoon, as the Episcopal News Service noted, "The sun came out at least a little bit, to the delight of golfers, walkers, and gatherers of autumn leaves." In the midst of these activities, the "thorny issue of women's ordination to the priesthood" was raised. Bishop C. Kilmer Myers addressed his fellow bishops and argued against the ordinations. The bishops concluded that something definitely should be done, so they commissioned yet another study.

The women meeting in Alexandria were outraged. They wrote to Presiding Bishop John Hines and told him that none of the women would participate on the committee because the time for study had passed. Nearly all of the women signed off on a letter that demanded action, and they called on the "bishops immediately to ordain to the priesthood women deacons." But as the women began gaining strength, so did those in opposition to women's ordination. Stanley Atkins, the Bishop of Eau Claire, galvanized the American Church Union, strong opponents of the cause. Other groups organized, including the Coalition for the Apostolic Ministry, the Society for the Preservation of the Book of Common Prayer (opposed not only to women's ordination, but to changes associated with the church's understanding of homosexuality, abortion, divorce, and the prayer book), and the umbrella group the Coalition of Concerned Churchmen.

Hiatt joined forces with Emily Hewitt to write and publish *Women Priests: Yes or No?* It was a strikingly clear, compact, and accessible argument for the ordination of women to the priesthood. The girl who had written "The Domestic Animal" had grown into a woman and had applied feminist ideas to the subject of the priesthood:

> We have somehow arrived at the notion that the best way to order society is to divide the tasks of living into two spheres, masculine and feminine. The most convenient way to do this is to circumscribe what is proper for one sex and to make everything else the realm of the other sex. In the case of our society, we have circumscribed what is proper for women and left the rest for

men. The problem we now face is that the old patterns are changing and we can no longer be as clear as we once were about what sex should do what.

Emily Hewitt would drive from New York to meet with Hiatt in her Philadelphia apartment and the two women would sit facing each other, with typewriters between them. They wrote the book in the summer months of 1972—with Heyward (who was working in Pennsylvania for the summer) reading through chapters—and sent it off to the publisher by December of that year.

Hewitt was a student at Union Theological Seminary along with Heyward, Marie Moorefield, and Barbara Schlachter, and was born in Baltimore, Maryland, in 1944. By 1953, her father had contracted a form of leukemia that would quickly kill him. Hewitt was close to her father, a medical director at a small hospital in Baltimore. "I was old enough to have read to him the night before he died," she said. "We had very similar tastes . . . he and I would occasionally do things together like go out and see the horses at the farms north of Baltimore." Both her brother and mother suffered from mental illness. About a year after her father's death, Hewitt found her teenage brother after he had taken an overdose of his mother's sleeping pills. She was able, that time, to save him.

As a high school student, Hewitt attended Roland Park Country School, where she fought—successfully—to stay after a visiting aunt and uncle wanted to remove her from her home and place her in a school in New England. At Roland Park, she remembers an exchange the class had with one of the teachers. The teacher had asked the students who among them, they believed, would become the most successful. The students gave the name of two of their peers who were particularly well-mannered, but the teacher chose a class clown, a "notorious class cut-up." She chose her because she believed this particular student would not buckle under authority. "It was the first time I heard an idea that would become a major theme of the sixties and seventies," Hewitt wrote. "It unsettled me. It was not lost on me that I was not Miss Faissler's model."

Hewitt left home to attend Cornell University in New York. During her junior year, her brother committed suicide. Her grandmother died later that year, and her mother had begun making suicide attempts. While working at the University of Florida, Hewitt's mother disappeared for a time, but an uncle found her and set her up in an apartment in Atlanta. Hewitt last saw her the Christmas of her senior year at Cornell. That spring, she received a letter from her mother saying she couldn't afford to come to her graduation. She enclosed five dollars as a graduation gift. "I felt terrible about getting it,"

Hewitt remembers, "because I thought, God, I hope this doesn't keep her from having something she would enjoy." About a week later, her mother was driving through Atlanta traffic to have coffee with a family member when she had a car wreck and suffered severe brain trauma. She would die later that summer. With no immediate family left and having just graduated from Cornell, Hewitt was trying to decide what to do next in her life. She considered Harvard Business School, but settled on Union Theological Seminary.

The seminary is on Broadway on the Upper West Side of Manhattan, a few blocks north of Columbia University, which sits between the seminary and the Cathedral Church of St. John the Divine, one of the largest Gothic Cathedrals in the world. In fact, the whole atmosphere of the Cathedral has a larger-than-life feel to it. Where other churches have songbirds flying around the gardens, peacocks roam the grounds of St. John the Divine. Where other churches might have a waist-high fountain sitting in a patch of ivy, St. John's fountain is the size of a small house and features a "somnolent moon," "a joyous sun," nine giraffes—one resting its head on the bosom of the archangel Michael, and the recently decapitated Satan whose head dangles underneath a giant crab's claw. Other churches pray over Spot and Rover and Boots during the blessing of the animals, but at St. John's, Edie Falco comes down the aisle carrying a kangaroo, followed by a camel decorated with a wreath of flowers. It's the sort of place where, in the late 1960s, Madeleine L'Engle served as a volunteer librarian and Duke Ellington—who lived nearby—performed one of his Three Sacred Concerts. In the early 1980s, at the beginning of yet another phase of the Cathedral's construction, the famous aerialist Philippe Petit, who in 1974 had walked across a wire between the Twin Towers, crossed a hundred and fifty foot wire over Amsterdam Avenue and presented Bishop Paul Moore with a silver trowel to honor the event.

Moore had a memorable and tumultuous career, more often than not, showing tremendous courage in the areas of Civil Rights, the Vietnam War, poverty, and most especially gay and lesbian rights. As noted earlier, it was Moore who ordained Ellen Barrett to the priesthood in the late 1970s, with Heyward serving as Barrett's presenting priest. And what started out as a mutually fond and admiring relationship between Heyward and Moore—something with a father/daughter feel to it—eventually ended up in fragments over the issue of women's ordination.

Heyward entered seminary in the late 1960s, where she was heavily influenced by her teacher C. Eric Lincoln, an African-American man who had been raised by his grandmother in Alabama, had picked cotton to support his family, and had managed a nightclub in Memphis. He had even been the road manager of a baseball team: the Birmingham Black Barons. Lincoln went on to earn degrees from Le Moyne College, Fisk University, the University of Chicago, and Boston University and to become friends with Martin Luther King, Jr., and Malcolm X. When student protests broke out at Columbia University and across the world in the spring of 1968, Lincoln encouraged his students to put down their books and support the protesters. Heyward, other students, and other faculty members at Union agreed. Heyward was arrested and put into holding for a few hours. She later said that it wasn't a particularly courageous moment in her case, but one that raised her consciousness. For the next month, Union operated as a free university, without exams. Heyward recalls classes meeting in the rotunda or in coffee houses. Four students might attend or a hundred might show up. "People taught what they wanted," she said.

If that spring was a tumultuous period politically for the world (the assassination of King occurred during the riots), the prior fall had been a memorable one for Heyward personally. In November, around the Thanksgiving break, she had experienced an emotional breakdown and was taken to a psychiatric ward in the nearby hospital. She was overwhelmed by the city, but even more so by the level of sexism she had found at the seminary. "I didn't have the language for it," she recalled. Along with two other men, she had been assigned to a small parish near the seminary. "They were allowed to preach and be involved in the adult education," Heyward remembered. "I was put with the children." Though she would later work closely with disabled children in her retirement, she believed at the time that she was being "shunted aside" by the church. "Those early years at Union were very formative for me," she said, "in terms of participating in the Philadelphia ordinations."

After the spring session of 1968, Heyward left New York for nearly two years to work in her home parish in Charlotte, North Carolina. Her parents were both from families prominent in the Old and New South, her father a direct descendant of a signer of the Declaration of Independence and her mother the daughter of a tobacco company owner. In 1962, while a junior in high school, she was "chairman" of the Youth Commission of the diocese, which for the first time, had elected a black student among its ranks. When it came time for the commission to meet at a camp near Winston-Salem, North Carolina, the bishop sent word that since the group now had a black member, it could not use the segregated facility. The commission pushed the issue, but the bishop was adamant, even though ostensibly an opponent of segregation. The commission continued to push, "threw a fit," as Heyward remembered it, until the bishop disbanded the group. Nine years later, when Heyward approached this same bishop for ordination to the priesthood, he turned her down. He said she had a problem with authority.

When Heyward reentered Union after two years of working in her home parish, she returned with a renewed sense of focus and clarity. Besides reading and commenting on drafts of *Women Priests: Yes or No?*, she joined the Women's Caucus on campus which was working to bring feminist theology into the classrooms. She joined a consciousness raising group that met in the room of doctoral student Linda Clark during the height of consciousness-raising activity in the city that gave birth to New York Radical Women, New York Radical Feminists, and the Redstockings. Her group, like many others around the country, structured their meetings around questions mimeographed by the Redstockings. On Sunday nights, eight to twelve women would meet over wine or tea and systematically go through the mimeographed sheet. Clark said that the process broke down barriers between the women and helped them to realize they were not alone in their experiences. It is difficult for women today to understand, Clark recently pointed out, that women weren't talking to one another. "So we would read one of these questions and then we would go around the circle and people would talk."

Not surprisingly, the women at Union analyzed their experiences in seminary. "We dealt with unconscious patterns," Clark said, "we were all bringing into our academic work and our vocations—whether we were actually going to become ministers or whether we were going to become Sunday school teachers." Clark pointed out that the women realized they were breaking out of known patterns, but she added, "We were holding all that information inside ourselves because we thought . . . we were the only ones frightened by what we were doing." Those Sunday nights were a time for the members of the group to process what it meant to be women in "the male-dominated" seminary, including their anger about the sexism they were confronting. Clark described one of the topics that came up for discussion:

> There was this one woman who was applying for a job. There weren't a lot of women in the room when they were trying to make this decision and one of these men said, "Well, we can't hire this woman because she is ugly and no

man is . . . going to take her courses." Somebody who had heard about this
would come back to this group and say, "Do you realize what these people are
saying about us at these meetings?"

Along with the consciousness-raising group, Heyward had also found
strength in the field of psychotherapy. One of her earliest exchanges with Paul
Moore occurred over Heyward asking for financial help with both the cost of
school and the cost of therapy. He wrote back saying that it wasn't customary
for the diocese to help with graduate school expenses. Nor did they normally
pay for therapy. "If we did," he added, "we would be bankrupt overnight."

On December 10, 1972, Heyward wrote Moore about her preparation for
going into the Louisville Convention, including spending ten days in Philadelphia discussing strategy with Hiatt, Schlachter, Carol Anderson, and other
women who were considering ordination. Though she was forthright with him
about the angst they were experiencing, her tone with Moore was nonetheless optimistic. "I'll say this for the struggle towards women's ordination," she
wrote her bishop, "as hectic, hassling, discouraging, often infuriating, as it is,
some mighty good solid bonds are being built among people who share this
common concern." Those bonds would grow stronger and stronger until the
"sisterhood" that those who would become the Philadelphia Eleven had created
became nearly impenetrable. And not because all eleven always agreed about
strategy or theology, but because they refused to let outside forces divide them
in their purpose.

In the letter to Moore, Heyward mentioned her time together with him in
New Orleans, when she, Anderson, and Schlachter had been invited to speak
to the wives of the bishops. The occasion was the House of Bishops' annual
meeting. According to Schlachter, their talks had been highly successful for
several reasons, not the least of which was that the wives had a particular type
of access to the bishops: "The women were instrumental in pillow talk with
their husbands," Schlachter recalled. She related a story Bishop Otis Charles of
Utah told about himself and his wife Elvira in New Orleans:

> He [Charles] was trying to get out of the shower and all of the sudden these
> two arms grabbed him and held him in the bathtub and said, "You are not
> getting out until you listen to me. You men have to do something about
> responding to these women and their call. Now, get going!"

"There was," Schlachter added, "a swing in the House of Bishops after that."

Years later, Heyward would recall Anderson's talk to the bishops. Anderson was the only one of the three to have been ordained a deacon at that point, so they all agreed that she should be the one to give the talk to the House of Bishops. "The first thing she said," Heyward remembered, ". . . is that she was happy to be speaking to them and she wanted them to know that she was neither the wife, nor the daughter, nor the mistress of any of them. And I remember thinking," Heyward laughed, "Holy Shit, why did she say that? Total silence fell upon the place." Anderson later explained that she was making a reference to the numbers of prostitutes in the area around the hotel, but Heyward interpreted her words differently. "We had been told by so many people," Heyward said, ". . . my wife doesn't want to be ordained, my daughters aren't seeking ordination, what is your problem?" At that 1972 meeting in New Orleans, the bishops voted 74–61 (with 5 refraining) that women should be allowed to become priests and bishops.

For the most part, then, it seemed as if the momentum was moving in the direction of the supporters of women's ordination as the convention in Louisville approached. More and more women were being ordained as deacons. And in forty diocesan conventions that had met between the General Conventions, twenty-seven had taken affirmative action on women's ordination with the others being either divided or against. Schlachter said,

> We had thought it would have been a shoe-in in Louisville, that we just needed to talk to people about the rightness of our cause and these men would say, "Well, my goodness, sisters, yes of course, you should be ordained." And actually . . . a lot of the men were beginning to share [their power].

But "a lot" would not be enough.

Also, the supporters of women's ordination had not realized to what extent the opposition had organized, nor did they expect the opposition to be able—at the beginning of the convention—to keep the vote by orders change (as proposed three years earlier in Houston) from being ratified. In Louisville, the divided votes would continue to count as negative votes. To complicate matters, the Presiding Bishop John Hines, a supporter of women's ordination, was stepping down. As his replacement, the House of Bishops chose a conservative bishop, John Allin from Mississippi, to head the church. In an unprecedented move, the House of Deputies nearly refused approval of the nomination, meeting for hours in executive session to debate the bishops' choice. Historian Pamela Darling speculates that the response by the deputies "probably strengthened the resolve of the various conservative factions."

As the debates over who would lead the church were occurring, some of the women were struggling to find their place in the convention. As females breaking into a male vocation, they felt the strain of trying to define themselves in a largely unwelcoming culture. Some believed that they had to be feminine enough to be thought of as "real women" but assertive enough to push their cause forward. Heyward wrote that the politicking began to wear on her, making her feel plastic and mechanical: "We must smile, be friendly, dress fashionable enough to be 'ladies' and appropriately enough to be 'clergy.'" She added, "Like Miss America contestants we must be on our best behavior." Heyward felt extremely apprehensive about her role and would come to believe that it was the wrong strategy for her. "I have never been comfortable flirting, conniving, or using cunning to win dates, offices, or honors. I could not do so to win ordination."

After the tense moments surrounding the naming of a new Presiding Bishop, the House of Deputies took up the issue of women's ordination. They debated for two hours and then voted against the resolution:

LAITY (57 NEEDED TO PASS)	CLERGY (57 NEEDED TO PASS)
Yes: 49	Yes: 50
No: 37	No: 43
Divided: 26	Divided: 20

Using the divided vote, the opposition had defeated women's ordination. Furthermore, there were more votes in favor of the opposition's position in Louisville than there had been three years earlier in Houston. Angered by the decision, the chairman of the House of Deputies, John Coburn, initially allowed no one to respond. Finally, he gave the floor to Don Belcher who had worked closely with Hiatt in Pennsylvania. Belcher told Hiatt, "In God's eyes, you are already a priest."

The women were devastated and gathered in one of the apartments of the Convention Center. Ann Robb Smith remembered it as "the darkest moment of the struggle—a time of anguish and despair." And she recalled Hiatt walking around the room, giving everyone hugs and, "like a mother to her injured child," telling them that everything was "all right." Darling writes that "it was a stunning defeat, and brought about the first phase of the campaign, when everyone played by the rules of the conventional political game, to an end." With all her calm assurances, the game had changed for Hiatt, too. An older woman

approached her about the vote, saying that she now thought that the ordination of women would become a "perennial issue for General Convention" in
the same way the seating of women delegates had been from 1946–1970. It was
not a wait Hiatt was willing to endure:

> I resisted the call to ordained ministry in my own life for a long time because I
> felt I had better things to do than fight the Episcopal Church. When I owned
> my call, I tried in very ladylike and reasonable ways to convince the church
> that women could be and, indeed, were called. Finally, it became necessary to
> act on the call despite the church's desire to delay.

But the women were unable to come to an agreement about the most effective way to bring about change. Hiatt described a meeting of women seminarians and deacons held a few weeks after Louisville. It was "acrimonious and
frustrating," she recalled, with "the women blaming each other for the defeat
(e.g. if So and So had not worn a mini-skirt; if someone else had not nursed her
baby; if yet another would only cut her hair or lose weight or shut up, etc.)."
Hiatt wrote that the younger women who had not been active in strategizing
about the issue or lobbying for the cause of women's ordination were willing
to let a group of older men work it out for them. "The men of course advised
patience, charm, and letting them plan the strategy 'for you girls.'" Hiatt and
others were distraught over the turn of events:

> While the young women hung on to their every word, the women who had
> worked for the change at two conventions quietly died inside. I decided I
> would not be part of such a humiliation only to see it repeated by new women
> every three years for the foreseeable future.

"Sue Hiatt, long leader to them all, was withdrawn," historian Heather Huyck
wrote. "Her rejoinder to the other women had been, 'Don't ask me to do more.
Don't say you're sorry. Go out and organize.'" It was also a moment when a
break occurred within the Episcopal Women's Caucus, when a more radical
group no longer willing to wait for the church broke from those within the
Caucus who were more inclined to follow the rules. Schlachter referred to it as
a break between the "good girls" and the "bad girls." One of the self-described
good girls, she later came to believe that the actions of the "bad girls" had been
necessary to bring about women's ordination to the priesthood.

Hiatt and others began to look for a means of becoming ordained without the backing of the General Convention. They discussed their issue with

lawyers Henry Rightor and William Stringfellow. Rightor was also a priest and a professor at Virginia Theological Seminary, and Stringfellow a remarkable lay theologian. Both confirmed that the canons of the church did not forbid women's ordination and that where the pronoun *he* occurred in the canons, it referred to both men and women.

In November, a meeting was held in Paul Moore's New York apartment with seven men—including a handful of the bishops in favor of women's ordination (Moore, Robert Spears of New York, DeWitt, Ogilby, and William Mead of Delaware)—and Hiatt, Heyward, Hewitt, Anderson, Schlachter, Bittner, Schiess, Marie Moorefield (another of the eleven), and Julia Sibley. The meeting did not go well. The women walked out in frustration, angered that the bishops were unwilling to use their power to ordain them in their individual dioceses. Technically, the bishops did not need the approval of the General Convention to ordain. In fact, as the women pointed out, the bishops had not asked for the convention's approval to ordain either African-American or Native American men. They just began ordaining them. Of course, this point is not meant to indicate that it was an easy process for African-Americans or Native-Americans. Nor is it made with the intention of ignoring centuries of dehumanizing of both groups, of physical and emotional abuse, of land theft, of murder, of the callous separation of families, and of slave labor, nor with the intention of ignoring the tremendous influence the Episcopal Church has exercised in the United States in the maintaining of laws intended to keep white supremacy in place, laws supported by both white Episcopal men and *women*. It is, however, to say that when bishops began ordaining men from groups outside the dominant power structure, they did not insist on a change of canons that would need the approval of the General Convention. Instead, they chose to read and interpret the canons in a more inclusive way.

The meeting served as a "dramatic turning point in power relations within the church: a few strong women stopped being deferential to male authority figures." The women, Darling wrote, began following "their own consciences," and while they were low in numbers, their change in direction "proved to be one of those moments after which nothing is quite the same again."

Then in December, five of the women eligible for ordination—with the approval of Bishop Moore—decided to publicize their case during the ordination of five men at the Cathedral Church of St. John the Divine. As scripted—and with the support of the five men—the women were to participate in every part of the service, except for the laying on of hands. It was to be a staged event

in the spirit of theater that the Cathedral so lovingly embraces. And it did
begin as a type of protest theater embedded within the ordination ceremony
of the men, moving smoothly except that Marie Moorefield came down with
the flu prior to the event and was unable to participate. But before the service
was over, that which had been symbolic had taken on a life of its own, and the
women and a large part of the congregation had walked out of the service and
out of the cathedral. They were joined by the bishop's chaplain Walter Dennis,
an African-American man who laid down his crozier and followed the others.

The five men had been ordained as deacons in June along with Heyward and Schlachter, so the two women would have been on course to have
been ordained with the men if the vote in Louisville had been different. The
other three women—Emily Hewitt, Julia Sibley, and Carol Anderson—had
been ordained as deacons between eighteen months and two years earlier.
During the service, all of the deacons took the Oath of Conformity in a side
chapel. When the men took the oath, their voices were broadcast over the
loudspeaker, but the speaker was intentionally silenced when the women
took theirs. Then everyone entered the procession and moved into the nave.
The men were presented individually, the women as a group. Moore asked if
anyone knew of "any impediment or crime because of which we should not
proceed" at which point Heyward stepped to the lectern and read a prepared
statement. "If the service proceeds without us," she said, "the sacrament of
ordination will be used to perpetuate injustice. It will be an outward and visible sign of the intentional sin and division of the church." And then once
again drawing on the experience of African-Americans, Heyward added,
"The sacrament will be debased just as much as it would be if black people
were excluded." (This comparison often put forward by the supporters of
women's ordination would come to anger some African-Americans in the
church and was one that many supporters, including Heyward, would later
significantly qualify.) When the time came to ordain by the laying on the
hands, the women didn't move. This is the point at which the script fell apart
or the moment when the actors stepped out of character and became themselves. They remained in place, on their knees, waiting for Moore to give
them a blessing, to lay his hands on their head, to ordain them. But he did
not. He told them to go in peace.

For Emily Hewitt, the moment marked a turning point in her life. She
believed that if Paul Moore in New York, a liberal bishop in a liberal diocese,
would refuse to ordain them, that they had little hope anywhere else. When she

walked out of the cathedral, she crossed the street and felt tears rolling down her face.

Traces of the event are still evident today in the Cathedral. A bas-relief cast in bronze and created by Dykstra Karns has been placed in one of the aisles. It shows the five women kneeling before Moore, whose hands are tied behind his back. A dove representing the Holy Spirit flies above the scene.

The following month, in January, the Archbishop of Canterbury made a trip to the United States and attended a service held in Riverside Church in Manhattan. Built by John Rockefeller, the imposing Riverside sits just behind Union Theological Seminary. Schlachter and Heyward were assisting at the service, but were also using the high profile event as a moment of protest. Both women were wearing red armbands. When Heyward gave wine to a young priest kneeling before her, he dug his nails into her hand, drawing blood and telling her, "I hope you burn in hell." Heyward was shaken by the event. It wasn't until her parents insisted that she get rabies shots that she was able to laugh about it.

In the meantime, the Bishop of Delaware, William Mead, who was becoming increasingly frustrated by the way the church was dragging its feet over the matter, told Hiatt that he would be willing to ordain her in Delaware. Hiatt began making plans to transfer to his diocese and to become the first woman ordained to their priesthood in the Episcopal Church in the United States. But it was not to be. In February, Mead died suddenly of a heart attack.

By June, three events happened within ten days of one another that gave Hiatt a means for pushing more strongly for the ordinations. The first occurred at the Commencement ceremonies at Episcopal Divinity School when the dean, Harvey Guthrie, announced he would resign if the trustees could not come up with money to hire an ordained female faculty member. The next event was a sermon preached by Dr. Charles Willie, the vice-president of the House of Deputies and one of the trustees at EDS. Willie, an African-American and grandson of a slave, was a noted professor in Sociology at Syracuse and on his way to teach at Harvard in the fall. On June 9, 1974, he stood at St. Mark's Episcopal Church in Syracuse, New York, and told the congregation that it was time for a courageous bishop to step up and ordain women. "Jesus taught us," he said "that unjust laws should be disobeyed when they conflict with the will of the Lord." Willie was preaching that day not only about the church's unjust treatment of women, but about its unjust treatment of minorities and its youth as well. He warned that any bishop who dared to follow the path of ordaining women would be "vilified and talked about" and that it would take both courage and humility on his part. "The church is in need of such a bishop today," he said.

A week later, the Very Reverend Ed Harris, dean of Philadelphia Divinity School, delivered a sermon at the ordination of five deacons, two women and three men. He called for the immediate ordination of women, proclaiming that "in Jesus Christ God has delivered us from all forms of domination and privileged access to power." And there in the congregation, sitting one row behind Bob DeWitt and listening closely to the words of Harris, was Sue Hiatt. When everyone stood to recite the creed, Hiatt leaned over to DeWitt and said, "Do you feel the swish of a gauntlet across your face?" After the service, Hiatt confronted DeWitt, Washington, and Harris about moving forward on the ordination of women. "She spoke quietly," Washington recalled, "but her words were like thunder." Hiatt, DeWitt, and Harris met the following day to organize a meeting that would pull together deacons, bishops, clergy, and interested lay people in order to plan an ordination service for the women. The meeting was scheduled for July 10, 1974, and it was there that the plans to undermine the church order were drawn out. The record of the event, today stored away in the archives of Union's Burke Library, was written in a sixty-nine cents Mead composition book covered with bright birds and daisies.

But there were other women, eight others who made up the eleven, who had to reach this point in relation to their own calls to the priesthood. Let's turn to their stories, beginning with the one who had flown with abandon into space on a trip that could have been the plot of a Jules Verne novel except, as the old saying goes, the truth really is stranger than fiction.

Chapter 3

THE DEACON'S TALE, PART II

Her granddaughter Kathryn said Jeannette had suffered from post-traumatic stress syndrome. Not as a result of piloting a six-hundred thousand cubic foot balloon filled with hydrogen nearly eleven miles into the stratosphere (higher than any woman had ever before traveled) while sitting in a gondola an eighth of an inch thick. Not as a result of unexpected cloudy weather during the flight, a scenario no one entering the stratosphere had ever encountered and "lived to tell the tale." Nor was the trauma the result of looking through the gondola's window as it rose through the clouds and seeing the balloon "swaying violently" in gale-like winds, nor from dropping too quickly through clouds after eight hours of flight, knowing neither her elevation nor speed, and landing roughly in a stand of trees on a farm near a small town in Ohio. In fact, after the landing, the mood of Jeannette Piccard seemed upbeat and gracious. When informed she had landed in Ohio, with the remnants of her balloon scattered through the trees, the American flag swinging from one of them, she joked with reporters and bystanders, "What a mess, I wanted to land on the White House lawn." She compared being in the balloon to being in "a magnificent cathedral," a place where you could "almost feel like part of eternity."

No, it wasn't the flight that had traumatized Jeannette Piccard. Kathryn believed that the effects of trauma had begun years before, when her grandmother was a child growing up in Chicago. Her family was an influential one, her father a noted orthopedic surgeon. Piccard had an identical twin sister named Beatrice. At the age of three, the two of them were playing outside, trying to light a cast-iron toy stove belonging to their eleven-year-old sister, who the day before had cooked baked potatoes for everyone. Jeannette and Beatrice (or Jane and Betty, as they were called) had decided that they, like their older sister, wanted to cook potatoes. They found a box of matches. With company in the house and the adults distracted, the two girls slipped away and began trying to light the stove. Beatrice's white starched dress caught fire and she ran.

As Jeannette watched Beatrice trying to escape the flames, she remembered thinking that her sister "wouldn't be able to live." Three days later, Beatrice died from her burns. "They had been very close, as twins—especially identical twins—often are," Kathryn said. In the last few years of her life, Jeannette told Kathryn that whenever she heard the siren of a fire truck or ambulance, the sound transported her back to that moment. Jeannette's mother kept the ashes of Beatrice on the mantelpiece, along with the ashes of two other sisters who had died in childhood. It was difficult on the family, Kathryn believed, even if the practice was not uncommon in its time.

Piccard's own mothering skills were brought into question when she announced that she would pilot her husband Jean by balloon into the stratosphere. The Piccards had approached the National Geographic Society for funding, but had been told the flight was too risky for a woman with three children. Though patriarchal in its decision making, the society was correct about the level of risk involved in such a flight. In the handful of stratosphere flights that had occurred in the United States up to that point, the first—in 1927—had ended when the pilot was forced to bail out with his parachute because his balloon was descending too quickly. Later that year, he attempted another flight, but when the balloon landed, he was found dead in the gondola. During the third attempted flight to the stratosphere, pilot Thomas Settle was forced to abort after twenty minutes, though a few months later he successfully set an altitude record for stratosphere flight. The fifth flight, which occurred in July of 1934, only a few months before the Piccard's October flight, was piloted by officers in the U.S. Army. It nearly ended in disaster when the balloon tore in midair and one of the pilots became stuck in the escape hatch while attempting to jump from the balloon in his parachute. Just moments after all three had all cleared the gondola, the remains of the disintegrating balloon exploded over the fields of Nebraska.

The risks weren't confined to the United States. Three Soviet men had been killed when their gondola had separated from the balloon and they had fallen to their death. Piccard grasped the level of danger and the potential for disaster confronting her, joking in gallows humor: "If there's some accident, don't bother developing the film," she said, adding, "the chemicals from our decomposing bodies will be enough."

Two of the Piccard boys (age eight and ten) were at the grounds of the Ford airport in the early morning hours of the day of the flight. Jeannette had hoped the flight would have been held in the summer when the boys were at camp, but delays moved it into the fall. Without the benefit of having the camp as a

distraction for the children, Piccard told her sons that the trip into the stratosphere would be no more dangerous than crossing the street. An old newsreel
of the event captures the four Piccards standing outside the gondola, Jeannette
smiling and patting her oldest son on the shoulders. The family turtle Fleur de
Lys had also been put into the gondola. Three hundred men were there to serve
as volunteers. Reports put the size of the crowd at forty-five thousand.

Waving to the crowd, Jeannette and Jean stepped into the round black and
white gondola that resembled a giant fishing bob. For the first time in the history of ballooning, TNT was used to disconnect the lines that held the balloon
to the ground, an innovation that made many nervous, given the presence of
seven hundred cylinders of explosive hydrogen. That morning, the charges did
not detonate simultaneously and the balloon began to "drift down and swing
on the one remaining ground line." The newsreel shows a group of men running towards the base of the gondola in an effort to push it upwards. Jeannette
released ballast to allow the balloon to rise above a line of cars and trees. The
camera cut to the two boys, the older one draping his arm over the younger's
shoulders. Both were waving. As the balloon moved higher, one of the boys
broke away and ran towards it, still waving. Piccard later said that she could
hear him yelling, "Goodbye, Mother."

Before they had risen to an altitude that required a closed and pressurized
cabin, Jeannette realized that a valve rope was out of position. She put on her
parachute and stood on a shelf at the door in order to reach the rope, expos-
ing her body from the knees up to the outside. Bits of lead ballast had spilled
on the shelf, creating the effect of standing on tiny ball bearings. She lost her
footing and slipped, though was able to regain her balance. She climbed back
in and closed the hatch. After the flight was over, the Piccards realized that at
the point she lost her balance, the two were probably over Lake Erie, where her
parachute would have been virtually useless.

The Piccards confronted a host of issues, including the heavy winds that
had created the problem with the rope. The landing was not without hazards.
Initially, Jeannette had difficulty lowering the balloon, but as they had antic-
ipated, once it reentered the fog bank it began descending much too quickly.
They attached a parachute to a heavy battery and threw it overboard, hoping to
slow down the descent. The effort was unsuccessful, so Jeannette released the
remaining ballast. When the Piccards broke through the clouds, they realized
to their dismay that they were heading directly towards a house. Jeannette was
able to maneuver around it, but decided to risk landing in an area filled with

trees. When the balloon hit, the two looked at each other trying to figure out how—"like Tarzan and his mate"—to make their way out of the tree branches. Suddenly, they heard a popping sound, the gondola broke away, Jean yelled "bend your knees," and they dropped the remaining fifteen or twenty feet to the ground. They were just outside Cadiz, Ohio.

The National Air and Space Museum holds a photograph in its collection that shows Jeannette standing partly out of the hatch, her head resting in her hands while she talks to a group of reporters, one laughing, some wearing overcoats and fedoras, and still others taking notes on her account of the flight. According to various news reports, she was either seen powdering her nose, eating a sandwich, smoking a cigarette, checking on the condition of Fleur de Lys, surveying the damage, or cracking jokes about the White House. Jean had a few small fractures in his ribs and ankles and had covered himself with a blanket, taking a moment to rest.

In her last post-flight entry, Piccard wrote, "Everything is over, everything that is, except the gathering of our equipment and the fragments of our once beautiful balloon." Of course, everything was not over. She was only in her late thirties and still had much more work to do, including realizing a vocational dream she had held on to since the age of eleven when she had felt a calling to be an Episcopal priest. In 1916, as a student at Bryn Mawr College, she wrote a paper in which she argued the point that women were "mentally, morally, and physically" fit for the priesthood and should be admitted as priests to the Anglican Church. When she first arrived at the college, M. Carey Thomas, the school's president expressed to Piccard her belief that the Episcopal Church might change its policy before Piccard's graduation from the college. And while the president was encouraging of Piccard's desire to become ordained, guest priest Father F.C. Powell—who spoke at the college and later became a friend and spiritual confident of Piccard's—discouraged her from the pursuit. In later years, after Piccard had become a mother, he advised her to redirect her spiritual desires, arguing that as a mother of three boys she had been given the opportunity to prepare one of them for the priesthood. Piccard later came to the realization that the call to the priesthood belonged to her, not to her sons.

In 1932, Piccard received an offer from Bishop Philip Cook of Delaware to guide her through the course of study required to become an Episcopal priest. Piccard was ecstatic, at least until Jean made known his dream of pursuing a trip to the stratosphere. Piccard wrote that she wept at the news, knowing that her call would once again be postponed for the sake of family responsibilities.

But in the late 1940s, the rector of her church in Minneapolis, the Reverend Daniel Corrigan, began to encourage her to take a more active leadership role within the church. Corrigan would later become a bishop and, in his retirement, be one of the ordaining bishops in Philadelphia. When Corrigan left Minneapolis, Piccard slowly began to transfer her church home to St. Philip's where the African-American rector, the Reverend Denzil Carty, had been drawing comparisons between the African-American struggle for Civil Rights, the oppression of Jews, the discrimination of southern European immigrants, and the church's view of women. Historian Sheryl K. Hill notes that Piccard had become "emboldened" by Carty's position and that she began "to challenge Episcopal Church canons and traditions." The extent to which she would be willing to increase the stakes of that challenge would become evident at the Philadelphia ordinations. She would begin making contacts: corresponding with Hiatt and becoming friends with the twenty-seven-year-old Alla Bozarth.

Bozarth was originally from the West Coast, raised in Oregon, but met Piccard during their struggles in Minnesota as deacons of the church. Bozarth's father had been a radio personality in Hollywood, a poet with a show called "Of Words and Verse," who, because of his work in radio, often met with prominent figures (including Eleanor Roosevelt), occasionally even inviting them into the family home. When she was three, her father left his radio career and began his studies towards becoming an Episcopal priest. "I consider it a capital injustice," Bozarth wrote in her memoir *Womanpriest*, "that the first three years of my life, which I don't remember, were among the most glamorous." Still, Bozarth absorbed her parents' love of writing, art, theater, and dance, and like her father, began publishing poetry in her early adult years.

Bozarth and fellow ordinand Carter Heyward both wrote memoirs within a few years after the ordinations in Philadelphia, even though Bozarth was the youngest of the eleven and Heyward herself was only twenty-eight at the time of the ordinations. The titles of both books—*Womanpriest: A Personal Odyssey* and *A Priest Forever*—point to an overriding emphasis by the two writers that they were born to be priests, had been preparing for the calling for their whole lives, and would die priests whether or not the Episcopal Church gave them its stamp of approval. Heyward writes about being a five-year-old in North Carolina and playing with her imaginary playmate Sophie Couch. Sophie told Carter that she wanted to be a priest and informed her, in fact, that they were both already priests. In *Womanpriest*, Bozarth explains that she was one of a long unbroken line of clergy on her father's side, had been the "mascot" as a child at her father's seminary, had assisted her father with parish calls, and that by the age of fifteen, had begun her own early efforts at ministry through her father's vocation. By that point, she had also made a commitment to becoming a nun:

> By the time I was fourteen I had decided that I wanted to give my life completely to God, and the only way I knew to do this was by becoming a nun. Given my intense nature, once I'd made the decision, I wanted to act on it immediately. My poor parents—they had a fourteen-year-old daughter who wanted to be a nun, and not only did she want all this, but she wanted it *now*, without further delay. My mother thought I was just going through some phase of religious mania, and my father just thought I was enduring an outrageously romantic attack of adolescence.

Her pleasure reading during these years—the sixteenth century's Teresa of Avila and John of the Cross—was hardly standard fare for a 1950s American teenager. Even her teacher at the Catholic high school, Sister Rosaire, "an intensely contemplative person, a spiritual comrade of Thomas Merton," was taken aback by an answer Bozarth had given in class. Sister Rosaire had asked the students to name a great piece of literature they had read, and as Bozarth writes, "I popped up with *The Summa Theologica* of St. Thomas Aquinas." Sister Rosaire, Bozarth recalled, "teased me forever."

Bozarth's mother was born into the Russian aristocracy just before the revolutions of 1917. Her grandmother was able to take one child and escape through Poland into Canada while placing her daughter (Bozarth's mother) and a son safely in Moscow. The young Alla was raised hearing stories of her mother's escapes in hay-drawn wagons and hidden behind crates on trains, with soldiers rifling their bayonets within an inch of her throat. At the age of fourteen, her mother applied gray in her hair to look old enough to attend design school, received her certificate, acquired a worker's visa, and with her younger brother, left Russia in a ship for Canada to rejoin her family. On the ship, she nearly died from an appendicitis attack. She moved to the United States to work in the theater, met a Russian prince in the Morningside community of New York City, and married him. Because of his "delicate constitution," the two moved to California. He died in 1945 and her mother went into a deep period of mourning before meeting Bozarth's father. The young poet and radio announcer fell in love with the Russian princess, "whose grief as a young widow added to her exotic mystique." As Bozarth writes, she was "conceived on Mariposa ('Butterfly') Street across from the Biltmore Hotel in Los Angeles" and was born on Ascension Day in May of 1947. Ascension Day. The day alone would have made the friendship between Bozarth and Piccard irresistible.

Bozarth's birth was not an easy one. She suffered a cerebral hemorrhage during the ordeal, dislocating her left eye from its socket which led to six separate surgeries over the course of her childhood. She recalled the intense nausea and the vulnerability she felt with both eyes bandaged during the weeks after the surgeries. She remembered being in a crib—around the age of two—in a teaching hospital after one of the surgeries:

> I remember the doctor coming in with a bunch of students . . . and taking the bandages off to show the students and I could see them. I couldn't much open my surgical eye, but I could see them with my healthy eye, that uninjured eye. And they all had white caps and white masks and were standing over me. You can imagine, you're very small and you're looking up and encircling you are these specters, with their faces covered and their heads covered, except for their eyes. That was a traumatic moment for me.

From the age of fourteen, she was also plagued by debilitating migraines and what was quickly becoming a severe case of fibromyalgia.

Bozarth loved her parents and knew that they loved her, but the couple struggled in their marriage, having both suffered tremendously during parts of their childhoods. Though she felt loved, she also felt, at times, like the designated adult in the family. Still, both parents had performed meaningful work within and beyond the boundaries of the church, her mother resettling over two thousand refugee families and her father working to secure plumbing, electricity, and other necessities for migrant families. "They were like rockets—they just burned themselves up in their lifetimes," Bozarth said. "They accomplished so much, did so much good, and were such larger-than-life personalities for good and ill, both of them." She was twenty-five when her mother died and in her thirties when both her father and her husband, Phil Bozarth-Campbell, died.

Bozarth met Campbell in seminary in the fall of 1970. She had begun her studies in 1968, initially planning to work towards her bachelor's degree at Northwestern while concurrently completing a master's degree at Seabury-Western Theological Seminary. She had been accepted to both and was prepared to begin the process when the dean at the seminary asked to meet with her. At the meeting, he told her that "he had no intention of allowing any more women into the seminary at that point . . . and that he didn't think any woman had 'brains enough' to earn two degrees at once." Bozarth decided to study privately for ordination while she also doubled up on her degree at Northwestern, effectively rolling five years of education into sixteen months. When she stood for exams, she was tested in the same manner as the men, passing her "ordeal by fire," as the examiner had called it. But that year at the Houston Convention the canon law on women changed and the chancellor of her diocese in Oregon urged the bishop to require her to begin the entire process again. She submitted, but "did not submit well," her relationship with the bishop damaged by what she believed to be "unreasonable and unfair" requirements.

Bozarth married Campbell the year after they had met, but the couple found themselves almost immediately working through the strain created by the sexism implicit in his being allowed ordination to the priesthood while she was rejected. In fact, the institution of marriage itself was for Bozarth a shock to her sense of self-identity. "If the Episcopal Church had opened my eyes to sexism," she wrote, "society's stereotype of marriage became the college text for the subject." She and Phil both decided to change their last names to Bozarth-Campbell, but, still, the expression of sexism that created the most strain on the marriage was contained in the church's policy on ordination. It was an issue that the couple encountered on a daily basis on campus. Furthermore, on occasions when priests asked Alla to help with the service in the campus chapel, the dean would make a conscious choice to move away from the section of the altar where she was serving. And in the case of her bishop, she felt that he had supported her privately, but had publicly worked against her ordination.

She attempted to deny her calling, but compared it to "burying the truth in [her] bones," and, in the end, found the attempt unsuccessful: "The calling would not go away. Though I tried to leave it, the call never left me." By this point, Bozarth had been waiting for over two years to be ordained, spending the time working towards a doctorate in speech at Northwestern. Phil had been a deacon for only six months. But the votes in Louisville against ordination had not only destroyed their plans of being ordained together, they had also brought the tension within their marriage to a point of crisis:

> Phil needed the affirmation of ordination as much as I did. I couldn't ask him
> to suppress his own vocation until the Church could accommodate mine. Yet,
> emotionally, the thought of his being ordained a priest without me was more

than I could bear. I tried desperately not to make him feel guilty about a situation that held us both in a vise, but confusion and grief muddied my intentions. Our marriage underwent a dance of death.

With the help of a therapist and a compassionate priest, they were able to work through their disappointments. Then a call provided a vocational opening for Bozarth. Katrina Swanson, another of the eleven, phoned to see if Alla wished to participate in the coming ordinations in Philadelphia.

Swanson was living in West Missouri with her husband George, an Episcopal priest, and their two children, William and Olof. Besides being married to a priest, Swanson's father and great-grandfather were bishops and her grandfather was a priest. Her father, Edward Randolph Welles II, had recently retired as Bishop of West Missouri and was writing a memoir for family and friends. He began with a story about his father and mother and one of the few times he had ever seen his mother cry. It was a September day in 1910, and someone had come to the house to warn the family that a group of men were planning to tar and feather Welles' father and then run him out of Chickasha, Oklahoma, on a rail. His crime: an hour earlier he had given Holy Communion in his church to an African-American man. The family escaped, quickly taking a train to a small town up the line.

Katrina Swanson's great-grandfather had served as the Bishop of Wisconsin. He built a cathedral in Milwaukee and wore a tall mitre, actions that drew criticism from the more Protestant-influenced branch of the Church that he was acting much too Catholic. In fact, debates about the nature of the Episcopal Church, about its Protestant (low church) and Catholic (high church) roots, were creating intense divisions within the denomination in the nineteenth century. The debates became so rancorous that a legend developed in the Milwaukee area concerning them: a fight broke out in a saloon in the city; in order to stop what was developing into a riot, the saloon owner jumped on a table and yelled, "Gentlemen, gentlemen, remember this is *not* an Episcopal convention."

Swanson came from a family with that "bigger-than-life" quality that Bozarth said described her own parents. It was the type of energy that prompted Bishop Ned Cole to say they should be called "Wells Fargo." *The Episcopalian* borrowed the comparison but added to it, describing the family as *the Welles Fargo Express.* It was a type of energy that made Swanson's father a natural runner, a track and field star at Princeton. "I must have had a remarkable sprint," Welles said, "because I won so many races in the final few yards. . . ." Even reading the correspondence generated by Welles and Swanson can be an exhausting undertaking. They eliminate most of the margin space (often scribbling side notes in what little margin remains) while recycling old school worksheets and leftover stationery. On one side of the page, you find Swanson discussing how to organize for the ordination of women and on the other side a graded mimeographed worksheet from one of her son's assignments in elementary school.

Colorful was one word that had been used to describe the Welles family. *Controversial* was another. Then there was *vigorous* . . . and *lively*. Maybe the descriptors were referring to the New England sea captain in the family, born on the Fourth of July—the original one in 1776. He returned from sea to find a new altar rail installed in the church, one with a row of crosses lodged between the supports. A supporter of the more Protestant branch of the church, he took his cane and knocked out every one of the crosses, complaining that they were "too Romish." It should be no surprise that one of the matriarchs of the family was a friend to Carrie Nation, the nineteenth century temperance leader who with her hatchet destroyed saloon after saloon with her comrades, voicing the command, "Smash, ladies, smash."

Swanson had not always been in support of the ordination of women to the priesthood. To a large extent her opinion was changed by a stay in Botswana and a relationship with Mrs. Lekgaba who ran a fleet of British lorries that transported both people and goods around the outskirts of the Kalahari Desert. Lekgaba had been raised in the Anglican tradition, had a father and a brother who served as priests in Rhodesia, and while she basically managed the church she attended, she was forced to hire men to preside at the services, men Swanson described as "abusive" and "alcoholic."

Even if Swanson had to be brought on board concerning women's leadership roles within the Episcopal Church, there were signs early on that her sympathies would lead in that direction. On her seventh birthday, January 1, 1942, not quite a month after the Pearl Harbor attack, Swanson had the unusual opportunity of meeting and shaking hands with Franklin Roosevelt and Winston Churchill. Learning that Churchill was in Washington, Welles had sent an invitation to the Prime Minster and to Roosevelt, asking them to attend a service at Christ Church in Alexandria, the parish Welles was serving. After the service, at the moment of the handshake, Welles recalled that Katrina had "stole[n] the show." Photographers began shooting and captured the moment of the handshake, Katrina holding out her hand to Roosevelt with Churchill and the other dignitaries smiling down. Behind Churchill in the photograph, barely visible, stands Eleanor Roosevelt. The headline read, "Little Girl Meets Roosevelt and Churchill," but what Katrina told others, what she remembered most vividly, was that she had met *Mrs.* Roosevelt on her birthday. There was one concern for the Welles' family in relation to all the handshaking going on at the service. Four hours later, Katrina came down with a case of chicken pox. "We worried," Welles wrote, "lest the war leaders' efforts would be impeded by their coming down also with the chicken pox!"

After Swanson returned home from Botswana, she called her father and asked for an appointment to see him. He told her that she didn't need an appointment, though she argued that given what she was about to tell him she believed she did. She wanted to be ordained, and she wanted to tell him personally. She informed her father that even as a child she had wanted to be a priest, but believed it would be impossible, that only boys could achieve that goal. Welles was supportive and the two of them worked out a plan for her studies. In his memoir, Welles carefully lays out the course of study his daughter underwent, by whom she was supervised, and the tests that she had passed in order to be considered eligible for the priesthood. The question of the Radcliffe graduate's qualifications would come up both publically and privately in the years surrounding the ordinations.

While Swanson had been assigned to call Bozarth to ask if she would be willing to be irregularly ordained, Betty Bone Schiess was on Hewitt's list of those to call. In fact, Hewitt recalled that her phone bills were expensive during that period of organizing, sometimes running to three hundred dollars a month. Nearly thirty years after the ordinations, in 2003, Schiess published her own memoir, one quite different in tone and message from Bozarth's and Heyward's books. At the time of her writing, Schiess was entering her eighties and had for all practical purposes left the church. Where Heyward and Bozarth's earlier memoirs had emphasized the many ways they had been born to be priests, Schiess admitted to having had no such grand goals. In fact, she spends the first few chapters showing how unlikely it was that she would end up in the priesthood. She did not attend church as a child, never once pretended to be a priest, was not the least bit concerned about whether she was not allowed to be an acolyte. She worried more about her dance recitals and the fact that Peter Rabbit was played by the headmistress' son while she was stuck in the role of a pea—no doubt a valid complaint, but not one concerning the Church. She thought little about God. She noted that the religious education she had received in high school had not affected her, and she admitted that when she served as chaplain for her Tri Delta sorority, she read the same devotion again and again. "So far as I could tell," she wrote, "this did not affect the sisters very much."

Living in Syracuse, Schiess became involved in the church because she was seeking a community to help with raising her children. "There is too much cheerful trivialization of parenthood," she wrote, and "too little is understood about the enormous responsibility of parenthood." She thought the Church's teachings seemed harmless enough, the Nicene Creed so beyond understanding that it would not affect their daily lives, the Book of Common Prayer arcane, though full of interesting language like "it is meet and right so to do." She liked the church's belief that "under God we are all equal" and wanted that message taught to her children. That is how her involvement in the Episcopal Church began. Her husband Bill was elected to the vestry, a position not then open to women. Schiess became involved with various fund-raising projects organized by the women of the church: bake sales, rummage sales, and prize-winning contests. Sometimes, she remembered, the money was willingly handed over, sometimes less so; often they could not determine where their money actually went. Her husband reported that the members of the vestry discussed ways they could "get the money out of the women."

In the meantime, the couple became actively involved in the Civil Rights Movement. When the desegregated Grace Episcopal Church in Syracuse received a bomb threat, Schiess and her family moved their membership to the church in a show of support. Schiess and several other women wanted to travel with the men from the church to the Selma-to-Montgomery March in 1965, but were told by one of the organizing priests that no one really cared what women did or had to say. "Some people gasp when I tell this story," she wrote, "but the observation was absolutely correct." She did go to Jackson, Mississippi, for the Meredith March against Fear, but when an African-American man approached her and told her to go home, she came to the conclusion that as "a middle-class white woman from the North" she was about "as much use to some southern blacks as to the Episcopal Church."

She was beginning to draw connections between the Civil Rights Movement, the war in Vietnam, and the rights of women. Later, reflecting on these years, she wrote that motherhood as defined by the culture actually concealed the most important work she could have done as a mother:

> There are not enough cookies in the world to undo war. . . . Nothing, absolutely nothing, motivated me more to become a feminist than this awakening to the fact that to play a traditional mother role was to abandon motherhood.

And then in 1968, Betty Friedan spoke in Syracuse. Soon afterwards, a chapter of the National Organization for Women was convened there, and Schiess became closely involved with its work, including recommending to the members of the chapter that they oppose a new practice in the Episcopal Church that would allow lay*men* (or male church members) to administer the chalice, but not laywomen. NOW went to work on the matter and was successful in taking its position to the national level within the church. For Schiess, the success was a turning point for her, one that moved her towards seeking ordination to the priesthood. "My thinking went like this," she wrote,

> If I were absolutely unsuccessful in making it possible for women to be ordained, then it would be clear that the church collaborated in the diminishment of women. We could leave in good conscience. . . . If we were successful, it would cleanse the Episcopal Church of one last remnant of institutionalized misogyny. As for a personal "call," this effort to relieve the Episcopal Church of its misogyny was, is, my call.

And so Betty Bone Schiess entered Colgate-Rochester Divinity School in 1968. She would study to become an Episcopal priest.

The year after Schiess entered Colgate-Rochester, she was followed by Merrill Bittner. Bittner had been raised in South Pasadena, California. Her parents were not church-going people, but thought their children should have a church home. They were planning to take them to the nearby Congregational Church, but happened to drive across town one Sunday to attend St. James Episcopal Church. The four-year-old Bittner loved it, so much in fact that when the family later returned to the Congregational Church, Bittner began screaming that she wanted to go back to St. James. For Bittner, the story served as confirmation in her adult years that she had been intimately bound to the Episcopal Church since her early days. St. James was a type of home for her, a "home away from home." She added quietly, "As much a family for me as my family."

Still, growing up in South Pasadena had its rewards. The coast was an hour away, the mountains off in the distance. She learned to play a mean game of tennis. Her backyard was filled with trees, a working and beautiful laboratory for a young girl who had fallen in love with biology. She decided she would become a teacher of the study of life. Later, she traveled to Ohio, to attend school at Lake Erie College, where she earned a degree in Biology. Like Emily Hewitt, she suffered a major loss in college when her mother died of cancer during her first year.

After graduation, Bittner found herself choosing between two directions of further study: the University of California at Santa Barbara to do graduate work in Marine Ecology or Bexley Hall Seminary, which had only recently merged with Colgate-Rochester. She had developed an interest in theology as a result of her studies in biology, though with an added twist. She had loved biology because it was a study of life, but in theology she had found a discipline that honored the "celebration of life."

Bittner had not entered seminary with the idea of being ordained, but was deeply moved by the Houston General Convention in 1970. She watched Phyllis Edwards at the Convention, the first woman ordained as a deacon in 1965. At that point in the history of the Episcopal Church, men were called deacons; females, deaconesses. The women were given a different course of study and their title certainly did not serve as a bridge to the priesthood. Unlike the later case of the Philadelphia Eleven and their bishops, Edwards and her ordaining bishop, James Pike, faced the wrath of the Church alone. Pike was suddenly confronted with charges of heresy for his views on the Virgin Birth, along with his position on other doctrinal matters. When Bittner saw Edwards sitting in a circle at the Convention, she believed she was looking at, if not a broken woman, certainly one whom she would describe as "hurt." Observing Edwards' demeanor moved Bittner to speak at the Convention. In her talk, she found herself affirming her belief that the Church needed women ordained to the priesthood. She spoke up, she later said, for women like Phyllis.

After the Convention, Bittner changed her vocational goals, deciding to become ordained as a deacon. Her news did not receive a warm welcome in her home church of St. James. One clergyman was "non-supportive," another adamantly opposed, and the members of the congregation, those who had comprised her home away from home, were not forthcoming in support either. Even her father opposed her decision, though he later had a change of heart and asked her to preside at his second marriage. But in these early years of her attempt to follow her calling, her mother died, her father was in opposition, and she had lost the support of her church family.

After seminary, Bittner was hired part-time by the Church of the Good Shepherd in Webster, New York, and part-time by the Rochester Women's Jail Project, a project she co-founded with DeCourcey Squire, one of eight people who had recently been tried and found guilty in the Flower City Conspiracy. The eight had been accused of ransacking offices in the Federal Building in Rochester. Seven of the eight served twelve to eighteen month sentences, though their convictions were overturned on appeal after the sentences were served. In 1973, during an interview for the *Courier-Journal* about her work in the jail system, Bittner told the reporter, "You can't talk to a hungry person about God until you give him a piece of bread." Bittner had worked out the dual position in Webster with the help of her bishop in Rochester, Robert Spears, who had written to her in July of 1972, affirming what he believed to be her call to the priesthood. He also expressed his admiration of her:

> You continue to reflect what seem to me essential attributes of a person who proposes to exercise ordained ministry—sensitivity, humility, enthusiasm, strength of purpose. I rejoice!

Spears was one of the most liberal bishops in the Episcopal Church and at this point before the convention in Louisville, Bittner's chances of being ordained by him seemed promising.

At the end of the decade of the 1960s, when Bittner and Schiess were beginning their seminary training at Colgate-Rochester, Alison Cheek was completing her studies at Virginia Theological Seminary in Washington, D.C. Cheek had begun her training in 1963, the first year VTS had opened its doors to female students. There were only two women and Cheek recalled that they were treated with "fear and suspicion." She had four children at the time, ranging in ages from five to thirteen, and was allowed to complete her degree over a six year period. When asked on her seminary application what books she had recently read, she listed the sort of works expected to be on the bookshelves of incoming seminary students, like those by Albert Schweitzer, whom she had studied fervently. But she also listed *Mike Mulligan and His Steam Shovel*, the 1939 children's book by Virginia Lee Burton that she had read to her own children.

Cheek grew up Alison Western in what she called an idyllic environment, on the southern coast of Australia, near the city of Adelaide in the small, contained rural community the inhabitants referred to as "The Marion," home to a post office and a general store. Her family owned an eighty-four acre orchard and vineyard and grew peaches, plums, nectarines, apricots, and table grapes. Cheek would walk the orchard with her father, learning how to prune, to plow, to irrigate, and to distinguish between types of buds. She learned not to spit chewed licorice root on the ground because it could root and spread. She learned about seasonal changes, absorbing a belief that would come to serve her well in the coming years: after winter would come the spring. When she visited her grandparents, she walked the coastline with her adoring grandfather, a shy but scholarly man who recited poetry to her and introduced her to Zeus and Athena and to folk tales from Germany. They identified sea shells together.

She was a precocious child. Once, when a minister was invited to a family meal, Alison was asked by her father to say the blessing. She happily did so, reciting:

> Eat away, chew away,
> Munch and bolt and guzzle,
> Never leave the table 'til
> You're full up to the muzzle.

The verse was from the children's book *The Magic Pudding* by Norman Lindsay. Not impressed by their youngest child's nimble use of literary allusion, they turned to her older brother Malcolm for a second effort at a blessing of the meal.

As with so many others, life changed for her and the family with the coming of World War II. Malcolm left for Europe to serve in the Australian Air Force. On his twentieth birthday—she was seventeen—the family threw him a party in his absence. Cheek wrote him a lighthearted letter about the occasion, playfully formal. "On the day, the 16 December, 1943," she began, "a party has been held at 'Oakleigh', Marion, in honour of one, Flight-Sergeant Malcolm Western who is 20 years old to-day." She described the dining hall that "was decorated with long red and green festoons and silver bells," his photo draped in the bells hung "tastefully from his cap." They sang "Happy Birthday," followed by a "lustily" rendered version of "For He Is a Jolly Good Fellow" that "lifted off the dining room roof." His father delivered a toast and then "Miss Alison Western rose and delivered a touching speech which completely broke the audience who dabbed their eyes with crepe serviettes. . . ." She mailed off the letter, but he never received it. It was sent back to her with a package of letters. Her brother had been shot down over Berlin that night. His body was never found, though his watch was recovered in a German shop and sent to his parents. His mother never recovered from the shock of her son's death. "She thought the Christian thing was to be brave," Cheek said, and consequently, "never had anyone to confide in about it." Her father, she continued, "had the good sense to have a breakdown over it." Cheek read to him throughout the period of his depression, attempting to raise his spirits, feeling that the roles of parent and child were being reversed. When he recovered, he became active in the youth work of the local church, offering to other young men the help he might have otherwise given to his son.

Cheek was a student at the University of Adelaide during the war, where she met and later married her economics tutor Bruce Cheek, who had a dream and a career goal of reducing worldwide poverty. The two moved back and forth between Australia and the United States while he pursued his work at Harvard and at the Australian National University, eventually settling in the Washington, D.C., area where he accepted an appointment for a position at the World Bank. During this time, Cheek began seminary, completing advanced studies in the field of pastoral counseling. Between 1969 and 1973, she held several positions, including Lay Assistant Minister at Christ Church (where Welles had invited the Roosevelts and Churchill). In 1973, she opened a private practice in psychotherapy. But in the summer of 1974, she received a phone call from deacon Nancy Wittig (who had also attended Virginia Theological Seminary) concerning the ordinations in Philadelphia.

The Cheeks were having coffee in the living room after dinner when Wittig's call came in. The two women made small talk at first, asking about each other's spouses. Then Wittig came to the point, telling her that she wanted to speak with her under the seal of the confessional. "Okay," Cheek replied quietly. Wittig revealed to her the plans for the ordinations. Cheek described experiencing several intense reactions at once, all the while speaking calmly and rationally with Wittig, asking questions and gathering information. She later described her thoughts at that moment:

> My heart was leaping up and shouting, "Yes, oh, yes;" my body was registering symptoms of panic; my head was beginning to calculate the risks. The news was shocking. It was utterly unexpected.

Cheek asked Wittig what she thought would happen in the aftermath, and Wittig answered that the bishops would probably be rapped on the knuckles, maybe even deposed. For certain, she believed, the women would be deposed. Cheek suddenly had an odd sensation—she described it as something like a *click*. She had experienced the sensation once before, when she was twelve and had just been told that her grandfather had died. She believed it was a sort of acknowledgement, the recognition that the end of an era was over. "It was a wrenching moment," she wrote about the news of the ordinations, "but something deep inside me recognized the inevitability of it." She hung up, telling Wittig that she would call her soon with an answer, then walked back to the living room, sat next to her husband on the sofa, and discussed the situation with him. Given her visa requirements, being deposed could have meant being forced out of the country.

"I'll support you," Bruce said simply. He would leave his position and leave the country with her. The next day she called Wittig to tell her she was onboard. "Oh," Wittig responded, "I've already sent your name in—I knew you would."

Nancy Witting had been one of those, like Heyward and Bozarth, who could look back on her life and say that she had been preparing to be a priest from the early days of her childhood. She remembered being a child of seven or eight and taking her father's linen collar, part of his Navy uniform, and reversing it, turning it into a priestly one that she used in her own parish, a group of teddy bears she would line up in her room. Her early years, like those of Cheek's, were somewhat idyllic, spent partly on a five hundred acre dairy farm in Loudoun County, Virginia. Her father had decided that if he survived World War II, he would buy a place in the country, somewhere to raise his family. "It was a wonderful way to grow up," Wittig remembered. She helped raise calves. She milked the cows. She drove the tractor as men threw bales of hay onto the trailer. Wittig also spent much of her childhood traveling the world, following the assignments of her career Navy father. She lived in Germany, Italy, Japan, and England.

Wittig's parents were concerned about issues of justice and attempted to educate their children, keeping copies of Martin Luther King's "Letter from a Birmingham Jail" on the coffee table and discussing current social inequities. Wittig remembers the bombings in Birmingham in which four young girls— Addie Mae Collins, Cynthia Wesley, Carole Robertson, and Denise McNair— were killed at the 16th Street Baptist Church approximately five months after King had written his letter from the jail. A teenager herself at the time, she was teaching Sunday School when the bombing occurred. That act "was evil," she later said. "How could people do this and still think they [were] Christians?" She was, however, motivated by the nuns and priests she saw marching for Civil Rights and demonstrating against segregation and other forms of white supremacy. "That was the church I wanted to be a part of," she said.

She entered Virginia Theological Seminary and after her first year, believed she had been called to the priesthood. She later told a reporter from *People* magazine that the call had not come as a bolt of lightning, but rather as a strong feeling she had experienced that she could help the church and that the church could help her. The article in *People* created an image of her that was 1970s cool and hip:

> There is an almost ethereal quality about Nancy Wittig. Her long, straight, sandy blond hair falls over the clerical collar she wears to work every day, usually along with Levis or gaily-colored pants. She wears no makeup, and the only sign of her inner tension is her ceaseless cigarette-smoking.

The photograph above the article captured an aspect of the women-as-priest scenario that could prove as threatening to the home as to the church. In the photograph, Wittig is standing in the kitchen, one hand on her hip, wearing her clerical collar and a watch with a thick, heavy leather band popular at the time, watching her husband drop tomatoes into a large pot of sauce cooking on the stove. He was wearing a striped apron. His hair disheveled, he appeared overworked. She seemed in charge.

She was, however, coming to feel powerless in the context of the Church, believing that her work as a deacon was self-destructive:

> I felt like I was dying, being sucked in and being a part of my own oppression. As a deacon and a woman . . . I was a token reinforcing the notion of women, that man officiates, woman is silent and obedient. I stood there, silent, saying in effect, "This is what it comes to, baby!" I could no longer do that.

She became involved with the issue of women's ordination, helping Sue Hiatt organize the first meeting of the Episcopal Women's Caucus at Virginia Theological Seminary in 1971. She was at the heart of the movement and had come to believe in her early days of seminary that the church hierarchy wasn't "shooting marshmallows" at the women who wanted to be priests. It was "throwing rocks."

As in the case of Wittig, some of the members of the Philadelphia Eleven (and of the four who followed them in Washington) found themselves in front of cameras more often, or featured more frequently in news articles, than the other members. A few, like Bozarth and Alison Palmer of the Washington Four, were raised by parents familiar with the culture of the media and felt comfortable within its boundaries. Palmer, as we will see, sought out reporters when she believed she needed to state her case to a more broadly defined audience. Some of the women were consistently participating in events (delivering sermons, presiding over the Eucharist, speaking to groups, publishing memoirs, etc.) that captured the attention of photographers and reporters. Others, like Sue Hiatt, tended to stay in the background, or "to lead from behind," as Heyward referred to Hiatt's leadership style, though none of the women avoided the media completely, nor necessarily wished to be ignored entirely by the press. One of the ordained priests, Marie Moorefield, declined my request for an interview. With deepest respect for her position, I have limited the discussion of her role in the story to that time and to those places surrounding the ordinations.

Chapter 4

THE GATHERING

The single page of notes was marked confidential. The participants were identified only by abbreviations—D, H, M, O, Wa, & We. The notes did not indicate where the meeting occurred, only that on March 4, 1974, six bishops had gathered to discuss the possibility of ordaining women as priests. They took an informal vote, finding out who would be willing to ordain women before the next General Convention, to be held in Minneapolis in 1976, and who would be willing to do so afterward. They wondered if one entire province might be willing to ordain or if three or more dioceses within that province would step forward. They wondered if ordaining women without the approval of the General Convention would hurt the cause of women's ordination. They asked themselves if the ordinations would be valid and, if they were valid, would they be irregular.

Except that drawing a distinction between "valid" and "invalid" ordinations is absolutely fundamental to the discussion of women's ordination, the fine points of the topic would probably be best left in earlier times, in the days of the intense debates concerning how many angels could dance on the point of a needle. Still, here are the few broad points we need to know about the question of validity. In the Episcopal Church, the ordination of a priest occurs by the laying on of hands of a bishop who has been ordained through a long line of Apostolic Succession. In other words, bishops—who were to carry on the work of the apostles of Jesus—have been ordained in the name of the Holy Spirit through this chain of hands since the days when the apostles were spreading the Gospel. While much has been written both to support and to negate the historical actuality of the unbroken line and while many argue that the actual succession has more to do with the continuity of Christian experience and teaching than with the physical laying on of hands, the idea of an unbroken line continues to carry great weight. In this sense, ordinations are a sacrament, a gift of the Spirit, bestowed by the laying on of hands and, like baptism, they cannot be repeated. Also, opponents to women's ordination argued that Jesus had appointed only men as apostles and concluded that only men could serve the sacraments and that only men could be ordained as priests or bishops.

Sometimes, valid ordinations are considered irregular. In such cases, the ordinations may not have fulfilled one of the church's discretionary regulations or standards, but can be regularized through a simple process of licensing by a bishop. In the case of the Philadelphia Eleven, several aspects of the ordinations contributed to their being irregular, including the fact that their own bishops—those from their individual dioceses—had not ordained them and that the then current Bishop of Pennsylvania had not given approval for the ordinations to occur in his diocese.

Notes from the March meeting illustrate the way the bishops were coming together to attempt to work out the intricacies of what it would mean to ordain women without the approval of the General Convention and indicate an awareness of their own power and authority in the ordination process. At the end of the notes, which were most likely taken by Bishop Edward Welles, father of Katrina Swanson, is a fragmentary statement that reads,

> Further consensus: to make some announcement *before* Minneapolis, but try to get more bishops on board first and not stir up opposition to [*sic*] far ahead of time!

It is not clear why, then, that on the same day, Welles wrote Presiding Bishop John Allin to tell him about the meeting. Though he did not mention the possibility of irregular ordinations, Welles pleaded with his friend to resist delaying women's ordination with a call for more study of the issue:

> But, please, dear Jack, I hope *you* will operate on a time schedule that does not seriously contemplate "further study" under any guise *after we reach Minneapolis*. The women are agonized but not only the women deacons! I say no more at the moment, except that I honestly do not believe we can much longer deny half the People of God the possibility and opportunity to share in the fullness of Christ's priesthood if truly called!

What he does not mention to the presiding bishop is the possibility of ordinations occuring well before Minneapolis. Perhaps at that point he had hoped they would not occur. In the informal polling the handful of bishops had taken at the confidential meeting in March, Welles had voted *no* to ordaining women before the General Convention. In fact, he did not decide to participate in the Philadelphia ordinations until the last possible moment. And even then, it would take a direct confrontation from Cheek, the inspirational words of his young grandson, and the quiet solitude of a late summer's midnight to tip him into the ordination camp.

Several years later, in his memoir *The Happy Disciple*, Welles revealed the names of the other five bishops who had attended the March 4 meeting. They were Robert DeWitt, Paul Moore, Lyman Ogilby, John Walker of Washington, and Charles F. Hall of New Hampshire. William Mead of Delaware, the bishop who had agreed to ordain Sue Hiatt, had died only the week before. Of these bishops, Moore (along with Welles) voted to wait until after the General Convention of 1976 before ordaining women. Walker and Ogilby said they would be willing to ordain women before Minneapolis, though only with the support of other bishops, presumably from among those not yet retired. The notes combined with Welles' memoir give a contradictory picture of how Hall would have voted before the convention, but they are clear that he and most of the others would have ordained women after Minneapolis no matter how the convention decided the issue. Only Moore and Ogilby would not commit on that point. Of the six bishops, DeWitt was the only one willing to move forward with irregular ordinations, though according to Welles' later memoir, "Bishop Moore said that if three retired bishops ordain some of his women deacons, he would not take it as an affront." Though that position would remain to be seen, the statement indicates that at some point the possibility had been raised that three retired bishops might be willing to preside over the irregular ordinations. Welles, however, apparently did not consider himself among that number according to both the notes from the meeting and the account from his memoir.

Later, DeWitt speculated on the reasons why bishops who were supportive of women's ordination "balked" at their opportunity to act when they had the power to do so. He listed peer pressure, their position as defenders of the faith, an unwillingness to move too far ahead of the mind of the church, and an unwillingness to "create more trouble" when there were constant administrative issues to address in the diocese. For some, the move would put them out of the running for Presiding Bishop. DeWitt concluded,

> Bishops are people, too. When a man has served his best, how careless dare he be about jeopardizing a full pension by risking deposition?

Even so, the risk was one DeWitt would be willing to take. A few others would follow his lead.

In February, not long before the meeting between the bishops recorded by Welles, John Allin—who had just assumed his new position as Presiding Bishop—decided to call a meeting of the women who wanted to be ordained to the priesthood. The meeting would be held at Seabury House near Greenwich, Connecticut. In the 1940s, the Episcopal Church had acquired the nearly hundred acre estate with a twenty-five room colonial house to be used as a home for the Presiding Bishop, as a hostel and conference center, and as a "spiritual capital" for the church. On the day of the meeting, a snowstorm had moved in, making travel to the meeting difficult. In fact, almost everything about the meeting was difficult. Hiatt remembered the Presiding Bishop as being "insensitive" and "insulting." Schiess wrote that when Heyward was delayed by the weather, the Presiding Bishop was particularly dogmatic and authoritative over the issue of her tardiness, pounding his fist on the table and exclaiming about how he treated his men who were late. Schiess' husband, a doctor who was in another room reading medical journals and a copy of *I'm Okay, You're Okay* stood and prepared to leave, assuming it was his wife who had created the disturbance. Schiess was particularly upset by one of Allin's comments; he told the women that where he came from (Mississippi) people thought that the women simply wanted "to wear fancy clothes, with ruffles at the wrist." Schiess said that although the women had agreed not to overreact to anything Allin might say, she informed him that she had had her fill of ruffles at "Miss Botts' dancing school."

The patience of Piccard was also tested. The seventy-nine-year old who had piloted a balloon into space finally had enough of Allin referring to the women as girls. She banged her cane on the floor and said, "No, Sonny boy, not a girl. I'm old enough to be your mama! You're the age of one of my sons," and then she turned towards one of the women and added, "Actually, he's the age of my miscarriage." Obviously, the Seabury meeting would do little to precipitate a meeting of the minds on the issue of women's ordination.

When Piccard returned home to Minnesota, she attended the ordination of Phil Bozarth-Campbell. Alla Bozarth recalled that during the ordination, Piccard provided a moment of healing for the couple and their marriage. Phil's ordination was planned to serve as both a celebration for him and recognition that, for Bozarth, the doors were closed to the exercise of her priesthood. She would stand in the doorway at the rear of the church during the service. The two distributed a statement to the congregation that elucidated their position within the church:

. . . this sacrament represents not simply the fulfillment of many years of preparation, academic and otherwise; much more importantly, it represents the fulfillment of a *calling* which demands the commitment of one's whole being. The process of hearing, questioning, doubting, understanding, affirming, and finally answering God's call is one of the most exciting and significant processes of any person's life. . . . This service tonight is, in many ways, a tremendously happy and fulfilling event. Yet at the same time, we feel a great sense of tragedy, waste, and injustice that we cannot both be publicly affirmed in our vocations to the priesthood. . . . The church has always represented the wholeness of God to a broken world. . . . It is to this concept of wholeness that we commit ourselves. We call upon you to commit yourselves to this wholeness.

During the service, when Phil Bozarth-Campbell was examined by the bishop, Alla Bozarth responded to the questions from the rear of the church. At this point, Piccard—who had not yet come to know Bozarth well—rose from her pew, moved towards Bozarth, and stood beside her. When the priests and bishops began the ritual of the laying on of hands, a group of women joined Piccard to lay hands on Bozarth. The moment sealed the friendship between the two women and gave Bozarth a moment of "healing power" that served as a turning point for her, "a passage from crisis to the quiet waiting." It was Piccard's "generosity and kindness and tact" at this event, Bozarth later recalled, that "made Jeannette and me absolutely as one."

Back in New York, Carter Heyward had mailed DeWitt a letter in early May explaining what was happening with her Standing Committee (a bishop's council of advice that, among its other duties, recommends candidates for ordination). Both Heyward and Emily Hewitt were serving at St. Mary's Church in Harlem, close to Union and to the Cathedral Church of St. John the Divine. The members of the vestry at St. Mary's had sent Paul Moore several letters, including one informing him that they fully supported the ordinations of their three deacons (the two women and Doug Clark) and that they hoped he and the members of the Standing Committee would change their position in relation to women's ordination and allow all three deacons to be ordained in a service scheduled for May 17 at St. Mary's. They politely warned Moore and the Standing Committee that the issue would not go away regardless of the decision made by the hierarchy:

No matter what the final decisions of the Bishop and Standing Committee regarding the May 17 service of ordination at St. Mary's, the Congregation will continue to be vitally concerned with and vigorously pursue the issues involved and most particularly the ordination to the priesthood of I. Carter Heyward and Emily Hewitt, members and pastors of St. Mary's.

In her letter to DeWitt, Heyward wrote that the rector at St. Mary's had informed her that Moore was furious over the exchange with the church, calling one of the letters "chicken shit" and having some choice words for the two women as well. But Heyward seemed to take the controversy in stride, ending her letter:

> What a world! Damnest and most glorious packages of tears and laughter! Guess that's what it's all about.

She did not, however, take her invitation to preach at Clark's ordination quite so sanguinely. She wrote Moore to confirm that she would be delivering the sermon at the service and to say that, to her knowledge, no one had planned to use the ordination as a moment of protest, though she acknowledged that she knew no more than he on that account. She ended the letter with a note of regret that the two of them were in disagreement over the issue, adding, "But, Paul, what is the choice? Tell me."

The sermon Heyward delivered was hard hitting and direct. She began by defining a priest as someone in a larger context of a "priesthood of believers," of lay people and clergy "committed to helping brothers and sisters recognize the God that moves through them." But in the process of defining the priesthood, she took direct aim at the concept of Apostolic Succession:

> The ordained priest is said to be part of the "Apostolic Succession," supposedly—although not actually—an unbroken succession of men who have been ordained as priests. A succession rooted in Jesus' charge to Peter that he be "the rock" on which the church be built. Continuity is meaningful. Irresponsible allegiance to tradition is not. Both Doug and I have trouble with the sort of ecclesiastical irresponsibility that would lead us, or you, into believing that an ordained priest has actually been somehow "zapped" by God and set apart from the rest of the Christian community, usually on a pedestal. We have trouble with such a notion because it is arrogant and idolatrous. It rings of insecurity and ego-tripping on the parts of priests who see themselves this way. . . . This pedestal view of priesthood deprives all Christians of having to assume responsibility for their own lives, their own faith, and their own priesthoods.

While Heyward and Hewitt were struggling with their diocese in New York, DeWitt was working to round up more bishops for a possible irregular ordination. One bishop not present at the Washington meeting in March was Daniel Corrigan who, like DeWitt, Welles, and Hall, was retired. In June, in a letter written by hand on legal pad paper, Corrigan informed DeWitt that he was ready to join him, "ready to cross the rubicon or Jabbok or whatever," as he phrased it. He asked DeWitt a series of logistical questions and ended his letter with a personal reflection:

> This [is] a hard letter to write! But it is so—unless something happens before Minneapolis, nothing will happen there.

He is raising a point here that Hiatt and other supporters of women's ordination would also argue: at the earlier conventions, it had been easier for the deputies to ignore the women than it had been to support them and, that by acting in Philadelphia, the women could potentially turn the tables at the next convention in Minneapolis.

Corrigan was a veteran of World War I, in the submarine service and later a merchant Marine. He had been a peace activist who had protested Vietnam, had marched with King on Washington and sat with him during the "I Have a Dream Speech." He worked on behalf of Native Americans and spoke in favor of the rights of homosexuals. *The Philadelphia Daily News* described Corrigan as a "lean, leathery man who" sounded as if "he might have been speaking around a Western campfire." In early 1974, Piccard had sent a letter to Corrigan, who had once served as her rector in Minnesota, to reestablish contact. She also told him about Bozarth, all the while bringing the topic of women's ordination back into his line of vision. When defending his decision to ordain women, Corrigan reflected on the convention at Louisville and on the comments that had been made to him indicating that the vote there had not been about only one convention or about women having to wait a few more years, but that it had actually carried much greater weight. There had been "many declarations" made to him after that vote, Corrigan wrote, "to the effect that 'this is out of the way, at least for a generation.'"

Also discouraging to the supporters of women's ordination was a list circulating from the committee whose task it was to set the agenda for the House of Bishop's October meeting in Mexico. On March 15, the committee released the agenda, which did not include women's ordination as a topic of discussion. At the House of Bishop's meeting in New Orleans in 1972, the topic of women's ordination had "appeared to override all other deliberations." But that was before the negative vote in Louisville. The prediction made to Corrigan seemed to be holding true—women's ordination had been pushed "out of the way." Heyward later recalled that the cultural and historical moment for change seemed to be slipping away from the women as the nation itself began to move in a more conservative direction.

By the time DeWitt had called Corrigan to ask him to be an ordaining bishop and to join him and the other organizers on his farm for the July 10 meeting, Corrigan had already received through the mail the June sermons delivered by Charles Willie and Ed Harris that had helped to galvanize both Sue Hiatt and DeWitt. Corrigan told DeWitt that he would be there.

• • •

At this point, we return to that sixty-nine cents Mead notebook. It belonged to Ann Robb Smith who used it to take notes at the July 10 meeting. By then, the questions being raised didn't so much address *if*, but *when* and *where* and *how*. Maybe it's just a coincidence that the first name in the book, located at the top of the inside cover, is Betty Medsger (their press agent), along with her phone number. At the very least, the placement of her name is symbolic of the role the media would play in the next month, indeed in the next few years, and the extent to which the organizers realized its importance.

According to Smith's records, six of the eleven were present: Sue Hiatt, Nancy Wittig, Emily Hewitt, Betty Bone Schiess, Katrina Swanson, and Carter Heyward. The Advocate's rector Paul Washington was there, as well as David Gracie, who would be in charge of security at the service. At that point, three retired bishops were planning to ordain the women—Bob DeWitt, Charles Hall, and Daniel Corrigan—and all were in attendance. Edward Welles was still debating his decision, but he was there along with Bishop Lyman Ogilby, who had replaced DeWitt as Bishop of Pennsylvania. And, of course, Medsger was there. All in all, a little over twenty people attended. They discussed such issues as security and liturgy. They thought about whom to invite and when to announce the event. They discussed possibilities for a preacher and decided to ask Charles Willie. They wondered how many eligible deacons to call, how many to ask if they were willing to be ordained. Emily Hewitt pushed for a safety in numbers approach—the more women to share the coming responsibilities and the more to deal with the public outcry, the better. So they approached every deacon who was eligible for ordination to the priesthood. They discussed

their fears about security issues—about the threat of bombs—and whether their
need to do what they felt to be right took precedence over those fears. They
discussed less critical issues, such as whether to use a guitar in the service, which
they decided against, concluding that they should keep the service as traditional
as possible. At the bottom of one of the pages were three simple words that
would turn out to be enormously significant to all involved: "concern for aftermath." Apparently, this worry was left to be sorted out at a later date.

Finally, the organizers discussed the public statements they were planning
to release on the day of the event. The statement from the eleven was circulated
among "friends in the struggle" and included women seminarians and deacons,
the Episcopal Women's Caucus, and other organizations working for women's
ordination to the priesthood. Some in the groups who were to receive the letter
preferred to delay action until the 1976 convention and believed irregular ordinations would set back the cause.

> Dear Friends,
>
> God willing, on Monday, July 29, the Feast of Saints Mary and Martha,
> three retired or resigned bishops will ordain to the priesthood eleven
> women deacons from eight dioceses of the Episcopal Church. We know
> this ordination to be irregular. We believe it to be right and valid. We are
> anxious to share with you who have supported the ordination of women to
> the priesthood the reasons we take such action now.
>
> Enclosed is an open letter from the ordaining bishops. We rejoice in
> their courage and feel privileged to join them in this act of Christian obedi-
> ence. We are certain that the Church needs women in priesthood to be true
> to the Gospel understanding of human unity in Christ. Our primary moti-
> vation is to begin to free priesthood from the bondage it suffers as long as it
> is characterized by categorical exclusion of persons on the basis of sex. We do
> not feel we are "hurting the cause," for the "cause" is not merely to admit a
> few token women to the "privilege" of priesthood. We must rather re-affirm
> and recover the universality of Christ's ministry as symbolized in that order.
>
> We do not take this step hastily or thoughtlessly. We are fully cognizant
> of the risks to ourselves and others. Yet we must be true to our vocations—
> God's irresistible will for us now. We can no longer in conscience answer
> our calling by saying "Eventually—when the Church comes around to
> accepting us."
>
> We welcome your support; we earnestly request your prayers. Above
> all, we urge you to continue the best way you know how in the struggle to

bring closer to reality the Pauline promise that "there is neither male nor female for we are all one in Christ Jesus.

Your sisters in Christ,

Merrill Bittner	Marie Moorefield
Alla Bozarth-Campbell	Jeannette Piccard
Alison Cheek	Betty Schiess
Emily Hewitt	Katrina Swanson
Carter Heyward	Nancy Wittig
Suzanne Hiatt	

The bishops released an open letter explaining their reasons for presiding over the ordinations:

On Monday, July 29, 1974, the Feast of Saints Mary and Martha, God willing, we intend to ordain to the sacred priesthood some several women deacons. We want to make known as clearly and as widely as we can the reflections on Christian obedience which have led us to this action.

We are painfully conscious of the diversity of thinking in our Church on this issue, and have been deeply sobered by that fact. We are acutely aware that this issue involves theological considerations, that it involves biblical considerations, that it involves considerations of Church tradition, and that it raises the vexing question of amicable consensus in our household of faith.

We are convinced that all these factors have been given due consideration by the Church at large, and by us. We note that the House of Bishops is on record as being in favor of the ordination of women. We note that a majority of the clergy and laity in the House of Deputies is also on record as being in favor, even though an inequitable rule of procedure in that House has frustrated the will of the majority.

All of the foregoing factors, by themselves, would not necessarily dictate the action we intend. Nor, even, would this intended action necessarily be required by the painful fact that we know pastorally the injustice, the hurt, the offense to women which is occasioned by the present position of our Church on this issue.

However, there is a ruling factor which does require this action on our part. It is our obedience to the Lordship of Christ, our response to the sovereignty of His Spirit for the Church.

One of the chief marks of the Church is its being the community of the Resurrection. Ours is a risen Lord. He was raised in the power of the Spirit so that we might participate, however inadequately, in His triumph against sin and separation, proclaim the good news of His victory, and occasionally ourselves walk in newness of life. His Spirit is the Lord of the Church. Hearing his command, we can heed no other. We gladly join ourselves with those who in other times and places, as well as here and now, have sought obedience to that same Spirit.

This action is therefore intended as an act of obedience to the Spirit. By the same token it is intended as an act of solidarity with those in whatever institution, in whatever part of the world, of whatever stratum of society, who in their search for freedom, for liberation, for dignity, are moved by that same Spirit to struggle against sin, to proclaim that victory, to attempt to walk in newness of life.

We pray this action may be, as we intend it, a proclamation of the Gospel—that God has acted for us, and expects us, in obedience, to respond with appropriate action.

> The Rt. Rev. Daniel Corrigan
> The Rt. Rev. Robert DeWitt
> The Rt. Rev. Edward Welles, II

After the July 10 meeting, the women began making phone calls to other deacons who would potentially be interested in joining them. Swanson called Bozarth, who remembered the precise moment of the call: 5:00 p.m. on July 11. "How would you like to be ordained to the priesthood before the end of the month?" Swanson asked. Bozarth jumped and screamed, "Yes," noting that she realized in midair the question had gone beyond asking if she was ready to be a priest. She was being asked if she wanted to become a prophet. "I came back down and said, 'Oh my God. *How?*'" From there, she began to count the potential costs to those closest to her: her newly ordained husband Phil, her father who was an Episcopal priest, her mother-in-law who was president of the Minnesota Episcopal Church Women. Swanson and the others who had made the calls had been careful to warn the women that they were likely to be deposed as a result of the ordinations. Bozarth took a few days to think over her decision. She was sustained, though, by the support of her family and friends.

On July 19, something happened that no one was expecting and it opened the floodgates of responses to the coming ordinations. Bishop Ogilby released a statement to his diocese informing clergy and parishioners of the event. He had called DeWitt beforehand and told him that because so many rumors were floating around about the possibility of the ordinations occurring, he believed he had little choice but to inform his clergy. Ogilby's statement was relatively mild, expressing that while he had not given "consent to or approval for" the ordinations to occur in the Diocese of Pennsylvania, he nonetheless supported "the Christian conscience of the persons" involved and believed the ordinations would be valid but irregular.

Heyward wrote that from that point until the service in Philadelphia, her phone at Union rang constantly, in seeming rhythm with the traffic lights outside on Broadway. *The Philadelphia Inquirer* ran a story about the ordinations, revealing the date, time, and place: 11:00 a.m., July 29, the Church of the Advocate on Eighteenth and Diamond Streets. The eleven informed their own bishops in their home dioceses. Heyward, Moorefield, and Hewitt sent a telegram to Moore who had taken his children to Italy after the death of his wife Jenny. He called DeWitt from overseas and said, "You are out of your mind!" In his memoir, Moore recalled his relationship with DeWitt and how he had felt about his old friend's decision to preside over the ordinations:

> We had been through many battles together. . . . I trusted him. I liked his way of going ahead if he felt he was right, whatever the consequences. This was the first time we had really differed. I was angry and hurt and feeling very, very far away.

Moore wrote a letter to Heyward (and sent a carbon copy to Moorefield and Hewitt) arguing that she was making a "grave mistake" and that he wished she had "resisted the temptation to slide towards radical action which is so natural a tendency for those emotionally absorbed in an issue." He regretted that she had placed another "difficult barrier" between them and that the ordinations would "turn so many against you and probably split your allies right down the middle."

Swanson could not reach her bishop, Arthur Vogel, who was out of the office until early August. Bozarth met with her bishop in a cold air conditioned restaurant on a scorching day in Minnesota. He had bought a newspaper which he had sitting on the table, folded up. The newspaper had carried the story about the coming ordinations, but Bozarth was relieved that he had not yet seen it. Cheek's bishop, Robert Hall of Virginia, called an emergency meeting of the Standing Committee and asked its members to take a vote on whether he should ordain her. "I felt it would cause less disorder in the church to go that route," he later said. The Standing Committee held the fate not only of Cheek's ordination in their hands, but potentially that of women's ordination in general. A *yes* vote on their part may have made Philadelphia unnecessary. The Standing Committee almost pulled it off. But by a vote of 5–4, the committee voted against Cheek's ordination. Philadelphia was still on.

On July 23, Allin sent a telegram to the women, pleading with them to cancel the service:

> For the sake of the unity of the church and the cause of ordination of women to the priesthood I beg you to reconsider your intention to present yourself for ordination before the necessary canonical changes are made. Am deeply concerned about the relationship obstacles which can result within your diocese as well as within the church as a whole.

In a response to Allin, Cheek placed the ordinations into the context of the larger women's movement:

> Women are striving to define themselves, name themselves as whole persons. This, it seems to me, goes to the heart of the Gospel. The attitudes and actions of the Church have damaged women. . . . A church unified at the cost of damaging and oppressing women has no gospel to preach.

Edward Welles also communicated with Allin during this period, sending the Presiding Bishop a long letter on the twenty-second explaining his decision to participate (though Welles would vacillate on his decision up until the last moment) and noting his regret that the conflict was creating tension between him and Allin. But Welles was also feeling personally rebuffed by Allin. On June 17, Allin had called Welles to tell him that he and his wife would be traveling throughout New England during the month of July and had hoped to make a stop at the Welles' home in Maine. Welles encouraged the visit and a few days later, his wife Catharine sent a letter by airmail reinforcing the invitation. The day after the Presiding Bishop phoned, Katrina called her father to invite him to the July 10 meeting at DeWitt's farm and on the twentieth, DeWitt himself called Welles to issue the invitation. Later that day, Welles mailed a letter to Allin stating that he was "as eager as you to keep the lines of communication open" and informing the Presiding Bishop of the meeting scheduled for July 10. At the end of the letter, he included directions to their Maine home. "There was," Welles later admitted, "a sad breakdown in communication at this point." The Allins never responded. The Welles waited at their home hoping that they might show. When the time came for the July 10 meeting, Catharine, still waiting, stayed behind in Maine and her husband went to Pennsylvania. Welles informed the gathering at the DeWitt farm that the Presiding Bishop knew of the meeting and, ever hopeful, raised the possibility that the Allins might be at his home as he spoke.

Not until after Ogilby broke the news about the ordinations on July 19 did Allin call Welles. On the twentieth, the two of them talked for over an hour by phone. Allin admitted to being hurt that Welles had agreed to preside at the ordinations without warning him. Welles replied that he and Catharine had been waiting for the Allins to arrive at their home and that the Allins "had certainly disappointed them."

After the call with the Presiding Bishop, Welles received another call from DeWitt informing him that Charles Hall had withdrawn as one of the ordaining bishops. Allin, in the meantime, issued a statement to the media on the twenty-fourth, in which he pleaded with the ordaining bishops to give the Church one more chance in Minneapolis. Allin was also continuing to apply personal pressure on Welles. The two spoke again on the twenty-third, with Allin accusing Welles of being "unfair," arguing that "the possibility of deposition or even a trial and suspension is out of tune with our times" and that "ecclesiastical trials just aren't held these days." As it would turn out, the Episcopal Church would not mind stepping back through time and dusting off those options.

Things were moving in other states as well. In the Diocese of Rochester, one newspaper reported in April that the Committee for the Whole Ministry of the Church had been buying up the orange ribbon in town. The ribbon was being bought and given to people to wear in support of women's ordination. The movement's leader, Anne Exley, was quoted, "Equality for women in the church, to my mind, means not only ordination, but equal opportunity for jobs; salaries equal to those paid by men; also equal numbers of women on elected and appointed groups—with women in a darned good share of chairperson roles!" Merrill Bittner was on the steering committee for the group. On July 25, a story ran in Rochester's *The Times-Union* that Bittner was to be ordained the following Monday in Philadelphia. Her bishop Robert Spears expressed his shock at the prospect of the ordinations: "It's unthinkable that procedures . . . are being bypassed," he told the reporter.

Of course, the Anglo-Catholic factions against the ordinations were mobilizing. On the twenty-sixth, the American Church Union (ACU) issued a statement to the press that they were considering seeking a restraining order based on the misuse of church property. In his comments to the press, the executive director of the ACU portrayed the women as somewhat passive and duped: "The victims will be the women who will not leave the service as priests of the Episcopal Church but as vagabonds." *The Philadelphia Inquirer* reported that Reverend Clayton Hewett went into seclusion to begin a fast, depriving himself of food and water. In a letter to Ogilby, he wrote, "We have reached a new low point in the life of the church." And he wanted those involved to be "dealt with in the severest manner which the church has at its disposal." A group of around a hundred lay people and priests met in the Rosemont area of Philadelphia to organize a protest and to begin gathering signatures for a presentment, or formal allegation, that could lead to an ecclesiastical trial. What had seemed to the presiding bishop several days earlier like a relic from another time suddenly became a viable and realistic option, complicated by the fact that at this point, Edward Welles still held the position of honorary vice-president within the ACU. They opened their session with a prayer, asking that the Lord deliver them from "all sedition, private conspiracy, and rebellion, from all false doctrine, heresy, and schism." They left the meeting with a petition to deliver at the ordinations two days later. And they took a vote to see how many of those attending believed that Ogilby had not responded strongly enough. About half of those present raised their hands.

The ACU wasn't Ogilby's only concern. He was receiving calls from all over the country asking him to stop the ordinations. But in the midst of threatened court action by the ACU, he issued another letter to the diocese on the twenty-sixth, this one much more formal and authoritative in tone than the one he had released earlier. It warned that the bishops would be in violation of the canons and constitution of the church. The ACU dropped its plans for legal action as a result of the letter and instead issued a Bill of Particulars, five points they raised against the ordinations, including the bishops' collegial agreement in Louisville to refrain from acting independently in the matter. They also pointed out that there existed "no provisions for the ordination of women to the Priesthood within the One, Holy, Catholic and Apostolic Church."

Heyward and Wittig had been in charge of arranging an event the night before the ordinations when the eleven, their bishops, family, and friends could spend time together at the DeWitt farm. "The atmosphere was electric," Schiess wrote. For many, it would be the first time they had been introduced to one another. At 3:00 p.m., a group of around one hundred began coming together in an old stone barn for chicken wings and wine. Heyward recalled the sights and sounds of the party, of being comforted by the sparkle in Piccard's eyes, of watching her father and Schiess' husband laughing together on the porch, of listening to Witting's husband criticizing the church roundly over its treatment of his wife, and of hearing a booming prayer by Welles. When Bishop Welles prayed, she wrote, "One has the feeling that the Lord is bound to take notice." At 5:00 p.m., they gathered to ask questions and to discuss their fears, their reasons for participating, and their "random thoughts" about the next day. Bozarth spoke immediately and forcefully, drawing on the prophet Jeremiah, who had been called upon to speak even though he did not believe in his own ability to do so. Welles still had not decided whether to participate in the ordinations. His ten-year-old grandson stood up and said,

> I'm William Swanson. My mom's going to be ordained a priest. I hope my grandfather is going to do it. I think we all have to pick up our Cross and follow Jesus."

But Welles attempted to persuade those in the group to wait until Minneapolis. When the others proved unwilling, he withdrew as one of the ordaining bishops.

After meeting in a large group, the participants split up and the three bishops met with their individual ordinands. Schiess remembers Corrigan asking the members of his small group one last time why they wanted to proceed. Then he told a story about why he wished to go forward. He said that when he arrived at his first parish, he decided to join a service club at the request of some of the members of his congregation. On the night of the initiation, the members blindfolded him and asked him "to swear to never do anything to help women, Jews, or Negroes." He recognized the voice as one of his parish members. But Corrigan knew that the women's action would exact a price. Hiatt wrote that on the night of the gathering, Corrigan laid out for them the responsibilities and the rights of a deposed priest.

As the evening moved on, Cheek was becoming increasingly frustrated with Welles, her ordaining bishop, who had decided to meet in the small group with Cheek, Wittig, Swanson, and Hiatt. Whether or not the Lord had taken notice of Welles, as Heyward claimed, Cheek had certainly been paying attention to his indecision. She had already had an eventful morning, telling the church she served in Annandale, Virginia, that she was planning to be ordained the next day in Philadelphia. She asked for comments and people "popped up like asparagus," including one woman who stood, shaking because she had not been used to speaking in church. The congregation was supportive, though when Cheek arrived at the farm later that day and told DeWitt what she had done in her home church, he held out his arms as if she had allowed herself to be crucified. At any rate, Cheek was in no mood for equivocation at that point. "Ed Welles had been dickering and dithering," she said with a laugh as she remembered the story years later. "But," she added, "my language was bad":

> He [Welles] didn't know whether he was going to do it or not. And I had this long day and I said to him, "I wish you'd shit or get off the pot." To give him his dues, he said, 'I can't, I'm constipated.' And then when he met my bishop at the meeting of the House of Bishops, he told Bishop Hall that I'd helped move him.

Years later, Cheek recalled that Welles would be a "wonderful" bishop to her through the years, praying daily for her family and completely supporting her during the controversies that would follow.

At the end of the night as people were cleaning, Bishop Tony Ramos of Costa Rica walked through the door, with a grin on his face. Ramos, age thirty-six, was known for his willingness to fight for a wide range of social justice issues. He had been a classmate of Hiatt's in seminary and had spoken for women's ordination on a panel at the 1970 convention in Houston. The retired bishops convinced him, however, that he would be much too vulnerable as an ordaining bishop in Philadelphia, so Ramos did not take part in the official ordinations, though he did serve as a supporting bishop at the service.

After returning to the townhome where he was staying with Swanson and family, Welles spent time alone thinking about his decision. It was midnight, and he sat to reflect and pray. He realized that though he wanted to wait until Minneapolis, he thought the chances were good that the vote would once again be negative because of the voting regulations in the House of Deputies. He believed that God wanted the church free from "discrimination and injustice" and that the "world did need women priests now!" He went downstairs to let his daughter Katrina know his decision, and then he called DeWitt.

The Corrigans had stayed overnight at the farm with the DeWitts. After Daniel Corrigan had retired to bed, he found that he couldn't sleep. He thought that DeWitt would still be awake, too, so he made his way downstairs. The two bishops spent some time talking together in the kitchen. Corrigan pulled out an edition of Robert Frost and read "West-Running Brook" and then "The Road Not Taken." Then they parted, Corrigan wrote, "quietly to bed—to sleep." He didn't say whether the call from Welles had disturbed the quiet.

Chapter 5

"THAT GREAT GITTIN' UP MORNING"

"Monday, July 29, 1974, was a strange and enchanting day."

Charles Willie

Merrill Bittner pulled an old home movie off her shelf, an 8 mm that had been converted to a VHS. It was a short film without sound that some now-forgotten soul from Rochester had made of the July 29 service at the Advocate in Philadelphia. The filmmaker caught only a few scenes, including the procession, a protestor waving his arms in anger, the ecstatic crowd, and Charles Willie in his black robe at the lectern.

But there was one more clip on the recording which is, in its understated way, unforgettable. For a brief moment, no more than a few seconds, the scene shifts from the church to the interior of a moving car. A young unidentified woman (Bittner said it might be her, but she couldn't be certain) is at the steering wheel. The person filming appears to be shooting from the passenger seat. The sun is just beginning to rise, a dazzling orange in a deep indigo sky beyond the driver's side window. That is the scene in its entirety. Yet, there is something jolting about it because in it is wrapped just about everything. Some of what it evokes is particular to time and place—Janis Joplin on the radio, a coffee mug on the dash, a pack of cigarettes lying on top of a service station map in the glove compartment, Kerouac packed away in a suitcase.

The rest is more difficult to put into words. Maybe it is the delicious tension of a young girl leaving home. Maybe it is much older and darker, another retelling of the ancient need to slay a dragon. Maybe it is unfiltered joy and innocence and a giant leap of faith into the exciting unknown, though it could just as easily be the gnashing of teeth and the tragic loss of a true love. Either

71

way, we get the sense that some cosmic curtain has just opened up to show you what it looks like when someone wakes up and heads out to change the world, and not in the ways normally available to us, like planting a garden patch or reading a book to a child—ways that give the world a chance to adjust. At that time in her life, Bittner was somewhat philosophical about it: "Sometimes opportunity chooses you instead of you choosing it."

• • •

Barbara Harris was busy answering the phone at the Advocate. It had been ringing off the hook all morning. A woman called, hysterical, wanting to know if the service was actually going to be held. "You people," she screamed, "are going to split the church." Harris replied, "Madam, this church is split already. That's why we're having this service."

The women and the bishops had agreed to gather at 9:00 a.m. When they arrived, they went to the basement of the church, the site where they had planned to escape if problems arose during the service. They put on their vestments and the women signed the Oath of Conformity, no small undertaking because of the promises it demanded. In fact, Heyward had been disturbed by signing the oath when she had been ordained a deacon the year before. The parts most concerning to her were those that discussed doctrine, authority, and the nature of Scripture. As found in The Book of Common Prayer, the bishop asks the ordinand:

> Will you be loyal to the doctrine, discipline, and worship of Christ as this Church has received them? And will you, in accordance with the canons of this Church, obey your bishop and other ministers who may have authority over you and your work?

The ordinand answers:

> I am willing and ready to do so; and I solemnly declare that I do believe the Holy Scriptures of the Old and New Testaments to be the Word of God, and to contain all things necessary to salvation; and I do solemnly engage to conform to the doctrine, discipline, and worship of the Episcopal Church.

The deacon Heyward worried that she could not faithfully promise to follow the oath to the letter of the law. In a panic, she phoned DeWitt, who told her to meet him the next day in New York's Penn Station, where he got a chuckle out of her predicament. Then he changed her way of looking at her vocation, convincing her that "in the larger scheme of things in God's world, the Oath of Conformity in the Episcopal Church does not rank very high!" He said, "First . . . to affirm the Bible as the Word of God doesn't mean that it's the only Word of God; second, to say that it contains all things necessary to salvation doesn't mean that everything it contains is necessary to salvation; and third to promise to conform to the doctrine, discipline, and worship of the Church means only that, as with any vow, you'll do your best, ask God to help you, and use your common sense."

Jeannette Piccard had also helped give the issue perspective, writing to the women and explaining that since the word *disciple* (in this case, one who follows Jesus) is a root of *discipline*, then showing discipline in the church is to follow the call of Jesus. And showing discipline did not allow for prioritizing church order over that call. Ordination, in the eyes of the eleven, was absolutely essential to following their calls. "Ours was a case in which, as women," Alla Bozarth wrote, "disobedience to the letter of the law was the only way in which we could express our obedience to the Spirit of Christ." So in the basement of the Advocate that morning, when they were handed a black Faber fountain pen, they signed their names to the Oath of Conformity.

While they waited there for the eleven o'clock hour, gifts began arriving from various sources. Emily Hewitt and Heyward were given silver crosses by the rector of St. Mary's. A Roman Catholic priest from Ohio sent his own cross for one of the ordinands to wear in the service—Katrina Swanson was designated. Sue Hiatt was given two different stoles to wear, one made by her friends in Philadelphia and another presented by Edward Welles, her ordaining bishop. Alison Cheek received flowers from her husband Bruce, though she was actually feeling quite "sad" and "detached." She was certain she would be deposed and then deported. "I loved the church, dearly loved it," she said, "and I thought that, if I were deposed, I would be ruined at the center of my being." Her only consolation on that day was that she would leave with her "integrity intact."

Bittner had worn her purple tennis shoes with the orange laces. In fact, about a third of the crowd of two thousand was wearing orange ribbons, handed out to everyone courtesy of the Rochester delegation. Many of the protestors against the ordination wore blue ribbons, and some wore buttons with the word *No* written across them. Finally, white ribbons were available for those who were in favor of women's ordination, though not through the irregular ordinations that were about to occur.

Understandably, nervous thoughts were running through the minds of the eleven. Some concerned ethical questions, as in the case of the Oath of

Conformity, but others were more practical. Heyward remembered struggling to knot the cincture around her waist correctly. Hewitt, who was not entirely comfortable in large crowds, asked Bittner to stay near her in case she fainted. She had never fainted in a crowd before and never would later in her life, but the photographs of the event show a gap in the line where Bittner had moved in close to her friend, just in case. One of the eleven remembered that she and a few of her colleagues were cautiously joking about the possibility that their periods would start during the service, in that hot church as they were standing in their white robes in front of the crowd and cameras. In a situation where some of their more vocal opponents were screaming about the way these "priestesses" were contaminating the church with their sexuality, the women's concern loomed particularly large that day.

As the eleven o'clock hour neared, the group gathered with their lay and ordained presenters and began their journey upstairs, moving slowly up a spiral staircase and hearing the music coming from above. Linda Clark, in whose room the consciousness-raising group met at Union, was serving as one of the organists. At some point in the early part of the procession, Moorefield lost a contact lens, and for this reason, Hewitt actually did end up on the floor, searching around for the lens. "I had good eyesight," she later explained, but even so, she never found the lens and Moorefield went through the service without clear vision in one eye. As the group continued upward, they heard Paul Washington addressing the congregation, though they were unable to make out the individual words. When he finished his remarks, they heard a disconcerting roar from the crowd.

The roar surprised Washington, too, who was standing in his white robe and wearing a pair of black reading glasses that Buddy Holly might have worn. He was welcoming the two thousand and offering the crowd a metaphor for why organizers felt compelled to proceed immediately with the ordinations. "What is a mother to do when the doctor says, 'Your baby will be born on August 10,' when on July 29 she had reached the last stages of labor and the water sack has ruptured?" he asked. And then the congregation was directed to the opening hymn. What Washington had not realized what that the hymn was "Come, Labor On." The crowd erupted into laughter. And thus began the ceremony.

Still, even that moment wasn't a time of levity for everyone. For Schiess, the connection of the ordinations to her own difficult pregnancies led to feelings of panic and to a moment of prayer:

As we were filing in, I was overwhelmed by the number of people there. "Come, Labor On" was the hymn, and I had the same feeling as I did going into hard labor when I was bearing children: "If, dear Lord, there is a way out of this, I want out. I didn't mean for it to get this far. Help!" And then the feeling that there is no way out, that this is it. It wasn't just stage fright. It was realizing what a really big thing this possibly was.

The processional, even though it began at the side of the church and was shortened for security reasons, took longer than expected. Heyward was blinded by camera lights as she and her presenters wove their way through the people. With the crowd shoved in on one side of them and the photographers trying to gain position on the other, the eleven looked more like rock stars at a concert than deacons presenting themselves for ordination. Washington was disappointed that they had decided to enter through the side. Both he and Harris wanted a longer processional, but Harris acquiesced to the shorter route, recognizing, as she admitted later, that the church had "its share of crazies." In the days before the ordination, Washington kept an ongoing dialogue with Hiatt over the matter of security, calling her once at 3:00 a.m. to discuss what it meant to trust God. He "took the attitude that God would protect us," Hiatt wrote, "while I was of the mind that 'in this world God's work must truly be our own.'" Because of safety concerns, Hiatt would not allow her family to attend the service. Nonetheless, by the time she had arrived at the church, she had no doubts within herself that she would follow through with her plan. The woman who as a girl had told her mother emphatically that she could change the world, was moving forward with what she described as a "steely determination."

As they continued in the procession and into the laughter, shouts, and applause of the crowd, some of the other women saw their fears dissipate. When the bishops walked in, the applause grew even louder. With his height and the added effect of his grandfather's mitre, Welles stood out above the crowd. Seeing the bishops, Ann Robb Smith turned to Hiatt and yelled, "They're going to do it, Sue. They're really going to do it. The Holy Spirit has grabbed them by whatever hair they have left and they're actually going to do it!" They were all processing towards the altar where a frontal had been made in red, black, and green by the women of the church, with a paraphrase of a verse from Galatians written in felt: "In Christ there is neither male nor female, bond nor free, Jew nor Gentile. We are one."

Then everyone sat for Willie's sermon. He was a good choice for the occasion. Later listeners compared his sermon to one of Martin Luther King Jr.'s, who was a friend of Willie's, the two having met when they attended Morehouse College together. Willie said that both he and King owed a great deal of their rhetorical style to the way they had been taught at Morehouse. Here is how effective Willie's message and rhetorical style were: even though he relied heavily on the complex language of German theologian Martin Buber in his sermon, even though he explained the process of vote by orders and described the deputation of the General Convention, quoted from the *Convention Daily* and cited his share of numbers and percentages, he still managed to deliver a sermon which inspired people in the congregation to break continually into roars of approval and rounds of applause.

He began by taking the event out of the context of the Church and placing it into a much larger one: "May God bless the harvest of this moment, so that it will not be a high moment in the history of the Episcopal Church but a holy moment in time." Still early into his sermon, he gave his reasons for being part of the ordinations. "I participate in this service today," he said, "not because I wanted to speak out but because I could not remain silent," clarifying that he spoke not as a Church official or as a professor, but as "a child of God who has decided to make no peace with oppression." He drew parallels between the Civil Rights Movement and the Women's Rights Movement, arguing that "both [were] freedom movements for men and women, and for blacks and browns as well as whites." He told the appreciative congregation that "unfulfilled hope tends to turn to despair and eventually into rage" and that it was time for "self-determination," not in the manner of "arrogant disobedience," but of "tender loving defiance." He asked, "How can a religious organization condemn sexism in the world and at the same time condone legislative actions which discriminate against women in the Church?" Then he confronted the General Convention directly in a statement that would have carried great weight given his position as Vice-President of the House of Deputies: "Let no one confuse the work of the General Convention with the will of God . . . they may or may not be the same." Alluding to the eleven, he told the crowd that no longer are "some women willing to cooperate in their own oppression." Then he wrapped up his sermon with several points, arguing that while collegiality had its value, it could not be put above "the affirmation of personhood" and that "a law which demeans personhood is a law unworthy of obeying." He concluded with a charge to the congregation, "Vow to make no peace with oppression, whether it is sexism or racism."

You would not have wanted to follow Willie's sermon, but the protestors had little choice. They were next on the program. Corrigan called upon them, "If there be any of you who knoweth any impediment, or notable crime" in any of the women to be ordained priest, "let him come forth in the name of God and show what the crime or impediment is." To some degree, the comments were relatively staid, with the exception noted earlier of the Reverend George Rutler who stood up and condemned the sight, sound, and smell of perversion (and sulfur) the ordinations were raising. He was, as Hiatt said, "eloquent if insulting." Rutler's eloquence earned him a sound bite on the national news that evening, though during the service his statement confused Schiess. She turned around to see who he was talking about. "Nobody was there," she said, coming to the realization that he was talking about her. "I felt faint," she said. She looked over at Bill Wolf, her priest presenter, who was laughing. She asked him how he could laugh at that moment, and he answered that in case the cameras were on him, he wanted everyone to know how silly he thought Rutler was. Bozarth thought that Rutler was "emotionally distraught." She was sitting beside her husband Phil who was her priest presenter. When Rutler attacked the bishops, telling them that they were offending these little ones and breaking the bond between Adam and Eve, Phil muttered "heresy." Bozarth thought to herself that "it was high time the bond were broken if it was based on domination and the kind of disrespect we had just witnessed." Willie watched and thought to himself that he was glad he and his wife had decided against bringing their children. And he wondered why Rutler didn't seem concerned that Willie wasn't a priest himself.

One other protestor stirred up things a bit—particularly among the Piccard household—by saying that it was a "travesty" to ordain Piccard, who at the age of 79, was beyond retirement age and would unfairly receive a pension. The executive director of the ACU also read his statement and presented the Bill of Particulars and, after another statement or two, the protesters were quietly escorted out of the church.

The epistle was then read by Kate Mead, widow of Bishop Mead, and a selection from the Gospel of Matthew was read by the Reverend Patricia Park, a newly-ordained deacon who would become a co-leader of the National Coalition for Women's Ordination to the Priesthood and the Episcopate.

When the ordinands stood to be charged, there was a scuffle in the press area. Something heavy, possibly a camera, had fallen and created a loud crash. For a moment, Bozarth wondered if she had been shot. "I knew you could be shot without feeling it," she later said. She looked down but didn't see blood on her white alb. Then she turned to look at her sisters, to make certain it hadn't been one of them.

The women had agreed prior to the event that when it came time for the laying on of hands, Piccard would be first. She had, after all, wanted to be a priest for longer than the rest of them had been alive. In fact, she first remembered informing her mother of her desire to be a priest when she was a young girl of eleven and her mother had come into her room one night, sat on her bed, and asked her what she wanted to be when she grew up. A priest, she answered. Her mother burst into tears and ran out of the room. "It was the first time I'd ever seen my Victorian mother run," Piccard said. At 12:20, Corrigan (who had once been Piccard's parish priest) and approximately one hundred other priests and bishops, including a few Roman Catholic priests, gathered in prayer and performed the laying on of hands. One of Piccard's sons had tears streaming down his face. Corrigan then ordained Schiess and Bittner, whom he had known at Bexley Hall Seminary when he was acting dean, and Bozarth. DeWitt ordained Hewitt, Moorefield, and Heyward. And Welles ordained Cheek, Wittig, Hiatt, and his daughter Swanson. After the women were themselves ordained, they could participate in the ordaining of other women.

The emotional and physical experience of the laying on of hands varied from woman to woman. Cheek was one of several who felt intense pressure, as if her neck was about to break. Others felt something deeply mystical, including Heyward who—after watching Moorefield move back—made her way to DeWitt:

> I stepped forward, catching the bishop's eye momentarily, and as if strangely transcendent of the time at hand, my whole life seemed contained within the moment: past, present, future. All that had ever mattered to me flooded within me, as a geyser of lifeblood or holy water.

After the laying on of hands, the women assisted the bishops in serving the Eucharist. Serving two thousand people was a slow process, but for many, a moving one. One elderly woman remained kneeling at the altar after everyone had left. Schiess thought she was having difficulty standing and went to help her. The woman, in tears, asked to be allowed to kneel there for a few more moments. It was the first time, she told Schiess, that she had felt included in the service, the first time that "she knew it meant her." Bozarth looked out across the crowd and felt a sense of reconciliation:

As I stood in the sanctuary during Holy Communion, administering the holy food with my sister priests, seeing the radiant faces of those many people who had come to make this moment happen with us, many things came together in my heart. I remembered the words of Jeremiah, and then the words of Jesus to the dead daughter of Jairus, calling her back to life: *Talitha Cumi*, "Young woman, I say to you, arise." And I looked at the beautiful faces of all the women present, reflecting the love and presence of the Holy Spirit. Compared to the light I saw in my sisters' faces, the dark words we had heard a few moments before had no power or truth whatsoever.

Barbara Schlachter was one of those people in the crowd. She was experiencing a complicated set of feelings, the day being at once one of the most "traumatic" and marvelous of her life. She had been out of the country during the recent planning stages and had arrived home two days before the ordination. She had literally just walked in the door, when she heard the phone ringing. The call was from Heyward who asked, "Are you going to be ordained with us the day after tomorrow?" Schlachter had been one of the five who had presented herself to Paul Moore in December.

"I was so stunned that it was actually happening," Schlachter recalled. She declined the invitation. From her perspective, there just wasn't enough time to make a life-altering decision. Still, she traveled to Philadelphia to attend the service. "It was an incredible, incredible service . . . I am so glad it happened, but it was so strange not to be up there with them. . . . I was traumatized by the sense of pull."

Other women were feeling a mixture of fear and joy over the event. Pauli Murray, who a few years later would become the first African-American woman ordained in the Church and who had confronted many dangerous situations in her life, including being arrested in 1940 for refusing to sit where a bus driver had ordered her in Petersburg, Virginia, wrote that as she took a train to Philadelphia that day, she experienced "sudden terror" at the thought of breaking a "tribal taboo":

> My panic was so great that I might have left the train at Newark had I not met two clergywomen from the United Church of Christ, whose obvious enthusiasm for the event calmed some of my fears.

But by the end of the service, she wrote, "the joyous spirit that enveloped the congregation swept away all my doubts as to the rightness of the action taken that day." Her most "cherished memory" was kneeling before Piccard and receiving a blessing.

Janice Duncan, who worked for the Diocese of Pennsylvania, returned early from her vacation to attend the service as a witness. She was afraid as she walked up to the church, frightened that someone would block the door or would order her to leave. No one stopped her, so she sat in the chancel and "tried to make [herself] small." But she was comforted and inspired by the intense sense of community within the church that day, and a sense of the Spirit that permeated the building.

In fact, that sense of spirit is something that comes up again and again as people attempt to describe what they felt that day. On the one hand, the organizers were hardly naïve in the ways of public relations and would have known that they would have to lay claim loudly and often to the presence of the Spirit in what they were calling a prophetic act. But there seems to be something else that they are attempting to express that goes beyond gaining the upper hand in presentation. Two points come up consistently when witnesses to the event tell of their experiences that day: (1) it was outrageously hot in the church and (2) many of them felt the presence of Spirit there, a feeling that seemed to have taken people off guard, as if they had been surprised by the intensity of the sensation.

After approximately three hours, the service ended with the recessional march moving along to a "lustily sung" hymn full of "alleluias," as Hiatt described it, and accompanied by more cheering and applause. On that Monday in July, the Episcopal Church was changed. The protestor George Rutler knew it and left the church, later becoming a Roman Catholic priest, a move he called "the best thing he'd ever done." The Episcopal Church had become for him like "Russia after the revolution." He called it "unrecognizable" and added that "the Catholic Church seemed to be stable against the political correctness of liberal Protestantism, which has now disintegrated totally." He went on to serve in various roles as a Catholic priest, including as a chaplain in a hospital and psychiatric ward.

Pamela Darling discussed the changes in the church brought about by the Philadelphia ordinations, describing the women's assertion of agency as being a "dramatic challenge" to the leadership of the church,

> Most shocking of all was the fact that—unlike the campaign to seat women in the House of Deputies—women had taken it upon themselves to act within the church without permission. The ordinations had to be performed by male bishops, but it was women who had laid the groundwork, raised the money, gathered the support, and persuaded them to participate. Although

the official reaction focused on punishing the ordaining bishops and male priests who invited women to celebrate the Eucharist, its intensity was rooted in outrage over the fact that women had seized the initiative, claiming and exercising power to bring about change on their own timetable.

The night after the ordinations, Paul Washington, who had believed he had found his life's work at the Advocate and had believed he had "been born" for such a ministry, realized he had left himself extremely vulnerable to the church hierarchy. And not only himself—the Advocate could suffer as well by having its budget cut as a punishment. He left the church profoundly discouraged. He soon received a call from his bishop, Ogilby, who informed him that he had violated the church's Constitution. Washington disagreed. Ogilby continued: "Yes, you violated Article VIII of the Constitution . . . I am going to have to admonish you."

"All right, Bishop," Washington responded, "I have no choice but to accept your admonishment. Thank you." Washington received a written notice that he had violated the Constitution. It was the least possible disciplinary action available to Ogilby. Over time, other priests would not be so fortunate.

The bishops of the new priests immediately began inhibiting, suspending, and/or admonishing the women. Bishop Arthur Vogel, who had succeeded Welles as Bishop of West Missouri, admonished Katrina Swanson and informed her she could not wear her clerical clothing or perform any clerical functions until she submitted to discipline or was tried in a diocesan court. Bishop Edward Turner of Kansas sent a letter to the chaplain's office of Topeka State Hospital where Moorefield served as chaplain and informed her that not only was he inhibiting her as a priest but also as a lay person. He went even further, telling her that she was unwelcome in the diocese: "Your scandalous participation in a so-called ordination to the priesthood makes you persona non grata in this Diocese."

Ogilby released a letter on August 1 that he instructed his clergy to read to their parishes. In the letter, he informed the diocese that he had admonished Washington and had received assurances from DeWitt and Hiatt that they would not exercise their ministries until their status had been clarified. While Hiatt agreed, she told Ogilby in a phone conversation that she was unwilling to wait indefinitely. She also noted that she had not waived her right to an ecclesiastical trial and asked Ogilby to put into writing the reasons she was being asked to refrain from acting as a priest. Bishop Frederick Wolf of Maine released a public letter calling the ordinations invalid and saying that he was "distressed by the irresponsibility of the bishops who initiated this tragic event." It would be a second letter—one he wrote a year later after being told of a tragic plane crash—that would send many in the church into an uproar about his position on the status of the Philadelphia Eleven.

The Episcopal Women's Caucus also released a statement that seemed to distance the caucus from the eleven, even though Hiatt and Wittig had organized its first meeting. In its August 2 statement, the caucus affirmed its earlier position that each woman must "move in her own way and take those actions which are in accordance with her own conscience." They "rejoiced" in the ordinations and called on the bishops to affirm the eleven women. But they also clarified their own role in Philadelphia:

> The Episcopal Women's Caucus, Inc. was involved neither in the decision nor in the planning of the July 29 ordination and no Caucus funds including those recently received from the Board of Theological Education were used.

Though not celebrating publicly at that moment, the eleven were speaking with the press. The twenty-eight-year-old Wittig said, "I've always been a nice, good Southern girl and never bent people out of shape, but I feel this is my time." Moorefield, age thirty, told a reporter that she believed it was "worth risking even something important" to her—her job as a hospital chaplain—in order to take a prophetic stance for the sake of a full ministry.

• • •

After the ordinations, Bozarth climbed back into her car with her mother-in-law Betty Campbell, president of the Episcopal Church Women in the Diocese of Minnesota and Bozarth's lay presenter in the ceremony. They had made the trip together from Minneapolis on funds provided by Campbell's aunt, pediatrician Dr. Alice Fuller, who had served as a World War I army nurse. In later years, she and Bozarth would sit together at a Steinway on a sun porch and, with four hands, play Beethoven's First Symphony. Fuller had been given a check a few months before Philadelphia and had put it aside, "waiting for a time of special need" in which to use it. When she heard about the coming ordinations, she realized the moment had arrived. She gave the money to Bozarth and Campbell. Driving along the interstate on that trip, Campbell told her daughter-in-law that the opportunity to be her presenter had been a life-altering one. "Though I'm in my mid-fifties," she said, "coming with you like this has made me a fully grown adult woman." She continued,

It's the first time in my life I've stood up to friends and family and announced that I was going to do something that I would have to defend, that would come under attack and criticism and possibly cost me some friends and the disapproval of some family members for going against the current. In this truly independent act, not worrying about what other people will think, I've become a fully grown and independent person.

The coming of age stories on the roads leading to and from Philadelphia were not confined to the young.

But the journey was only beginning. The next stop would be Chicago. On July 31, Allin called an emergency meeting for August 14 and 15 to be held in a hotel at the O'Hare International Airport. The women were waiting, giving their own standing committees and the larger church time to "act creatively" in light of their ordinations, though some were celebrating the Eucharist in private homes. On August 6 Willie wrote John Allin asking him to call a special General Convention so that the church could eliminate its practice of discriminating against women. "It could be our finest hour," he wrote. Not only did Willie believe that what happened next fell well short of the church's finest hour, it would immediately prompt him to resign his post as vice-president of the House of Deputies.

Chapter 6

THE BISHOPS' TALE, CHICAGO

If it hadn't been evident from the beginning that the bishops were going to have an image problem, the photograph taken at the House of Bishops emergency meeting in Chicago by a staff member of United Press International (UPI) would have driven the point home. In the background of the photograph, the Presiding Bishop is shown celebrating the Eucharist with his brother bishops in a reserved room in the O'Hare International Towers Inn. In the foreground, a large sign sitting on a pedestal reads "Bishops Only." To the side, separated from the bishops by the sign, stands Alison Cheek watching from a distance. Sitting below her is the seventy-nine-year old Jeannette Piccard.

In an era when "Whites Only" signs had only recently been thrown into city dumps or hidden away in the storerooms of hotels, restaurants, or movie theaters, the sign that the bishops used to keep others out of their territory was saturated and dripping with cultural significance and historical memory. It was the sort of move on the bishops' part that led to the coming onslaught from editorial cartoonists across the nation. In his cartoon *Punk*, Pat Oliphant, winner of the Pulitzer in 1967, drew a shriveled-up bishop praying on his knees. According to a newspaper lying across his bed, the bishop had just rejected women priests and is assuring the Almighty that His will has been done. On the wall in the bedroom hangs a framed poem: "God is a gentleman through and through/And in all probability, Episcopal, too."

Bill Mauldin, also a recipient of a Pulitzer, released a cartoon titled "Machismo" in the *Chicago-Sun Times*. In this cartoon, the Episcopal hierarchy is represented by a frightened bishop in his cassock standing on a chair. The drawing was meant to remind readers of the stereotypical images of women jumping on chairs to escape mice. Here, the "mouse" is a tiny woman dressed in black and carrying a briefcase with "lady priests" written across the front. And Mike Peters, who distributed through King Features Syndicate, drew a male priest in the pulpit expounding on the fact that women priests were nonsense, given that God had made men in his own image. In the next frame, a hand descends from the sky and whacks the priest with a giant purse.

John Allin had called the meeting in Chicago, interrupting the August vacations of many of the bishops, who had arrived—as Paul Moore wrote—angry and, at times, nervous; neither condition helped, he believed, by the environmental factors. To begin with, he observed, they had been "hermetically sealed from the world" in a room with the air conditioner running on high to counteract the August heat. They had been pulled away from mountaintops and boats, from vacation spots like Martha's Vineyard and the Florida beaches, and were now surrounded by "plastic potted plants" and busy wallpaper. While understandable on one level, this reaction from the bishops only further underscored their positions of privilege. And while perhaps not aesthetically uplifting, the hotel was an expensive one, unlike the cheap motel rooms the women had reserved for themselves. They had to drive to the hotel, Emily Hewitt remembered, to "sit where the boys were."

Of course, the primary reason for the bishops' anger was that the ordination that had occurred in Philadelphia. And over the course of the two-day meeting, their anger showed no signs of abating. In fact, in Moore's estimation, the bishops were angrier when they departed Chicago than when they had arrived. Edward Welles described it as a "hot anger," and one that "had not cooled enough to permit reason to function calmly."

Immediately after the ordinations, Hiatt had called Welles to thank him for ordaining her and to find out how he was faring. He was, he said, "desolate." He was worried that his old friends would be unable to recover from their anger towards him or from their beliefs that he had betrayed them. But he was not one to wallow, and he noticed that his feelings of desolation had faded within a few days and that after a week, were "gone completely and forever." With his wife Catharine by his side, he was ready to confront Chicago.

Nine of the eleven women traveled to the meeting and made themselves available to answer any questions the bishops might have for them. Charles Willie went though he was uncertain why an invitation had not been extended to him in the first place, given that he was vice-president of the House of Deputies and had delivered the sermon in Philadelphia. Theologians Harvey Guthrie, Edward G. Harris, and Hays H. Rockwell—all three of whom had attended the ordinations—also made the trip and three weeks later issued a report saying that they were "disturbed both at the content of what was done and the process leading to the final action." They were, they wrote more simply, "Appalled at what happened in Chicago."

The meeting was called to order at 1:35 p.m. on Wednesday. The suffragan bishop from Texas began with a devotional. Of no great surprise was the fact that the biblical readings—and their interpretations—seemed to present a God who would have given the bishops a big thumbs up for their position on the ordinations rather than a smack on the head with a purse. This would be no time for the spouting of rebellious words from Old Testament prophets calling for change; the bishops were gathered to reclaim law and order. The first reading, from the fifteenth chapter of the Gospel of John, began,

> I am the true vine, and my Father is the vinedresser. Every branch of mine that bears no fruit, he takes away, and every branch that does bear fruit he prunes, that it may bear more fruit. . . . Abide in me, and I in you. As the branch cannot bear fruit by itself, unless it abides in me. I am the vine, you are the branches. He who abides in me, and I in him, he it is that bears much fruit, for apart from me you can do nothing. If a man does not abide in me, he is cast forth as a branch and withers; and the branches are gathered, thrown into the fire and burned.

In another context, this chapter from John could have just as easily been read as supportive of the women, as supportive of people following their callings in the name of Jesus, abiding in the vine and bearing the fruit of their ministries. But in Chicago, the verses were read to send a different message, a warning that the price of pulling away from the corporate body of the Episcopal Church could be costly. For example, in his opening address Allin used words referring to the *corporate* (or to the *body*), to *order*, and to *collegiality* over forty times. Conversely, the word *prophetic* was used twice in one of the scripture readings, but was never alluded to in the speech. Nor was there discussion of the sense of call to the priesthood that the eleven women had argued as a basis for their ordinations. No talk about the morality in challenging unjust laws or practices or of following one's conscience. This was a speech about "conserving" and "protecting" the institution.

As one of the scriptural readings for his speech, Allin chose a passage from Ephesians that laid out the various gifts given by God. The passage promises stability to all who realize their place in the scheme of God's plan. In this plan, some were meant to be pastors and others teachers. The passage doesn't mention that the positions were handed out according to gender, but in this

Chicago meeting, the implication would not have been lost on the audience. To step outside of this order, as the reading was meant to suggest, would be to invite vulnerability and deception:

> Unto every one of us is given grace according to the measure of the gift of Christ. And he gave some, apostles; and some, evangelists; and some, pastors and teachers. . . . That we henceforth be no more children, tossed to and fro, and carried about with every wind of doctrine, by the sleight of men, and cunning craftiness, whereby they lie in wait to deceive. But speaking the truth in love, may grow up into him in all things, which is the head, even Christ: From whom the whole body fitly joined together and compacted by that which every joint supplieth.

Allin then quoted at length from the twelfth chapter of First Corinthians, beginning with verse four that lists the gifts of the Spirit and moving forward through verse thirty-one in which the corporate body again becomes central: "For as the body is one, and hath many members, and all the members of the body, being many, are one body, so also is Christ." This verse is followed by one similar in structure and meaning to the one the women of the Church of the Advocate attached to the altar cloth at the Philadelphia ordinations, or the "Philadelphia happening," as Allin called it: "For in one Spirit we were all baptized into one body, whether Jews or Greeks, whether bond or free." It's a clever twist on the Presiding Bishop's part, to turn the overarching message of the ordinations into one that, as he noted, confirmed "the corporate nature of the Church" and "the necessity of corporate decisions." He again quoted Paul, asking that the bishops be tenderhearted and forgiving and to put aside all anger and bitterness. Yet, the point he follows with argued that the bishops had a "responsibility to work in the midst of the Church" given the limitations of "unilateral decision making." While on one hand the speech was filled with thoughts about love and forgiveness, on the other it was provocative and pointed, drawing comparisons between those who had participated in Philadelphia and those who would eventually wither and find themselves burning in a brush fire of cosmic proportion.

Allin laid the ground rules for the meeting, pointing out that the House of Bishops was not a judicial branch of the Church, even while a group of bishops had been gathering signatures to launch a presentment (or trial) against Corrigan, DeWitt, and Welles. Allin argued that the job of the House was to "interpret the faith and doctrine" of the Church. They were not there, he emphasized, to discuss the ordination of women to the priesthood. They could, however, discuss—and even rule on—the validity of the women's ordinations in Philadelphia. That one task alone, ruling on the ordinations without discussing them, was enough to create confusion. But Allin told the group that they were there to answer one question: "What is the evaluation and response of the House of Bishops to the Philadelphia happening?" Or, as he phrased it, "When is a vow not a vow?"

Allin offered various ways they might proceed: to issue no response (though he thought that route irresponsible); to call a special General Convention to address the issue; to interpret, ignore, or delay the question of validity; to begin judicial proceedings; to "censure those involved," or, to "allow" the four bishops to remove themselves from the membership of the House of Bishops and "accept" their promise not to practice again as bishops. The three ordaining bishops and Ramos made no such offers regarding the final suggestion. Instead, DeWitt read to the House the open letter the four had written in July and added that they were truly sorry for offending "sensitivities" and for abrogating canonical rights, but added that the ordinations had been conducted with "informed conscience and good faith" and that they believed that what they had done "was right." Tony Ramos was allotted time to speak just after DeWitt finished. Ramos had acquired a reputation for speaking forcefully to the church when it had failed, in his eyes, to give matters of justice their proper due. His statement in this case was forthright, but he also seemed intent on lowering the level of tension among his fellow bishops:

> Right Reverend Sirs and Brothers, one thing I would like to make clear to all of you. If there is one thing I love it is this Church; if there is one thing that I am loyal to, it is this community of believers. But of all things, if there is one thing that I am committed to, it is the Gospel of our Lord Jesus Christ, whom all of us are called to serve and to witness to. At the age of 37, in the twelfth year of my ministry and the sixth year of my episcopate, during which time I have persistently worked to change structures of this Church, to liberate it from a colonial past, to make it face the issues with which our world confronts it, I would not have placed my episcopate in jeopardy if it had not been for a deep love and concern for this fellowship.

As for the women, they were standing in the halls waiting to be asked their opinions, though that was never to be. Moore wrote that he looked over at one of the women and watched her "following every word" of the proceedings:

Her life, at least her career, was at stake. It seemed bizarre that she was not allowed to speak for herself. But the privilege of the floor for the women had been voted down.

In fact, Cheek recalled that when the photo was taken of her and Piccard watching the procedure from across the "Bishops Only" sign, someone standing in the room was "shooing them away." Charles Willie was also turned away, so he borrowed a press pass and entered anyway. Catharine Welles had managed to make her way in and was sitting behind the seventy or so press members. Daniel Corrigan's wife Elizabeth saw her sitting inside and asked Betty Bone Schiess to try to find out if Catharine were experiencing any problems. Schiess went in and discovered Welles calmly taking notes on a Bible. When two priests saw Schiess enter, they walked over to ask her to leave. Schiess refused. The priests left for a moment and when they returned, Welles lifted a lace handkerchief from her purse, waved it at them, and said, "Go away, you naughty men." Once again, the priests walked away, at which point members of the press offered Schiess a pass in case the problem persisted.

Sue Hiatt was watching the event and knew early on what the outcome would be. By day two, she would be back in her motel drafting a statement. She warned the other women that the bishops would rule that their ordinations were invalid. "Impossible!" Alla Bozarth responded. "They can't do that." Nancy Wittig, in the meantime, was struggling with what she described as one of the worst migraines of her life. She was coming to realize, she later said, that when the canons referred generally to men, they didn't mean men and women. "They actually meant men."

After the speech by Ramos, the bishops divided into smaller groups to discuss the possibilities Allin had laid out for them. Moore remembered both confusion and anger being expressed as the discussions began in the groups:

> Our group chairman began: "Perhaps we should define the limits of our assignment. We are not here to discuss the pros and cons of women's ordination, or even whether the Philadelphia ordinations were valid or irregular or totally invalid. Rather, we are here to discuss what we should do about the bishops who broke ranks and how we should treat the eleven women who were ordained in Philadelphia."
>
> "But they weren't ordained, that is just the point."
>
> "Slow down, Bill. We are not here to discuss that."

"Well, then, please don't refer to that fiasco as an ordination. And anyway, I do not see how we can discuss what to do with the bishops or the women unless we decide whether they were really ordained or not."

"I think they were ordained. All the elements were there—apostolically consecrated bishops, a valid liturgy, and the intent to ordain. What more does *your* theology require?"

"Let me say two things. First, an action outside the ordered life of the Church, an uncanonical action, does not hold water. Second, the 'matter' of the sacrament was not appropriate. To baptize you have to use water, to celebrate the Mass you need bread and wine, to ordain you need an adult male."

"You mean it doesn't 'take' unless the recipient is a male?"

"To put it crudely, that is exactly what I mean."

"Boy, let's unpack *that* one," someone uttered under his breath.

Those seventy press members in attendance began sending back reports from Chicago. *The Washington Post* reported that suffragan Bishop Wetmore—who had been one of the three bishops to put forth a presentment against DeWitt, Welles, and Corrigan—had stood up and said that the ordinations had harmed the authority of the House and had jokingly added, "which many look to as the best club in the country." Unfortunately for the bishops, it was the sort of comment that fueled criticisms of their being more concerned about maintaining a boy's only club than about implementing justice. *The Post* noted that Allin later criticized the comment, stating that "if that's true, then there is a real need for renewal among us."

That evening, Bishop Charles Hall from New Hampshire, who had pulled out of the Philadelphia ordinations at the last moment, rose to address the House of Bishops. He told the group, "I have nothing but the deepest admiration for the spirit, the courage, and the conscience . . . of those who went through with it." And then growing poetic, he added, "A few must go too far, that many may go far enough."

More difficult to ascertain was Bishop Lyman Ogilby's position. He had been asked to clarify where he stood on the ordinations. He had apparently decided to lay his cards on the table in Chicago, to explain where he was "coming from." Then he delivered a page and a half, single-spaced report without once mentioning the Philadelphia ordinations, or women's ordination at all. In fact, the concept of ordination came up only twice, in the context of one that occurred in 1948 in the Philippines. There were references to some of his early role models, to the Philippine Independent Church, to Winston-Salem in North Carolina, to a pectoral cross, to the Anglican Communion, to Manila, to "streams [that] rise and flood, fall and recede," to the World Council of Churches, to the 1961 Concordat of Full Communion, and to the "sacramental and mystical, body of Christ" (which had never seemed more mystical than at that very moment), but nothing about women's ordination. In fact, he never even mentioned the city *Philadelphia*. It was a striking work in the art of evasion. His concluding statement merely added to the intrigue. He typed part of it in all caps, as if to emphasize that he could not possibly make his point with any more clarity:

> THIS IS WHERE I'M COMING FROM. And I pray in the Holy Spirit
> that this House will always move in this stream.

The discussion that seemed to carry the most weight with the bishops was the report by Bishop Arthur Vogel, Katrina Swanson's bishop. Vogel was the least friendly to women's ordination of the eight bishops who had the new female priests in their dioceses. His report, which he gave as spokesperson for the theology committee, argued that the ordinations were invalid based in part on a report written by Roman Catholic theologian Frans Josef van Beeck. But Vogel so thoroughly misrepresented van Beeck's views on the ordinations and his beliefs about the concept of validity that van Beeck issued a response in *The Journal of Ecumenical Studies* with the title "Invalid or Merely Irregular?—Comments by a Reluctant Witness." Van Beeck argued that he believed the ordinations in Philadelphia to have been valid, but irregular. But in Chicago, Vogel's argument worked, even though the report was not discussed by the members of the House. One bishop did ask if the House could have a written copy and a member of the committee answered *yes*, as soon as one could be transcribed and edited by Vogel.

Finally, the resolutions committee gave its report. Thirteen resolutions had been submitted to the committee during the Chicago meeting, but the committee dismissed most of them because they either raised the question of women's ordination or raised issues more properly suited for an ecclesiastical court. The committee presented its own resolution, so short and terse that one bishop said that the "brevity, given the complexity of the issue" and given the number of resolutions presented to the committee, was "an insult to the House." The resolution from the committee read:

Resolved, that the House of Bishops declared that priestly orders were not conferred on the eleven deacons at the service in Philadelphia on July 29, 1974.

After a moment of shocked silence, the protests began. The Bishop of Nevada stood up and said, "I'm flabbergasted." He argued that the resolution was "inadequate." Then Moore complained, "I don't know how I can go home if this house just flat ruled a resolution of that kind." He said that New York was a place in which women's rights were a serious issue. His concern was that the resolution "would be seen in the eyes of the world as an insult to the dignity of women." Robert Spears of Rochester called the resolution a "cheap cop-out."

The committee was forced into going back to the drawing board over lunch. Charles Willie used the break to talk with several of the bishops, including Moore, to encourage them to give the women an opportunity to speak. His advice was ignored, though the bishops informed him that instead of speaking with the women, the House was planning to offer the women pastoral counseling. Willie attempted to show them why that compromise was a bad idea, but to no avail. A letter from Heyward to Allin reveals just how insulting the women found the counseling option: "Your letter to my sisters and me strikes me harder than a slap in the face." She wrote that the eleven had support throughout the Church and that if the bishops truly wanted to help, they could start by affirming and regularizing the Philadelphia ordinations. "When this is done," she concluded, "I will be glad to sit down with you and others and figure out how *we* can be supportive of *each other*."

After the break, the committee presented another resolution, one passed by a large margin and declaring that the ordinations in Philadelphia had not been valid. But the manner in which the resolution was presented confused some in the House to the point that they had not realized that they had voted for invalidity. It is difficult to say what actually caused the level of confusion among the bishops concerning the new resolution.

Perhaps it was the fact that Bishop Otis Charles of Utah had proposed a resolution in the morning—one that had been read to the bishops—similar to the one the resolution committee had settled on over lunch. But, unlike the committee's revised version, Charles' original version made no reference to the ordinations as being invalid. In fact, the Charles' resolution had confirmed the women as priests.

Perhaps the confusion was the result of the loud, annoying air conditioning in the background that had hindered the debate. Or maybe the bishops simply wanted to return home or to their vacations or maybe they felt rushed after hotel management announced that the room would have to be cleared by 5:00 p.m. Edward Welles believed that some of these factors played a role. He also believed that the bishops had simply been "snowed" by misuse of van Beeck's theology. In any regard, the final resolution read:

The House of Bishops in no way seeks to minimize the genuine anguish that so many in the Church feel at the refusal to date of the Church to grant authority for women to be considered as candidates for ordination to the priesthood and episcopacy. Each of us in his own way shares in that anguish. Neither do we question the sincerity of the motives of the four bishops and eleven deacons who acted as they did in Philadelphia. Yet in God's work ends and means must be consistent with one another. Furthermore, the wrong means to reach a desired end may expose the Church to serious consequences unforeseen and undesired by anyone.

Whereas our Lord has called us to walk the way of the Cross through the questions and issues before us, resulting from the service in Philadelphia on July 29, 1974, and

Whereas the Gospel compels us to be as concerned with equality, freedom, justice and reconciliation and above all love, as with the order of our common life and the exercise of legitimate authority, therefore, be it

Resolved, That the House of Bishops, having heard from Bishops Corrigan, DeWitt, Welles, and Ramos the reasons for their action, express our understanding of their feelings and concern, but express our disagreement with their decision and action. We believe they are wrong; we decry their acting in violation of the collegiality of the House of Bishops, as well as the legislative process of the whole Church.

Further, we express our conviction that the necessary conditions for valid ordination to the priesthood in the Episcopal Church were not fulfilled on the occasion in question; since we are convinced that a bishop's authority to ordain can be effectively exercised only in and for a community which has authorized him to act for them, and as a member of the episcopal college; and since there was a failure to act in fulfillment of constitutional and canonical requirements for ordination, and be it further

Resolved, That we believe it is urgent that the General Convention reconsider at the Minneapolis meeting the question of the ordination of women to the priesthood, and be it further

Resolved, That this House call upon all concerned to wait upon and abide by whatever action the General Convention decides upon in this regard.

A roll call was announced. Bishop Charles called for more discussion, but when Allin asked if anyone in the House needed clarification, only three bishops indicated yes. The roll-call began. It soon became clear that the results would be a landslide that would go against the eleven, a vote that would declare their ordinations invalid. Cheek stood in the doorway absorbing stares that were both "powerful and daunting." She stared back. "In order to hold my gaze [I] had to have something going through my head. The biblical words, 'You have been judged and found wanting' helped me to hold it together." Recently she compared the moment to one three years later, at the death of her husband Bruce:

> Each "yes . . . yes . . . yes" felt like a thud, with a rare "no" breaking through. As I remember it now the memory of the thuds of shovel fulls of dirt on to Bruce's coffin rises up. I think on both occasions I was stunned.

As the vote came to a conclusion, she turned to look at Jeannette Piccard who had opened her arms like the crucified Christ. "I was startled," Cheek said. "But now I think enviously that at least she knew the extent and depth of her feelings."

Initially, the vote appeared to be one hundred thirty-seven, yes (for the resolution declaring invalidity); three, no; and seven, abstaining; but then bishops began asking what they had just voted on. Allin attempted to interpret the vote, saying that he understood that the House had just agreed that nothing had happened in Philadelphia. *The New York Times* reported on the confusion, Eleanor Blau writing that the statement concerning "necessary conditions" in the resolution "was not understood by some of the Bishops at first as a declaration of invalidity." Some of the bishops began changing their votes, moving the final tally to one hundred twenty-nine, yes; nine, no; eight abstaining. Welles, Ramos, Charles, Robert Spears of Rochester, and Charles Hall were among those voting no. Moore and Corrigan abstained. Ogilby voted in favor. If DeWitt voted, the records do not indicate it.

The bishops ended the Chicago meeting with a few other quick resolutions. They agreed to send greetings to President Ford. A few days earlier, deacon Patricia Park, who had read the Gospel at the Philadelphia ordinations, was photographed with the new President when he and the First Lady had attended a service in D.C. where she was scheduled to preach.

The bishops also reiterated their resolve to offer pastoral counseling to the eleven. And they added one more resolution directed towards the eight bishops with the new priests in their dioceses, though they continued to refer to the women as deacons. The resolution's first sentence seemed like a show of support; it's second, like a veiled threat:

> *Resolved*, that the House of Bishops at its meeting in Chicago express collegial support to the eight diocesan Bishops whose deacons participated in the service on July 29, 1974. We know that their respective actions will bear witness to the order of this Church and the charity and reconciliation of the Gospel.

In other words, the eight bishops were not to consider regularizing or licensing one of the eleven unless they wanted to incur the wrath of the House.

The bishops also took a moment to thank their Presiding Bishop for his leadership, giving him a standing ovation for his efforts. The three bishops who had threatened presentments against DeWitt, Corrigan, and Welles seemed appeased by the vote of the House and removed the presentment option off the table, though it would resurface soon after Chicago.

In her motel room, Hiatt had completed the statement released by ten of the eleven women (Swanson could not be reached by phone for confirmation). The statement expressed their "shocked and saddened" reaction to the vote by the bishops, questioned the theology behind the bishops' decision, and gave notice that the eleven would be exercising their priesthoods:

> [B]ecause we know ourselves to have been validly ordained, by duly consecrated bishops in the presence of nearly 2,000 clergy and laypersons, we cannot accept the decision of the House of Bishops. Each of us will make her own decision as to how and when to affirm the priesthood she knows to be hers. We ask the prayers and support of the clergy, the laity and women everywhere in our continuing effort to help the Episcopal Church deal with the ministry of women within our household of faith.

Charles Willie was visibly angered by the outcome of the meeting. He made a comment to a few people gathered around him to the effect: "It's the most blatant form of male chauvinism I've ever seen." One of the reporters heard him and asked if he would repeat the comment for the cameras. He agreed. They pointed him to the chair that had been set up for the Presiding Bishop's news conference. *The Virginia Churchman* reported that "as about fifty reporters waited before a bank of microphones to interview the Presiding Bishop . . . Willie came forward into the television lights." His comments received more press than Allin's would. *The Virginia Churchman* called it an "outburst"; the Episcopal News Service, a "stormy invective." Besides restating his comments about male chauvinism, Willie added,

> The laws prohibiting women from being priests are unjust! We know what happens when people follow unjust laws. . . . If you think the women ordained as priests are unlearned, we can send them to seminary. . . . If you think they're not holy enough, we can teach them to pray. But if you dismiss them from the priesthood simply because they are female, they can do nothing, because God Almighty made them that way. To question the ability of a woman to be a priest is to question the judgment of God Almighty.

In his 1979 memoir *Take a Bishop Like Me*, Moore questioned Willie's response in Chicago. "All the resentment he must have harbored for years was flowing out in angry rhetoric," he wrote. "For a Harvard professor," Moore added, "he sounded less than academic." To this day, Willie remembers the slight, down to the page number on which it occurs. Recently, he reflected on that time in Chicago and on his precarious position as an African-American man, saying that what Moore had failed to understand was that he was not going to be party to actions he believed were unjust:

> So he had to call me . . . an angry, young, black man. . . . What had happened to this nice, young, black fellow who is just angry now? I wasn't angry. I wasn't going to participate in anything that was naughty, and I'd tell them.

But Willie was also receiving pressure from the African-American priests who had worked hard to put him into the position of vice presidency.

> I got a call from a few black people who said, "Chuck Willie, stay out of that white woman's mess." That wasn't true with [everyone], but I said, "Well, Brother, injustice to anyone is injustice to everyone. I'll be there and I hope you'll be there. . . ." They kind of laughed and stopped and said, "Okay."

Willie said that after the Chicago meeting, he knew that the hierarchy within the church was "going to get" him. He resigned in a public and formal manner, with the media present, in a church in Syracuse. His resignation was not the only one prompted by the events in Chicago. On August 16, William Wolf, professor of theology from Episcopal Divinity School who had presented Schiess in Philadelphia, resigned in protest from his position on the Joint

Commission on Ecumenical Relations of the Episcopal Church. "The bishops," he wrote in his statement of resignation, "have expressed themselves less as fathers-in-God and more as outraged bureaucrats, as graceless legalists, and as arrogant males." They had used "a diminished collegiality," he argued, "that has excluded in advance one half of the human race."

In their report on the Chicago meeting, three of the theologians present in Chicago—Guthrie, Harris, and Rockwell—criticized the bishops in a number of ways, including for having made a decision (without adequate discussion) based on a faulty report from the theology committee, for allowing a presentment threat to influence the dynamics of the meeting, for failing to consult with theologians (or using "theological resources of the Church"), for confusing invalidity with irregularity, for ignoring the eleven women, and for making an immoral decision to avoid the real issue in front of the House, the "free access of both sexes to holy orders."

Heyward later wrote that the bishops had been looking for a way to invalidate the ordinations and condemn the ordaining bishops "without appearing to be Pharisaic legalists." The resolution they affirmed, she said, "contained a little love, a little vindication, a little anguish, a little soft brutality, a little pastoral concern, and a little legalism." She wrote Moore the day after Chicago to say that "had there been any question in my mind that the July 29 ordinations were inappropriate, witnessing the House of Bishops would have erased all doubt." And she was letting him know that as of August 16, she had ended her "agreement not to exercise priestly functions." Moore responded that he, too, was traumatized by the depressing event, but believed that any action on her part to end the agreement would only escalate matters and would force him into disciplining her.

There was other fallout. From Philadelphia, Paul Washington wrote Allin a letter questioning the Presiding Bishop's claim of emphasizing "reconciliation" and "love" in Chicago. To whom, Washington wondered, was he directing that love and with whom did he wish to be reconciled? William Stringfellow, a prominent lay theologian and lawyer, wrote in an article for *Christianity and Crisis* that the Chicago resolution was conceived in a "surrealistic" environment in which what was called "pastoral" would have been more accurately labeled "paternal." He pointed out that the room had moveable walls and could have accommodated more people. He criticized the bishops for acting beyond the confines of their power and for giving the press a false understanding of the role of bishops:

A wire service, for example, carried this lead: "The ruling body of the Episcopal Church yesterday declared invalid the ordination of eleven women to the priesthood, then withdrew formal charges against three bishops who ordained the women." There is not a single phrase in that story that is factually true: The House of Bishops is *not* the ruling body of the Episcopal Church; it did *not* declare the ordinations invalid; it did *not* withdraw any charges because it is not capable of *initiating* any charges. And the fault for the falsity of this and similar reports about O'Hare lies not with the press; the blame inheres in convening the House in the first place, in circumstances where it possessed neither legislative competence nor judicial power under the church's constitution and canons.

He wrote that what the Presiding Bishop had "dubbed a matter of urgency and emergency" was actually only a form of "mischief," the end result being that all the bishops had "uttered was a mighty curse."

If, as Moore believed, the bishops were angrier when they left Chicago than when they had arrived, the sentiment was shared by almost everyone else who had attended the meeting. Chicago had solved nothing, as one reporter noted. Even so, it had changed everything.

Chapter 7

THE PRIESTS' TALE

Historian Pamela Darling estimated that between the 1974 Chicago meeting and the Minneapolis General Convention of 1976 the eleven women celebrated the Eucharist in approximately twenty churches. The media followed the new priests around to most of the larger events, keeping the issue in front of the public and preventing the Church from quietly and systematically dividing and conquering them. The attention brought secular groups into the debate; in September of 1974, spokespersons for the Federation of Organizations for Professional Women, the National Women's Political Caucus and the Center for Women Policy Studies (CWPS) wrote a joint letter to Presiding Bishop Allin, noting that while they respected the Episcopal Church's private internal matters, the Church's decisions nonetheless had an impact on the "national public community." As such, they asked Allin to "account" for the differences between the bishops' decision at the Chicago meeting and [their] "calls to the nation's conscience" in matters concerning race, economic and military oppression, and other forms of "dehumanization." They called for the Church to dismantle its power structure disempowering women and to bring an end to the way it was responding to the eleven:

> We ask . . . that you take no further action to oppress or humiliate these eleven persons while you consider possible actions to allow women what is now blatantly reserved for men in your church—internal political power and public and symbolic/sacramental power.

As the letter indicates, the criticism the bishops received over the Chicago meeting did not quietly fade away after a few weeks. In a September newsletter from the Diocese of Missouri, the Reverend Claudius Miller wrote a stinging critique of the bishops and of the church at large, accusing it of acting "pigheadedly" towards women and mocking the bishops' show of self-importance in Chicago:

> The House of Bishops tells us that it had twice suffered "anguish"—intense inner pain and sorrow. At what? Being called back from vacation to sit at O'Hare for 24 hours? No person in his right mind wants *that* to happen to

him, but hardly a cause for "intense inner pain and sorrow. . . ." We are reminded by the Bishops that "our Lord has called us to walk in the way of the Cross." I know of no phrase in all of Christian history more cheapened by quick talk and little action than this.

After the August meeting in Chicago, the eleven for the most part abandoned their position of waiting for the church to act and began looking for ways to exercise their priesthoods; on October 1, at the National Cathedral in Washington, D.C., a plan to do so was developed that involved nineteen Protestant denominations, several Roman Catholic organizations, and a variety of ecumenical agencies. They would come together on October 27, Reformation Sunday, to participate in a service to celebrate women in the ministry. It would be held in New York City, and three of the newly ordained Episcopal priests—Jeannette Piccard, Alison Cheek, and Carter Heyward—would be the celebrants, the first time in North America that women priests in the Episcopal Church would preside at the Eucharist. As had been the case a few months earlier in Philadelphia, the press was intrigued and eager to cover the story. And as before, the leadership of the Episcopal Church was spurred into action.

Word of the service reached Paul Moore in mid-October, while he was attending the bishops' meeting in Mexico. In fact, on his first day there, he read about the coming service in the local newspaper and immediately wrote Heyward, arguing that she was "needlessly" heaping "bitterness" upon herself. Even with the concerns over women's ordination, the meeting in the Mexican resort—where the bishops wore Bermuda shorts and luau shirts—proved to be a much more pleasant experience for them than Chicago had been. They could joke more freely. When one bishop complained that the church's policies would drive away the women, another quipped, "Is that a promise?" In Mexico, the bishops continued to strengthen their commitment to collegiality, agreeing neither to regularize the eleven nor to allow more ordinations of other women, at least until after the 1976 General Convention. The majority, however, went on record as saying that they supported "the principle of the ordination of women to the priesthood."

DeWitt and Tony Ramos, who had experienced a "cool" reception in Mexico, were nonetheless encouraged by the bishops' agreement on women's ordination. Some of the eleven were less impressed. Piccard, Cheek, and Heyward released a statement that confronted the supposition that women could be addressed hypothetically:

Women do not exist merely "in principle." We are people and we are priests—
not an hypothesis, but a reality.

They also acknowledged the larger context of their ordinations, one made evident by the amount of attention they had garnered in relation to the place of
women within the broader church:

> . . . what has transpired in the Episcopal Church is not particularly an
> "Episcopal" problem. It is a problem facing the whole Christian church:
> fundamental to church life, women remain peripheral, ignored and invisible
> within its processes.

Heyward then composed a long letter to Moore acknowledging that there was
a political overtone to the work the women were doing (as when the Church
held a Eucharist at the Pentagon) and calling on the liberal bishops to stop serving as the eleven's most "devastating opponent[s]." She confronted him directly
about his concern over the bitterness she was heaping upon herself:

> I read that remark to mean that there are people bitter at me—and that
> you are one of them. . . . and that if I would just quit "doing things," the
> problem would resolve itself. Bitterness would probably subside. And we
> could live together as one, whole, Christian family. But, like grace, such
> reconciliation is not so cheap.

She wrote that their church was "split wide open," that "anger and bitterness
were to be expected," and that the anger and bitterness "would be more con-
structively directed against the structures—and their defenders—than against"
her or the other women.

The following week, Moore released a public statement saying that he
regretted that Piccard, Cheek, and Heyward "felt compelled to celebrate the
Eucharist" and that while he wished he could celebrate with them, he could
not participate in an uncanonical act. Two days later, he responded to Heyward, denying any bitterness on his part and assuring her that if she could have
heard him speaking about Emily, Marie, and her (the three of the eleven from
his diocese) to the bishops in Mexico, she would have known that he was not
bitter. He said, though, that he was more determined than ever to wait until
Minneapolis because he was convinced after Mexico that women's ordination
would be approved at the General Convention. He believed, he wrote, that regularizing their ordinations would "do very little good and would do a great deal
of harm." Then he added a more personal thought:

I worry about you once in awhile; you must be living under a great deal of tension. Take care of yourself.

Regardless of his disapproval, the service was on. Initially, it was to be held in a chapel of Union Theological Seminary, but the board of the seminary came out in opposition to the plan and the service was moved next door to the interdenominational Riverside Church (though many students, faculty, and staff members of Union signed a petition in support of the service). With the approval of Piccard, Cheek, and others, Heyward decided to designate most of the offering to the Presiding Bishop's Fund for World Relief and to earmark it for "hunger relief," a program Moore was launching the following week in conjunction with Allin's project.

On the night of the service, Riverside Church was "jammed," as the Reverend Jeanne Audrey Powers remembered. Powers was a United Methodist minister and one of the main organizers of the service. As some of the service leaders gathered to participate (Carol Anderson, Barbara Schlachter, Charles Willie, Linda Clark, Beverly Harrison, Rosemary Reuther, Betty Medsger, Patricia Park, and others), the three priests sat on a medical cot in a back room of the church talking with DeWitt. A few days later, Piccard wrote DeWitt, addressing him as "Bishop Bob" and thanking him for ministering to them at that moment. She ended her letter noting that had she been male, she would have presided over her first Eucharist fifty-two years earlier, but then, she wrote, "I would have missed all the wonderful things that God has permitted me to do while I waited."

Merrill Bittner attended the service but was doing her best to appease her bishop Robert Spears. She was on the phone, assuring him that she was not serving as one of the presiding priests at the service. Piccard had written Bittner a few weeks earlier, saying that she herself had been caught between "the devil and the deep blue sea" in Minnesota because she was continuing to work as a deacon in Minneapolis even though she had been ordained as a priest. At Riverside, Piccard was making a choice, though she did not say whether it was the devil or the sea she had chosen. Either way, the service, as DeWitt wrote the next day to his brother bishops Welles, Corrigan, and Ramos could not "have gone much better," and he noted that there had been no "counter-demonstrations." He gave a brief overview of his early concerns about the event, along with a closing thought from Piccard:

With me, you probably had wonderments about whether it was appropriate, "strategic," risky . . . I find it helpful to remind myself when I form such

questions that perhaps I am being a little paternalistic? In any event, I felt
much better about the whole thing after its completion than I did when first
hearing about it some several weeks ago. Someone asked Jeannette Piccard
what her next goal was after the service. She replied, "This is the goal."

There was a hitch, however, that showed up few days later. On October 28,
Piccard, Cheek, and Heyward mailed a $672 check from the offering to the
Presiding Bishop along with a copy of the service and a brief letter that spoke
of the "Spirit-filled occasion." Heyward later claimed that she first thought of
sending the offering to the Presiding Bishop for several reasons, though she was
aware of the "'oddity' of the situation." She believed that the need was apparent
and that the money would help launch Moore's hunger relief program. There
was also another reason: they wanted, she wrote, "To make a gesture indicating
our caring about the Episcopal Church and our being Episcopalians." Still, the
women must have been aware that by mailing the check under those circumstances, they were asserting their own place of power within the day-to-day
financial business and pastoral outreach of the church, as they had done the
night before in relation to its sacramental life. In any event, the Presiding Bishop
was not touched by the show of affection for the church nor was he willing to let
the women assert their leadership within of it. He sent the money back.

As it happened, a meeting about women's ordination was being held at
St. Mary's Church, Manhattanville, the Harlem church where both Heyward
and Hewitt had served as deacons. St. Mary's had also played a role in organizing the Riverside service. Heyward took the check to the meeting. Those
attending, Heyward later wrote, were filled with "unabashed outrage" over the
return of the check. One of them asked her for permission to inform the press,
and Heyward provided the go ahead. She then wrote Paul Moore requesting
that he give the check to the Presiding Bishop, believing that Moore would be
able to convince Allin that the money was not "tainted." Moore wrote back
informing her that Allin had agreed to accept the money. "I would not appreciate," he added, "any more publicity on this, however." Heyward responded,
"You're quite right—I cannot understand why all the fuss in the first place."

While this on-going correspondence was occurring between Heyward and
Moore over the offering, Moore publically released a formal reprimand of Heyward over the Riverside service, writing,

> As Bishop I directed the Rev. Carter Heyward to refrain from exercising
> priesthood. She deliberately defied this directive and in so doing alienated

herself from the regular life and discipline of this diocese. . . . I hereby formally reprimand the Rev. Carter Heyward for this action and inhibit the Rev. Alison Cheek of the Diocese of Virginia and the Rev. Jeannette Piccard of the Diocese of Minnesota from ministry in this diocese. . . . I do not use strong words lightly. I have been sympathetic and patient, seeking by persuasion and support of the cause to avoid this situation. However, the service of Oct 27 demands a response.

Episcopal priest Jorge M. Gutierrez and his wife Carolyn read Moore's reprimand in *The New York Times* and decided to send Moore a letter of their own, critiquing Moore's argument point by point, beginning with his emphasis on law and order:

> You concluded that additional ordinations must come only after legislation. Those words clearly echo past politicians decrying the demonstrations of the Sixties while affirming the equality of all and intending it for none.

Moore had written that the women had "jeopardized some delicate ecumenical relations," presumably meaning they were making discussions with certain leaders of the Catholic Church difficult. He did not mention, however, the interdenominational nature of the Riverside service and the fact that Roman Catholics had participated. In their letter to Moore, the Gutierrezes asked, "Must women stay down, so that you and other prelates can further ecumenical relations between churches that are in agreement about the subjugation of women?" It was, they argued, an "unholy alliance."

In the time between the Philadelphia ordinations and the convention in Minneapolis, this alliance between the Episcopal and Catholic Churches would also be directly confronted by Alla Bozarth, although Bozarth took the bold step of actually presiding over mass at St. Paul's University Chapel at the University of Wisconsin in Madison. DeWitt wrote her, having seen a photograph of her standing over the elements "emblazoned" on the front page of the *National Catholic Reporter* (NCR) (Bozarth had not known that the photographer and a reporter were present), "I am not at all clear as to how you did it," DeWitt wrote, "but I already know you are one not to be underestimated." Bozarth had not initially planned to celebrate at the Catholic chapel, but rather at the Episcopal Canterbury Club, whose congregation had invited her. But Episcopal Bishop Charles Gaskell placed what Bozarth referred to as "a medieval style interdict" on her, not allowing her "to set foot on" Episcopal Church property. The Episcopal Canterbury Club, Bozarth noted, "figuratively had to go to Rome [or to the Roman Catholic Newman Center on campus] to worship with a female Anglican priest."

DeWitt noted that he hoped she would "not suffer too much flak from this episode" and reminded her that many would be appreciative of her efforts. But no doubt Bozarth had angered the leadership of both churches. In fact, she remembered experiencing the effects of a "collective nervous breakdown" of "three Episcopal bishops and at least two Roman Catholic Archbishops." Catholic Bishop Cletus F. McDonnell told the *NCR* that (1) he completely disapproved; (2) if he had known beforehand, he would have "under no circumstances" allowed it; (3) his "Episcopal brothers" would not "appreciate" it; and (4) he would "be checking into it." Bozarth's response to the reporter from the *NCR* was that the early church had never intended that its ministry should divide people along lines established by hierarchy and that she believed "commitment to the good news [had] been replaced with a law and order mentality in the church. "Authority," she added, "in the corrupt sense of that word."

Bozarth's own bishop in Minnesota, Philip McNairy, called her in a few days later asking for the name of the Catholic archbishop in whose jurisdiction the service was held. He wanted to send an apology, so Bozarth gave him Cletus O'Donnell's name. "For some bizarre reason," she later wrote, "he sent the letter to Bill Cousins, Archbishop of Milwaukee." But from Bozarth's perspective, the mistake served a useful purpose since she had been asked to speak at a function for the Archdiocesan Sisters in Milwaukee in a few weeks. She felt "covered," having been "apologized for in advance." Not all went well at this event, however. After she had finished speaking, a woman from the John Birch Society rose from the back of the room and said, "The devil uses clever words and we have heard the devil here tonight." Bozarth was shaken by the comment, by its "icy air of malice." She told one of the Sisters "that it was probably time to leave," later adding, "I may have used somewhat more colorful language."

While those in New York City were preparing for the Riverside service, Katrina Swanson in Kansas City was being faced with suspension in her diocese of West Missouri. Swanson's bishop was Arthur Vogel, who had delivered the report from the theology committee in Chicago and had argued (and convinced the House) that the ordinations in Philadelphia were invalid. At the time of the ordinations, her husband, the Reverend George Swanson, was the rector of a church in Kansas City, where Katrina served as an assistant.

On August 12, 1974, three clergy and four laymen filed charges with Vogel and brought a presentment against Swanson. Their charges read that they were bringing "Katrina van Alstyne Swanson, a clergyman of this diocese for trial for offenses against the doctrine, discipline, or worship of this Church and for conduct unbecoming a clergyman." But Vogel and the Standing Committee decided to offer Swanson a deal. Her decision to take the deal would be the only true regret she had in the years following her ordination. On July 31, two days after the ordination, Vogel sent her a letter. He greeted her "in the presence and peace of Christ—believing that his Easter victory means the future is never closed to God's grace" and then told her that she could either accept suspension or "receive a judgment from an Ecclesiastical Court." She decided to accept the suspension. Years later, when reflecting on her decision with a reporter from *The Philadelphia Inquirer*, she said,

> I guess I felt that God was calling me to orders and, if the procedure went forward to trial, I really would be deposed and probably never be able to serve as a priest within the church. To be reinstated would have required the written consent of all the dioceses touching West Missouri—some of which still do not have women priests. I suppose I didn't have enough faith that God could pull off that kind of miracle. And I buckled.

But if she had hoped that her acquiescence would soften the diocese, her hopes would be disappointed. At the West Missouri diocese convention in November of 1975, women's ordination to the priesthood was, not surprisingly, a major concern of those attending, who passed a resolution on the issue to take to the 1976 General Convention in Minneapolis. The resolution stated that even if the General Convention accepted women into the priesthood, the approval "should not be construed to validate or regularize previous illicit ordinations. . . ." In other words, the Philadelphia ordinations would not be validated regardless of how the General Convention voted. At this diocesan convention, the West Missouri delegates to the House of Deputies at the General Convention were also elected with three of the four clergy delegates ready to vote against women's ordination. The lay vote split 2–2, essentially a negative vote in the House if a vote by orders were called for, and there was little doubt that it would be.

In the meantime, Katrina's husband George Swanson was being targeted by the leadership in the diocese who had decided to audit him in relation to a halfway house he had established. The papers announcing the audit were delivered to the hospital room where one of the Swanson's children was critically ill with Reye's Syndrome. "It was a gruesome time. . . . [with] a lot of dirty pool," Katrina Swanson told *The Philadelphia Inquirer*. Additionally, Vogel had informed Swanson that her only recourse in the diocese was to start the entire ordination process from the beginning, from before she had even been made a deacon. He ended his letter:

> This comes with all best wishes. You, your family, and your ministry remain in my prayers. In his service, Arthur A. Vogel

Swanson had been ordained a deacon by her father Edward Welles in September of 1971 and, as a male, could have been ordained a priest in March or April of 1972. In his memoir *The Happy Disciple*, Welles laid out the steps he and his daughter took in relation to her studies and to her physical and psychiatric exams and noted that she had passed all requirements to be ordained as a deacon. Welles retired as Bishop of West Missouri on December 31, 1972, to be replaced by Vogel. Swanson requested from Vogel that he allow another bishop to come into the diocese to regularize her, but he refused. By all appearances, he wanted the Swansons out of West Missouri.

In the neighboring Diocese of Kansas, Marie Moorefield was struggling with a decision: whether to get on with her calling as a minister by being ordained in the United Methodist Church or to stay and fight for her priesthood in the Episcopal Church. Her letters from that time give some indication of the types of issues she was confronting in a diocese with a bishop unfriendly to women's ordination, a bishop who informed her after the ordinations that she was no longer welcome in the diocese. Moorefield wrote Paul Moore that after Chicago, her hopes that the bishops might be able to reconcile "the integrity of tradition" with the "leading of the Holy Spirit" seemed "premature and perhaps in vain." She was applying for certification as a Supervisor in Clinical Pastoral Education and needed a "clear relationship with . . . ecclesiastical authority" and a "growing pastoral identity." Because of the "treacherous ground" on which she found herself professionally, she told Moore that she had to focus her efforts on her ministry to the people:

> The priority for me is being able to serve fully and freely as both pastor and priest witnessing to the Gospel among people who are struggling with the basic questions of life and to do so with the support and authorization of the Christian community of which I am a member. I do not feel that this is possible for me within the Episcopal Church at this time. . . . I sincerely hope that this transition will be able to take place before I am brought to trial and/or deposed.

The remaining ten of the eleven sent a statement of support for Moorefield to the United Methodist Church, affirming their "deep personal affection" for her and "great respect for her work." They expressed their regret that the Episcopal Church would lose her ministry and their dismay at the "brokenness" within the Episcopal Church in relation to "the full ministry of women."

Though she had written Moore that her "decision had been a long hard struggle in the making," Moorefield's decision would prove more difficult than even she had imagined. She found that she deeply missed certain aspects of Episcopal theology and practice and asked once again for Moore to regularize her. But it would be another ten years before she was received as a priest into the Episcopal Church.

While she did not change denominations to practice her priesthood, Nancy Wittig left her parish church, St. Peter's, in Morristown, New Jersey. She was pregnant at the time and felt that her health was being destroyed by the ongoing controversies within the parish. On August 25, a few weeks after the bishops' meeting in Chicago, she stood in front of the St. Peter's congregation and said that her decision to be ordained in Philadelphia had been a "painful" one and one that continued to carry risks. On a personal level, she worried about being rejected by friends. She worried about being expelled from the ministry. "I fear," she said, "the unknown." But even more, she feared the judgment of God if she had turned her back on the ordinations. Fear, she believed, whether her own or that expressed by the church, should not be the deciding factor in the debates about women's ordination to the priesthood.

Wittig had also been profoundly concerned about not surviving the ordinations in Philadelphia, and the risk of being hurt or killed had weighed heavily on her. It was her father, the career Navy man, who had made certain the police had come by the busload to the service. She worked through the fear and a year later would tell a reporter,

> I don't feel bound any longer by what might happen to me. I have a new freedom to live out what I have to live out, a new sense that I can't be hurt anymore.

But she also told this reporter that she was not going to place herself unnecessarily in harm's way. "I am no longer," she said, "participating in something destructive for me and for other people." It was the sort of growing sentiment that led her to resign from St. Peter's. She issued a letter to the Rector, Wardens, Vestry, and People of St. Peter's on October 25, a few days before she assisted in the Riverside service:

As a result of the attitudes and actions expressed at the vestry meeting of October 22, I am aware that there is a significant lack of confidence in me as a person worthy of the Christian ministry. In such an atmosphere, I find it impossible to carry on an effective ministry at St. Peter's. I can no longer submit myself to the gross confusion and fear of others because of its toll on my health.

Some members of the vestry had told her that they wanted her to avoid being "'sucked into' further controversial activity." Some implied she was not a suitable person to work with the youth of the church. One person wanted her to wear the stole of a deacon rather than that of a priest. And the vestry wanted her to promise not to sue the parish. She believed she could not make such a promise: "I wasn't suing them and I didn't plan to sue, but my integrity and the integrity of the clergy meant that I couldn't promise such a thing."

Betty Bone Schiess had no such compunction about suing the Church and hired a powerful New York attorney, Constance Cook. Serving in the New York State Assembly in the 1960s and early 1970s, the Republican Cook coauthored a pro-choice bill that was passed in New York in 1970, three years before Roe v. Wade. She would accept a vice president position at Cornell University, the first woman to hold that position at the university. She was both well-respected and well-connected. And she was an Episcopalian.

In mid-October, ten days before the Riverside service, Schiess sent Alison Cheek a letter in which she argued that since "the categorical exclusion of women to the priesthood and episcopacy is contrary to *all* doctrine of the Episcopal Church," the wrong people were being put on the defensive in relation to women's ordination:

> When we assume the position of guilty party we are, perhaps, contributing to the idea that we are responsible for crimes committed against us and the church. It is rather our Bishops, Standing Committees etc. who must somehow be brought to task for acting contrary to doctrine.

In her Diocese of Central New York, Schiess had been called in front of a Committee of Inquiry regarding the Philadelphia ordinations. According to her, Cook had written the chair of the committee asking for clarifications of the charges, but was given an incomplete answer. When Cook and Schiess arrived at St. Paul's Cathedral and were finally allowed into the room where the committee was to meet, Cook asked for permission to stay so that she could advise her client, but was refused. Schiess and the committee members sat at a round table as a court stenographer typed responses to what felt to Schiess like an "endless" number of questions. The committee finally decided to follow the lead of the bishops in Chicago and conclude that no ordinations had occurred on July 29.

Schiess pointed out that priests and lay persons could not bring presentments against bishops—only bishops could raise presentments against each other. She decided, therefore, to take the matter into civil court, and in a suit against the Diocese of New York and Bishop Ned Cole, she asked for protection of "constitutional rights and civil liberties to worship freely and to be employed without discrimination because of sex" under Title VII of the Civil Rights Act of 1964, which prohibited discrimination based on race, color, religion, sex, or national origin. In the suit, Schiess stated that she had been offered, in December of 1974, a position of priest associate with Grace Episcopal Church in Syracuse but that Bishop Cole had refused to license her for the sole reason that she was female. Schiess wrote in a complaint to the New York State Division of Human Rights that Cole had warned Grace Episcopal Church "that dire consequences might ensue" if the parish employed her as a priest. While Schiess acknowledged that the Human Rights Law of New York allowed religious organizations to limit employment for religious principles, she argued that, in fact, the Episcopal Church and the larger Anglican Communion had ordained women priests in Hong Kong who had presided over the Eucharist in the United States. Further, the House of Bishops had approved women's ordination to the priesthood in principle.

In the suit, she also took a bold step of arguing that what had been termed *collegiality* was actually a form of *conspiracy*:

> Plaintiff is informed and believes that the defendant Cole and the presiding bishop and several, if not all, of the bishops of the other ten female ordinands conferred and agreed together to prevent an ecclesiastical trial of any of the eleven women which might result in a duly adopted ruling of the Church that the ordinations were valid.
>
> Plaintiff is informed and believes that the defendant Cole, in furtherance of this conspiracy, prevented the filing of presentments or charges which might have resulted in trial and appeal to the final church judiciary. To date, none of the women ordinands have been tried.
>
> Said arguments ostensibly made in the name of collegiality were in fact and in effect a conspiracy for the purpose of depriving plaintiff indirectly, solely because she is a female. . . .

When Marjorie Hyer from *The Washington Post* wrote a story about the suit, she reported that Cook had admitted that the likelihood was low that the suit would be decided before the General Convention of 1976. Perhaps more importantly, when the General Convention opened its doors for business, a suit would be before the courts in which the concept of collegiality had been radically redefined as conspiracy and in which the plaintiff was asking for, among other things, thirty thousand dollars in damages.

Cook and the other lawyers for the eleven and for the ordaining bishops had maintained contact with one another to discuss the issues their clients were facing and to discuss possible strategies. On December 11, 1974, lawyer William Stringfellow wrote Robert Dewitt a five-page letter summarizing some of the opinions that had come out of the discussions and asked DeWitt to pass along the letter to others involved. Stringfellow believed that the bishops intended to stonewall as long as possible, that there was almost no chance that the bishops would regularize the eleven, that there was "some sentiment, which may be increasing, to eliminate the eleven priests, one by one," that the women should accept as many offers as possible to perform as priests, and that instead of leaving the church (which would only please the opponents and set back the cause of women's ordination) the supporters should participate in a Church-in-Exile, which had already begun in smaller pockets where the women were being invited to preside. The Church-in-Exile would remain part of the Episcopal Church, but would be a "new church within the old church," a part of the church that developed in reaction to "failed" leadership.

Within the next six months, that perception of failed leadership within the Episcopal Church would only grow stronger, perhaps peaking during a moment of tragedy that affected not only the church, but the larger nation as well.

Chapter 8

WIND SHEAR

Between the 1974 ordinations and the 1976 General Convention in Minneapolis, Sue Hiatt, Robert DeWitt, Ann Robb Smith, Charles Ritchie, and Don Belcher were meeting regularly in Philadelphia to stay abreast of what was happening in the aftermath of the Philadelphia ordinations. At these meetings, they would discuss issues such as how to acquire funding for travel, legal defense, and personal expenses of the eleven or how to implement strategies to move the church towards acceptance of women's ordination to the priesthood. At Hiatt's home on January 13, 1975, the group laid plans for a meeting of the eleven, including some of their supporters, to be held in February in Washington, D.C. And they also discussed the possibility that on January 17, Bishop Robert Spears of Rochester (Merrill Bittner's bishop) might announce his willingness to recognize Bittner's ordination. They showed cautious optimism over that development, recognizing that Spears was under "tremendous pressure" from opposing forces.

As the minutes from these meetings illustrate, Hiatt was continuing to organize the movement and was in constant contact with people connected to it, playing her role as a "leader from behind" as Heyward would describe Hiatt. Alison Cheek remembered that for months, she and Hiatt spoke on the phone nearly every day. But Hiatt's outreach was not limited only to the women. She carried on a correspondence with Edward Welles, who seemed to have a deep fondness for the woman he had ordained. In January of 1976, he wrote to her in a state of concern. He had heard that she had withdrawn from a conference in the Diocese of Olympia because James Wattley, a member of Coalition for the Apostolic Ministry (CAM), one of the groups committed to the all-male priesthood, had been invited to participate. Welles wondered if the time for dialogue were over. Hiatt responded to Welles in early February, clarifying her position. "Of course the time for real dialogue," she wrote, "is never over, but the possibility of such dialogue between us seems uselessly slim":

> I have grown tired of "debating" people who have no respect for me or my position and who do not recognize me as what I am. To talk about whether

women *can* be priests when I *am* a priest seems ludicrous. By even listening to such foolishness I deny my priesthood and allow the "dialogue" to be carried on exclusively on their terms. We are no longer (if we ever were) talking about the same subject—they want to discuss whether, we can only speculate when.

Hiatt had accepted the invitation to the conference with the understanding that the format of her session would not be one of debate; nonetheless, a week before the conference began, she received the program with Wattley's name added to her session. She called the organizers of the conference to ask why and was told by one of the conference organizers that they had been under pressure to allow "equal time" for the opposing side to give its position. Hiatt replied that if they wanted to give equal time, they should turn over their pulpits every other Sunday to women. Then she withdrew. In her letter to Welles, she related more of the story about her relationship with Wattley: "I have had some personal correspondence with Fr. Wattley over the years that makes his personal contempt for me and my vocation perfectly clear."

Welles was having problems of his own with those who disagreed with his position on women's ordination. He (along with DeWitt, Corrigan, and Ramos) was facing a Board of Inquiry that would determine whether they had broken canon law and should face an ecclesiastical trial. Even though the charges had initially been dismissed in Chicago, they were raised again by Stanley Atkins and ten other bishops. But in an 8–2 vote, the Board of Inquiry decided that some of the questions the case raised did not belong in the Board of Inquiry's jurisdiction and that the House of Bishops would have to decide if a bishop could—in order to follow his conscience—usurp the roles of Standing Committees, vestries, the General Convention, etc. The majority opinion of the board stated that much of what the bishops had been accused of would have been reason to send the case to trial, but because of the mixed nature of the accusations, the board had voted to send it back to the House of Bishops. This decision by the board infuriated some who wanted to see the bishops brought to trial. The Rev. Francis W. Read—Chairman of the Legal Committee of the American Church Union—argued, "No greater travesty of justice has ever been perpetrated in the name of Canon Law." He even went as far as to call the decision "sexism in reverse," contending that the decision "would not and could not have been justified in the case of ordination of men." One could argue, of course, that it would be difficult to imagine the board convening in the first place over the ordinations of eleven highly qualified men.

Besides her communications with the ordaining bishops, Hiatt was also in contact with other bishops within the church. In August of 1976, she wrote Robert Spears asking that he refrain from actions that would lead to Merrill Bittner being deposed. Hiatt had taken a "soft-glove" approach (as she scribbled in the margins of a copy of the letter she mailed to Bittner) which included praising Spears for his support of women's ordination. "Since before the Louisville convention," she wrote, "I have observed you to be among the most courageous and committed of bishops of the Episcopal Church," adding that she believed he had been the "boldest of the bishops" of the eleven. How Spears moved from being the one bishop who would seriously consider regularizing one of the eleven to the bishop willing to depose Bittner is a question not easily answered.

Bittner and Spears had initially enjoyed a close relationship, but like Carter Heyward and Paul Moore, their disagreements over the church's handling of women's ordination would create divisions between them that would never be completely mended. Today, Bittner keeps an 8x10 black and white photograph of Spears and herself in one of her scrapbooks, a photograph Spears had given to her on the day of her ordination as a deacon. In the photo, Spears is standing over her shoulder in what appears to be a church parlor. They are both looking at a booklet she is holding in her hands. He could have been a proud and committed parent and she a diligent, sincere daughter, intent on performing the task she had been given. On the back of the photo is an inscription that reads,

> For Merrill,
>
> As a remembrance of a great day—January 6, 1973
>
> > Love, peace and joy!
> >
> > +Robert R. Spears, Jr.

Bittner had become a popular subject for the press in the Rochester area. The staff from the *Courier-Journal* followed her work in the jails, writing an article in December of 1973 about how the only female deacon in the Diocese of Rochester was providing the women inmates with a host of services, from giving them artistic outlets to helping the women find homes and jobs after they had been released from prison. A comment by the reporter indicated that Bittner had already acquired a reputation for being concerned about the rights of women: "Her fight for the recognition of women's rights is being waged not only within her church, the Episcopal Church of the Good Shepherd in

Webster, but within the Monroe County Jail." Bittner recalled towards the end, when her health was failing and she would sometimes try to hide herself away in her home, members of the media would knock incessantly on her doors and windows, yelling, "We know you're in there, Merrill." Of course, the ordinations in Philadelphia only heightened the media attention.

Spears had not wanted Bittner to be ordained in Philadelphia and the day after the ordinations, he wrote a memo to the Standing Committee arguing that she was "liable for presentment" because he had "forbade her participation." It is possible that this move by Spears was taken to protect Bittner from other priests who would have likely raised their own presentments against her that could have spiraled out of Spears' control. But if Spears' act was intended to be protective of Bittner, the protective impulse would soon pass. He suspended her from her ministry until the Standing Committee could have a chance to advise him on the situation. On September 9, the members of the Standing Committee met and agreed to gather a group of "distinguished" theologians who could inform them as to whether the ordinations in Philadelphia had been valid. Taking issue with the House of Bishops' position in Chicago, the theologians came to the conclusion that the ordinations were valid, but irregular, needing ratification (another name for recognition or authorization) by the church, which could be as simple as a bishop signing a form. There was no cause, they maintained, for the eleven to be reordained.

With this analysis in hand, the Standing Committee voted 8–2 to advise Spears to correct the irregular nature of Bittner's ordination as quickly as possible. The story began running in the newspapers, and Spears said he would deliver a decision on January 17. Many people believed that he was going to take the step of recognizing Bittner's ordination, and as noted, even Hiatt and company in Philadelphia maintained a cautious optimism. Spears asked for prayers for guidance from clergy and laypersons in the diocese.

A few days before the announcement, Spears informed Bittner of his decision, telling her that he would be announcing that he would be unable to recognize her until receiving the approval of the General Convention. On the seventeenth, he told the diocese that he had consulted with the Presiding Bishop, other bishops, and experts in canon law from both sides of the issue and had concluded that authorizing Bittner's ordination would cause a backlash of "severe proportions" in the Church. He hoped that his decision to wait would prompt the Church into making "its ordained ministry inclusive of both male and female."

Bittner issued a statement of her own, one she addressed to the clergy of the diocese. She spoke of hope, new life, healing, and the need for wholeness. And she affirmed her resolve to remain part of the church:

> God willing, I shall continue to be a priest of the Church in your midst. I will not go away. What forms this ministry is to take, I do not know. I do know, that I am ready—a bit scared—but ready never-the-less, to proclaim life in the midst of death—in all its guises. I will call you brother, even if you will not call me sister.

Though many in the diocese showed support for his decision, Spears immediately began receiving criticism. The local radio station WHAM released an editorial stating that Spears' decision had been a cowardly one: "We find it difficult to believe that a bishop of a church which should be teaching its adherents the rightness of equality for women, should 'chicken out' on a decision that would put him squarely in support of the position of women as equals to men." Bittner, the woman who had assured Spears by phone she was not presiding at the Riverside service, decided it was time for her to begin exercising her priesthood. The church she chose, Calvary-St. Andrews in Rochester, had already laid claim to a history of providing a home to rebellious priests. Some seventy years earlier, the Reverend Algernon Crapsey had captured the attention of the media, his story appearing in newspapers as far away as Europe. Crapsey did not believe in a literal interpretation of the Apostle's Creed and did not mind saying so. He wrote his bishop,

> When I say of Jesus that He ascended into heaven I do not mean and cannot mean that with His physical body of flesh, blood and bone He floated into space and has for two thousand years been existing somewhere in the sky, in that very physical body of flesh, blood and bones. Such an existence would seem to me not glorious but horrible. . . .

Bittner's service at Calvary-St. Andrews had its share of media attention, including the presence of reporters, photographers, and television personnel. According to their reports, the service was a high-spirited one. The congregation was upbeat and enthusiastic. The opposition was fired up, too, and had a list of priests ready to sign their names to a presentment against Bittner.

A few months later, while this conflict was working its way through the channels of the church, Bittner was in an airport and happened to glance over at the newspaper rack where she saw her photograph on the front page beside a headline that read "Women's ordination tied to death." The story, she would discover, ran to section B, under the heading "Blamed in death." The article drew the connection between Bittner and the death of a bishop.

On June 24, 1975, Eastern Airlines Flight 66 took off from Louisiana, scheduled to land in the afternoon at the John F. Kennedy International Airport in New York. On board the flight was the Bishop of Louisiana, Iveson Noland, who was to join Presiding Bishop John Allin, Bishop Frederick Wolf of Maine, and others to plan the coming House of Bishops meeting and to discuss women's ordination. Not long before Flight 66 was to land, a DC-8 had nearly crashed on the runway after experiencing tremendous wind shear from a severe thunderstorm. Other pilots warned those in the air tower of the danger; nonetheless, the landings continued. Two more planes landed safely, but Flight 66 apparently lost control in the storm and crashed into the runway lights before bursting into flames. Most of the 124 passengers were killed, including Bishop Noland.

The following week, Bishop Wolf sent out a letter (that quickly hit the newswires) to the Philadelphia Eleven, to DeWitt, Welles, Corrigan, Allin, and to other officials in the church. In the letter, Wolf blamed the women both for the death of Noland and for the expenses the church had accrued from the debates around the Philadelphia "event." Below are selections from the two-page letter.

I do not apologize for sending this personal communication in xeroxed or mimeographed form. . . . The Diocese of Maine is not wealthy, and the Church has already spent too much money on you. . . .

As I trust you know, the Rt. Rev. Iveson Noland, the Bishop of Louisiana and the President of Province VII, died in an airplane crash. . . . You may not know, and I feel that you must, that he died on his way to that meeting of the Council of Advice. I do not hold you personally responsible for Iveson Noland's death. However, Iveson Noland would not have died in that plane crash if you had not done what you did in Philadelphia. That is a part, by no means directly so, of the consequences of your ecclesiastical disobedience and you have the right to be aware of this. . . .

Beyond those monetary costs, there has been the turmoil and anguish caused particularly by some of the women Deacons in your persistent defiance of the action of your Fathers-in-God in Chicago when your "ordination" to the priesthood was clearly declared invalid. . . .

If I sound angry, it is because I am. Anger is, in my judgment, still an occasionally necessary part of Christian Charity. I write this letter to you as a Baptised member of the Body of Christ, the community of reconciliation. . . . You are in my prayers. Faithfully,

+Fred Wolf

Wolf also pointed out that the church's lawyer had charged the church a fee in the "five-figure range" when the Board of Inquiry had convened over presentments against the ordaining bishops and that he believed the cost of the Chicago meeting to be in the neighborhood of one hundred thousand dollars.

Piccard responded quickly, writing Wolf that his letter seemed more like a cry of pain than one of anger and that he should not "flagellate" himself for convening the meeting in the first place: "I cannot believe that God struck down a whole planeload of people just to prevent Bishop Noland from participating in a meeting of the Council, whatever its agenda may have been." The Reverend Charles Pickett, the rector of Christ Church and St. Ambrose in Philadelphia, wrote to Wolf, concerned because he had received irate responses from other denominations, including a group of Roman Catholic nuns, after the story of the letter ran in the *Philadelphia Evening Bulletin*. The *Portland Press Herald* quoted a gracious Wittig, who said that Wolf had most likely written the letter in anger and that he might be feeling regret over it. In the same article, Schiess dismissed the letter for being "so absurd" she could not "take it seriously." The Reverend John Earl Lamb had read the story in *The Boston Globe* and wrote to Wolf, "Following your illogical reasoning the death of the bishop could be blamed just as well on the Wright brothers." Lamb added, "Frankly, I don't know why women have put up with second class citizenship in the ecclesiastical establishment for so many centuries anyhow." Paul Washington wrote Wolf, denouncing the bishop's letter, and mailed DeWitt a copy. DeWitt responded to both Washington and Wolf, writing Washington, "I felt all I could do with any appropriateness was simply to acknowledge to him that I had received his letter."

Forty years later, Emily Hewitt's reaction to Wolf is still remembered by some of the eleven, even though parts of it are mythical. The story is that when Hewitt received the letter, she wrote across the bottom of it, "Dear Bishop Wolf, I write you in haste that some yo-yo has gotten hold of your stationery." Hewitt recently said, though, that she never actually sent the letter, but would occasionally joke about it with the other women during moments in the struggle when spirits were low. In relation to Wolf's letter, she told the others, "You shouldn't spend a second worrying about this—we didn't murder that guy."

When a member of the media asked Bittner for her response, she said, "There is no response I can make to it other than to say I feel sorry for a man who lost a friend and was moved to express his sorrow in a letter like that." She received through the mail a copy of the story tying Noland's death to women's ordination. On this copy someone had added handwritten comments in blue pen, including a comment concerning how she needed to lose weight, and then adding, "I wouldn't walk across the street to hear you and a lot of other people in Webster [New York] feel the same way."

While trying to deflect the insults and name calling resulting from Wolf's letter, Bittner still had to consider what the church's response would be to the Calvary-St. Andrews service in February. When a presentment was made against her, Spears appointed a committee to advise him. In late October, the committee announced its position—that Bittner "was acting in obedience to her conscience rather than in disobedience to her Bishop, and that to act affirmatively on the presentment for a trial would do a disservice to the life of the Church." Spears agreed, though issued her a reprimand and wrote that he prayed the issue would be resolved by the General Convention.

By March, a frustrated and physically exhausted Bittner had decided to leave the church, a choice, she wrote, made all the more difficult because it felt as if she were leaving family. But she clearly stated in her public letter that she was not renouncing her orders:

> It is with both agony and joy that I wish to inform you of my decision to no longer affiliate myself with the Protestant Episcopal Church of the U.S.A. . . . This decision is, for me, the claiming of a reality that has informed my life for some time now. In effect, I have not left the church, the church has left me. Indeed, perhaps as a woman, I have always been of, but not fully in the church. . . . I am in no way quitting the task I was ordained to be about. I will not abandon the faith that has informed my life. I have no intention of renouncing my priestly orders or my vows to the Church of God.

Spears sent out a press release a few days later, writing that "if the Episcopal Church seems oppressive to her, the decision to leave is understandable." He regretted her decision, he noted, because she was the only woman of the eleven whose bishop had recognized her priesthood and he hoped that her decision would "not have a negative effect on the fundamental issue of permitting the ordination of women as priests in the Episcopal Church." In effect, he was blaming her for any potentially negative decision the Church might make on women's ordination. But he and the Standing Committee went a step further. In its May meeting, the Standing Committee decided to certify that Bittner had, based on her March letter, abandoned the church. Spears wrote Bittner and confirmed the charge of abandonment, inhibited her ministry for six months, and informed her that if she had not retracted the statement within six months, she would be deposed from the ministry.

Bittner arranged a meeting with Spears in his office to argue that he had misinterpreted her letter. The meeting did not go well. Bittner left angry, swearing as she left his office. Spears sent her the following handwritten letter:

> Dear Merrill,
>
> I am sorry for losing my temper—and also that you lost yours. In my own office I am at a disadvantage—I can't make a dramatic exit. If you want me to take you seriously as a friend and an adult, you'll have to do more than walk out whenever you feel like it.
>
> Bob

Bittner wrote a letter to her friends (copies of the letter have shown up in the various collections of the eleven), telling them that while she was feeling shaky, she was improving and looking forward to the next part of her life. She informed them of the plan to depose her and pointed out the irony of the abandonment charge:

> I am now going to be deposed for *not* celebrating the eucharist! . . . Amazing what I had to do to get recognition as a priest in this diocese—such recognition was certainly news to me!

Nevertheless, Bittner was about to begin something new . . . and healing, wanting to spend more time "being excited about new possibilities for the future" and less time on "grieving the loss of a major part of [her] life." She saved her money, bought a van, put a mattress in the back, called an old college friend, and spent the next year driving across the country.

Ever the adventurer, Piccard mailed her a letter of encouragement, writing that she should feel free on her trip to park her van in her backyard. "When you want to move on," she added, "maybe I'll go with you!"

. . .

The story of Fred Wolf deserves at least one more look since it raises questions about sexuality the church has been grappling with for decades. About a year before his death in 1998, Wolf arranged a luncheon date with Carter Heyward. At the lunch, he apologized for the letter. Since writing it, he told her, he had gone into a recovery program for alcoholism. And, he added, he had come out as a gay man. Heyward believed that Wolf felt a connection with her because she herself had come out publicly not long after the ordinations and had confronted her own addiction issues with alcohol.

Wolf, as Nancy Wittig had predicted in 1975, had come to regret writing the letter. He was afraid, Heyward said, that at his death, the letter would be how he would be remembered. The depth of his regret regarding the rhetoric he had used about women's ordination was reflected in a conversation he had once with the Reverend Elizabeth Kaeton. He told her that when he had stood to address the House of Bishops, he had asked the House to imagine the obscenity of "a crucifix with the corpse of a half-naked woman hanging from it." Remembering the moment with Kaeton, he said that he had misinterpreted the source of the obscenity:

> Never mind the obscenity of the crucifixion. . . . The real obscenity was me—a drunken, misogynist, self-loathing, closeted gay man, inadvertently exposing myself publicly in front of my brother bishops and God. Everyone knew exactly what I was saying . . . except me.

In his comment to Kaeton, Wolf draws a connection between his misogyny and his own self-directed homophobia. He is not alone in connecting the two. Scholars and other cultural critics have also linked homophobia with misogyny, arguing that LGBT people are perceived to be rejecting patriarchy's insistence on the dominance and privilege of straight men. It should be no surprise, then, that so many of the parishes in opposition to female priests have also intensely opposed the ordination of gay and lesbian priests.

Approximately a third of the Philadelphia Eleven have come out as lesbians over the course of their lives, but Heyward notes that at the time of the ordinations, those who then identified as lesbian remained closeted (except to others of the eleven and to Bishops DeWitt and Corrigan who were personally ordaining them), not wanting to give the opposition more ammunition for their arguments against women in the priesthood. The Episcopal Church had a relatively liberal and forward-thinking policy towards the LGBT community in relation to other Christian denominations, but given the vote-by-orders procedure that had allowed a minority within the Church to consistently vote down women's ordination and given the deep and widespread prejudice within the culture against gays and lesbians, the lesbian women within the eleven chose to wait for another day to fight that battle.

Wolf no doubt created anger and despair by sending the letter, but he also put himself through intense self-examination and attempted to make amends for what he came to believe was an obscene act towards the women of the church. The story of his life and ministry is perhaps fertile ground for discussions about sexuality, not only in the Episcopal Church, but in religious cultures throughout the world.

For the women, the decision to hide their identities at the ordination must have been a conflicting, if not wrenching, one. While taking the bold and dangerous move of being ordained in the name of achieving wholeness for the priesthood, they watched as lesbian women—whom this "wholeness" did not include—served as security during the ordination service at the Advocate, risking their own safety to protect not only the eleven but the crowd of two thousand. It would have been evident that day that wholeness would be a process, and not one brought to fruition simply through the ordination of women.

Even so, given the response from Episcopalians and others as a result of the ordinations, no doubt the issue of women in the priesthood was itself perceived as both a defining moment and one that had shaken the foundation of the church. In the next chapter, we will examine other letters written to (or about) the eleven, letters written both in opposition and support. In the case of some of these authors, the levels of obscenity they reached far surpassed anything that had been attained by Fred Wolf.

Chapter 9

LETTERS, SCARLET AND OTHERWISE

Finding themselves on national television and in the pages of major newspapers and magazines, the eleven drew the attention of people who wanted to respond to the ordinations, to the meeting in Chicago, to the various services the women were presiding over, and to other events associated with the movement. Their letters varied tremendously in scope of opinion. Some voiced anger, even rage. Others expressed support for the ordinations and spoke of having their lives irrevocably altered. Some wrote directly to the women themselves, while others wrote to newspapers and newsletters, particularly publications such as *The Episcopalian* or more regional papers like *The Virginia Churchman* (which was also receiving its own share of complaints concerning its sexist title. A change of title would take another decade).

These letters give insight into how people thought about the ordination in relation to a range of subjects, including power, community, law, and perhaps most strikingly, sexuality. Some framed the Philadelphia ordinations as an abuse of power in the style of Nixon and Watergate. In fact, that storyline was told in a much larger format—on the front page of *The Philadelphia Daily News.* The day after the ordination in Philadelphia, the paper led with the large headline "Abuse of Power" that ostensibly referred to Nixon, except that most of the front page was covered with a photo of Heyward and Schiess serving communion at the ordination. While some saw the ordinations as an abuse of power, others wrote letters that argued that the actual abuse of power stemmed from those who ran the institution of the Episcopal Church. These writers placed the acts of the eleven women and the four bishops into the context of civil disobedience.

The following examples of correspondence do not attempt to replicate percentages of those supporting or opposing the ordinations. In fact, those numbers could shift quickly and dramatically depending on what had happened in any given week. Edward Welles described his own experience with what he called his "incoming communications" (which seem to include phone calls) in the few weeks surrounding the ordinations. Before the ordinations, his communications ran four to one against, but a week later, they were only two to one against. After Chicago, they shifted to three to one in favor. This particular sampling of letters is included here in an attempt to shed some light on the *types* of responses the women were receiving in their mailboxes or as they opened their newspapers and their denominational publications in the approximately two years between the ordinations and the Minneapolis convention of 1976.

As illustrated in an earlier chapter, Merrill Bittner received her share of hate mail, including letters from the person who sent her fishing line with which to hang herself. But others also received letters that were particularly violent and were often connected to one or more issues concerning sexuality. In this context, the ordinations were not only about eleven women becoming priests, but about how their becoming priests raised fears of the church becoming, as one writer claimed, a "cesspool" of "whoremongers and pimps." Bozarth received an envelope one day that held a newspaper clipping, a photo of her wearing her priest collar and standing in an unemployment line. As she remembered years later, she was there to look for work, not to receive benefits, but the photographer thought the image would make a good story. An anonymous writer cut out the photo and mailed it to her, having written the word "sleazy" across it and castigating her for taking tax payer's money, adding that she should get a job as a chaplain in a brothel.

Cheek received a letter addressed to her as "pseudo priest" with *vox pox*, or the voice of the people, written on the envelope. It was eight pages of news clippings, primarily about the ordinations, with messages written across them in black marker. They read, "heretic; profligate; prostitute; dump the bitch; defile, defame, whoremonger, pseudo reverend self serving priest; fornication; welfare frauds, niggers and long-haired depraved bastards-bitches in dope; VD infested; down the drain—flush her; radical like women's lib; perpetuate promiscuity; adultery, mongrel, and defile, defame, and besmirch escutcheons of Episcopal Church." And that was just page one.

The sender went on to call the Church of the Advocate a "nigger brothel," to refer to the bishops as "Lucifer" and to Sue Hiatt as a "bitch in disguise" and, in an ending apparently designed to show their proficiency with words beginning with the letter *p*, railed against phonies, profligates, "permissive prostitutes," and "pretenders on the prowl."

There were other letters, more acceptable in polite company, instructing the women on how nice girls behave. One of the bishops pointed out the need for such advice, writing to Heyward,

> I am still deeply grieved over the fact that the Service took place. There must be a better way for committed Christian women to accomplish their purpose than to polarize and divide the church.

And almost a week after the ordinations, a woman from California wrote—in a page from the playbook of Bishop Myers' earlier statement about women priests—that the women and their followers should follow the example Mary had provided. Still, Myers had not delivered the low blow of comparing them to Henry VIII:

> You've had your way—Great!—squeeze every glorious moment out of it. Actually you're playing games. After all your church's founder Henry VIII was no more obedient than you, and no more pleasing to Almighty God. If you patterned yourself after the Mother of Him who came to redeem us you would be doing more good for your own soul and not bringing down to perdition those who now glory in your hollow victory. Did she, the mother of God set herself up as either equal or superior to the Apostles to whom he gave the rights of priesthood?

To *The Episcopalian*, a man from Florida wrote and employed a word meant to strike fear and loathing into his readers: he referred to the women as *priestesses*. It was a term often used by opponents of women's ordination to connect contemporary women priests to pagan rituals denounced in Biblical texts. He wrote,

> In response to the recent ordination of women as priests in Philadelphia by four bishops of our Church. I wondered what we were lacking. The four bishops have given us the answer—priestesses, of course! In Christ's day, when having women priests was a feature of the day's paganism, Christ rejected having the same. Yet in our day, when this practice has become almost non-existent, we proud Episcopalians have restored an ancient practice. Bully for us! I thought our example was Christ, His practice, teachings, and principles, rather than "what would be nice."

Several of the women received a letter from a priest in Wisconsin who resorted to shame as a means of discrediting the eleven:

> For shame, that one who names herself a Christian should allow herself to cause such strife in Christ's Body, The Church. Why not withdraw and let there be peace. I shall pray for you.

On the theme of shame, a woman from Massachusetts kept it simple, sending Cheek a plain piece of white note paper, trimmed in blue, with one-word written in red marker:

SHAME!

On the day that the Riverside service was conducted by Cheek, Heyward, and Piccard, a woman from Connecticut sent the three a letter that also set forth a traditional argument for a woman's proper place, much like the letters that referred to Mary as a role model. This writer, though, steered the argument in a slightly different, though equally traditional, direction—that women were actually superior to men and needed to follow their higher calling, regardless of the costs. To do otherwise meant to tear apart the family, the church, and society at large:

> I believe if women would understand their job, they would realize it is of the highest importance. They would assume their true responsibility and the crime rate would not be up, the elderly would not be in convalescent homes and children would have a real home. A roof over your head and material objects are nothing. God gave us a family to hold together, which reaches out to the community and thus across the world. We are the stronger and it is weak women like you who try to use God as an excuse for your own frustrations. You can't stand "man only" consecrating the bread and wine, but I ask you, which is more important—that one act or healing the country? Even to heal just one person has an impact that resounds.
>
> If you believe in Jesus, why don't you ask His forgiveness for wasting His time and disrupting our church, and do His work as ministers, as we are all supposed to do. It is easy to blame man for not wanting women as priests, and I know it is hard work to do God's will, but I did not hear Him say it would be easy.
>
> Man always keep a little of the small boy, but when women who have the greatest responsibility do not mature, it is pitiful. I pray you will rise above your pettiness, accept the fact that you are a woman, and be proud. Do the work of God so that you can receive heaven on earth and be happy and peaceful.
>
> I pray for you to listen for God's direction so that you can go forth and do His good works and become a whole person as He wanted all of us to be.

Of course, if women really were superior to men, one might argue that it would be more appropriate to refer to God as a *she* rather than a *he*. It is easy to dismiss the logic of a single letter or even a few hundred letters coming from homes across the country, but dismissing it becomes more difficult when it is argued by priests and bishops. Besides, when this writer states, "A roof over your head and material objects are nothing," she has written honestly, putting her finger on an aspect of this issue that was fundamental. She is ready and willing to concede financial security in the defense of what amounts to a Victorian ideal of a proper lady. Of course, one wonders if she were writing from a home with a roof or from a refrigerator box in an alley. And it is difficult to picture the "real home" she puts forth in which to raise children in these circumstances, but nonetheless, her letter is at least forthright about the costs of her position. It was a point seldom heard in the rhetoric of church leaders using Mary, or the more recent cult of domesticity, as a basis for their reasoning.

Not surprisingly, the women's movement, or "women's lib," was often blamed for the ordinations in Philadelphia, as in the case of another letter written in relation to Riverside.

> All my life I have belonged to and loved the Episcopal Church. I still do and will pray for it. God help it and us also. Now it is being undermined . . . by women's lib (so called). They call themselves Christian! And some Episcopalians! I am a professional woman—a trained teacher, librarian. . . . We don't need to become priests. We don't need that—or women's lib. I for one, along with many others, will have no part of it! . . . I am sorry about this but it cuts very deeply.

This woman, and the others who wrote letters about the impact of the women's movement on the church, were absolutely correct in their assessment that the women's movement had served as a major impetus in the ordinations. It is difficult to imagine the ordinations happening without the influence of either the women's movement or the Civil Rights Movement, and Schiess wrote emphatically that "it was Betty Friedan and the National Organization for Women that changed the Episcopal Church" and that neither the church nor NOW had acknowledged to what extent that were true. For Schiess, Friedan's *The Feminine Mystique* helped her to clarify her questions about having concerns as a middle-class white woman in the context of the Civil Rights Movement:

> I had read *The Feminine Mystique* and, like many women in my generation, I felt this was our book, our life. To admit this publicly was not easy. To say that we middle-class, middle-aged, married mothers were not "satisfied" sounded silly, trivial, in the light of the world's problems—most especially in the light

of the ongoing struggle of blacks. We learned about how to go about "seeking remedy" from the leaders of the Civil Rights movement of the 1960s, but
what business did we have applying it to ourselves?

Hiatt, as we've already seen, had been thinking about these issues for years, having written her paper "The Domestic Animal" in high school in 1953. And
Piccard had also argued in her second year at Bryn Mawr in 1916 that women
should be allowed to be priests. Still, Friedan's book addressed a large population of middle class white (and straight) women and undoubtedly had tremendous influence on a generation, on the women's movement, and on the
ordination of women in the Episcopal Church.

A fellow deacon in the church, a woman from Illinois, wrote to say that she
had been discriminated against many times by the church and that while she
agreed with the concept of women's ordination, she disapproved of the actions
of the eleven because they were assuming a "special privilege." And she was disturbed by the "vindictive" tone she had heard in their voices, particularly since
the Chicago meeting:

> Since the meeting has finished, what I have heard from some of your mem-
> bers in the papers, on the radio, and on the television, has made me angry.
> You have sounded defiant, angry, and demanding of ordination as your
> right . . . I now feel alienated from you. Your responses to the action of
> the House of Bishops sound resentful and vindictive. I realize as I write
> you, that this is a harsh statement. . . . I want to support all eleven of you
> in your efforts to become priests, even though you say you already are, but
> I can't if you remain defiant, vindictive, and resentful.

Other writers developed the theme, as in the case of this bishop from Georgia,
who sent a telegram concerning Riverside:

> I know nothing will dissuade you but your action tomorrow seems brutal
> and selfish. Still I pray for you and the others and for your bishops.

A priest from Connecticut referred to the women's acts as selfish and adolescent and took a swipe at the Congregationalists in his critique:

> You and I are not "do your own thing" Congregationalists; we are Episco-
> palian Christians by our own choice. It seems to me that, as such, we are
> subject to our Bishops. And, when and if our Bishops are wrong about an
> issue, we have these choices: conform (as promised in ordination), work
> with painstaking patience within the system, even though as individuals

we might not benefit from the hoped for changes, or enter a different expression of the Christian faith.

It seems to me that you and your colleagues have fallen to the rather adolescent "instant everything" demands, over an issue which at this time is not crucial for the church as a whole. Within the next ten years the General Convention surely would have approved the ordination of women to the priesthood, and I would welcome that move. It seems that your timing smacks of "causism" and selfishness, though I do not doubt that you acted according to your consciences; I think you[r] sincere acts are, however, with mistaken conscience.

And from Arizona, came a letter that suggested that the new priests, as well as "women like [them]," be removed from the church:

I must express my shock and disgust at reading in this morning's paper of your brazen defiant stand in celebrating Holy Communion at the Riverside Church. . . . Have *you* obeyed . . . or are you simply saying to your church *and* the entire world—"laws and rules of our church be damned— we are going to have *our* way"? Women do *not* remain "peripheral." There are too many wonderful, beautiful things for them . . . but women like *you should* be ignored and *removed* from the Episcopal Church. You are *all egotists* and a *discredit* to our church.

Heyward received a letter which attacked her egotism, but not because she desired to be a priest, but because, as the writer argued, the entire structure of the church was oppressive:

I have no hassles about women being priests—I have a lot of hassles about clericalism and the dependency it fosters among lay people in the church. I do really believe that women ought to have the right to be oppressors along with men—I guess I just wish women wouldn't join as oppressors.

The writer went on to express concern over a whole host of issues in the church, including "the powerlessness of the laity (most of whom are women)," the vulnerability of lay workers, janitors, and directors of religious education who lacked protection in the church, and the lack of a feminist consciousness in relation to the language used by the church. "I don't want to put you on the spot," the writer told Heyward, "but I do want to know what your stance is on all of this—so that I've got an idea of whether to expect feminism from women who do get in the power structure of the church."

Many of the letters brought up the issue of church law, their writers arguing—like the priest quoted above from Connecticut—that the women were operating outside the boundaries created by the structure of the church. For this reason, a priest from Buffalo, New York, wrote to rescind an invitation to Heyward, who was scheduled to preach in his parish in October:

> In pursuing ordination to the priesthood contrary to the laws and will of the Episcopal Church, you are separating yourself from the Body of Christ. While I support the ordination of women to the priesthood and will continue to do so, I feel you have taken the law into your own hands and have violated the principles upon which the One, Holy, Catholic, and Apostolic Church stand.

This theme was reiterated in a letter sent to *The Episcopalian*. A writer from Hawaii compared a line from Charles Willie's sermon in Philadelphia to a comment by John Ehrlichman, who spent a year and a half in prison for conspiracy and perjury in the Watergate scandal:

> I read that Prof. Charles V. Willie, preacher at the service during which 11 women deacons were admitted to the priesthood, characterized the ordination "not as an event of arrogant disobedience but as a moment of tender loving defiance." That pronouncement must surely rank with John Ehrlichman's justification of the illegal acts of the White House Plumbers as being excused by the god of "national security." Watergate has effectively demonstrated the harm and the evil that result from the abuse and misuse of power. It is indeed sad the Church has shown society that the Body of Christ also has in its ranks persons who have no regard for due process and established lines of authority.

In a later edition of *The Episcopalian*, a woman from North Carolina took issue with the prior letter, and in a show of support for the ordinations, wrote,

> Jesus broke many "church" laws to correct injustices he found. Peter and Paul broke unjust church laws dealing with Gentiles. The ordination of 11 women in Philadelphia broke an unjust law, and unjust laws must be broken so they can be lawfully changed.

The other letters of support that poured in for the ordinations ranged from poetry to longer and sustained prose arguments praising the women's willingness to take prophetic action. One person wrote a simple and anonymous note:

> The best of luck to you always. You are an inspiration to women everywhere. Love, A Homemaker for Equal Rights

A woman from California wrote to *The Episcopalian* to disagree with the earlier writer who argued that the women had abandoned the laws of the church:

> As we gathered in Philadelphia, we were not working outside the system, rather we were witnessing, leading ahead of the system. [All those who] participated in that service are servants of the Lord, deeply involved in every level of the Church's mission. Time will proclaim the prophetic faithfulness of that event. Those present felt the blessing of the Spirit radiantly among us during the experience.

This writer criticized the bishops' action in Chicago and reminded Episcopal readers of the beginnings of their faith:

> The House of Bishops' over-reacting in Chicago revealed its sexism by not being able to address the right question (What is God calling us to do now and how can we implement His will?); by being insensitive to the persons about whom they were deliberating by not ordering more chairs to be brought in so the women could sit through the long proceedings; by not allowing the persons involved to speak about their commitment, vocation, agony; by not counting these persons for the Eucharist not including them in the invitation to receive. Did they consider that Christianity began with an irregular conception and that the Episcopal Church in America began with an irregular consecration?

Many people wrote the eleven personally, thrilled with the ordinations and finding in them a means for transforming their own lives. The day after the Philadelphia service, a Virginia woman wrote Cheek,

> This evening's paper had the greatest news I've seen in ages. Wow! What an individual you are. I'm overjoyed at your courage and faith, your awesome and beautiful defiance. Your actions have caused what I hope is a permanent, catylistic [*sic*] change in me. It's rather like being struck by lightning! I do wish for you joy, satisfaction and richness of life in all you do. I also wish I knew where rebellious priests serve communion. What a remarkable feeling that would be. With unbounding admiration,

A woman from North Carolina wrote to say that the women had attracted the attention of a church leadership that had until then ignored them. Like others before her, she drew connections to Watergate:

> The church hierarchy is bothered by you now, but it wasn't bothered at all last year at general convention, when it voted for brutality to women,

called its vote a fluke, and declared the subject closed for the next three years. Courage! The nation endorsed morality last week; perhaps our church may, too.

In reference to the Riverside Service, Heyward received a letter from the Reverend Victoria Booth Demarest, whose grandfather had formed the English group that became the Salvation Army. Demarest herself was a writer and Congregationalist minister who was known to have delivered sermons in four languages. She had sent the eleven a formal and typed letter of support at the time of the ordinations, but mailed a handwritten note to Heyward in regards to Riverside:

> I wish I were there!! All my life I have fought for the right of women in the ministry and am glad I have lived long enough to see this day!! I wish some good angel would pay my fare to New York! . . . Yours in the good fight of faith.

A woman from a village near the Adirondacks had been reading a copy of *Ms.* when she was inspired to write:

> As a woman, I have always felt women have been unduly discriminated against in many professions, unfortunately including religion. As a gay, I know the discrimination can be thoughtless and brutal. I am very pleased and proud of the defiant stand you and the other women are taking against your church and discrimination. I will be watching with interest the outcome of your "illegal" ordination.

A woman wrote to Heyward after hearing her speak in Emory University in Georgia. Because of threats against her, Heyward had been asked to wear a bulletproof vest during the talk, but she declined. If the writer of the letter had known of the dangers involved at the event, she made no mention of it, focusing on the impact that Heyward had made on her:

> I did not expect to be so personally affected by your presence here. I was unaware of the ways that I have felt excluded from God's inner circle of love until I experienced being included—both by the obvious fact of your inclusion and by you, as God's representative, including me. Somehow I feel I've spent my life trying to be God's son, only to realize that I am God's daughter. I'm not sure what it means to me, Carter, but I feel a deep sense of healing and of oneness with God.

One man wrote to Heyward to thank her and to ask for prayers, assuring her that he would say a prayer for her as well:

I heard you yesterday on the Sherry Henry program. Being disabled and confined to home, the radio is my chief source of entertainment, and I enjoyed hearing you yesterday. . . . the very best of luck in your plight to be recognized as the priest you most rightly are. Thank you for reading my letter and please say a prayer for me as I will for you also. Take care of yourself and best of luck.

Some of the letters were much more lighthearted and playful. A woman from Ithaca wrote, "CONGRATULATIONS! Your ordination has been like a never-empty gin-and-tonic to me through this long hot summer." She continued,

I celebrate your courage, your wit, your humanity/divinity. Thanks for being you; each news release has been a needed breath of life—new—life.

And there was the poet who signed off in a Shakespearean vein as "The Bard," introducing a limerick to Heyward with a prediction about the church: "By degrading you and the other brave ladies ordained in July, the Church has uttered its own death sentence." The Bard might have been the first to agree that any prediction of the church's demise was, to borrow a sentiment from another iconic writer, "greatly exaggerated." He or she might also be the first to admit that any comparison to Shakespeare had also been overstated. The limerick:

There once was a lady named
Heyward
whom the bishops considered
quite wayward.
They panned feminism,
this started a schism,
and now their poor Church has
gone fray-ward.

And then there was a letter from Racine, Wisconsin, written in response to Heyward's being scratched while serving communion in New York. Again, the sender—or senders in this case—kept their identities hidden. The following was handwritten on a piece of mustard-colored paper with a gourd as a watermark:

Dear Rev. Miss Heyward: In today's *Chicago Tribune*, I read about that creep who hurt you while you were distributing Communion. Any guy who would do that is NOT a real man. My Hubby and my Pa say he should get a punch in the nose. Let's hope he gets what's coming to him. Sincerely, 3 folks for the Equal Rights Amendment

After John Allin sent the telegram to the eleven pleading with them to cancel the ordinations, Cheek replied to the Presiding Bishop, arguing that women were attempting to define themselves in the world as whole persons. She had attempted, she noted later, to be "reasonable and persuasive," telling Allin, "I am trying to be a faithful communicant in this church" and that "I have a lot of turmoil and deep grief around my decision." She took a humble approach, admitting, "I'm not very brave, and don't look forward to the hatred I'll evoke."

Then the two spoke on the phone. These forty years later, Cheek doesn't remember the specifics of their talk, just that she had taken the call on her bedroom phone and that she felt patronized during the conversation. She composed a letter to Allin that clarified her position. And she pulled no punches. If she had indeed not been very brave in the prior letter, she had certainly found her courage by the time she penned the following one:

Dear Brother,

After treating my sisters and myself as non-existent, non-persons at Chicago, and ignoring us entirely, you write us offering "pastoral concern" and ways to communicate with the House of Bishops. I cannot understand you. I still feel bruised from our telephone conversation and am determined to take better care of myself.

The issues seem clear. The church is not concerned with vocations, qualifications, the calls from parishes, simple justice and decency, the personhood of women; but clings to conservative, punitive, legal procedures, at variance with both the Gospel and civil liberties. It is ludicrous, amoral, intolerable, and what is there to talk about?

Decent human beings in the world outside the church just can't believe us. Our institution is incredible, a laughing-stock, a source of outrage and indignation to fair minded people. Forget about preaching the gospel. The credibility gap between word and action is too wide for any intelligent person to bridge. Moral leadership where it counts is sadly deficient. Pastoral concern and talk of love is a travesty when divorced from justice and power.

My communication to the House of Bishops is this: "For the love of God, stop being the deceitful community and take immediate steps to put your house in order."

If any of my sisters is willing to meet with you and/or any of the other bishops I would certainly like to be with them, but I should like to remind you that faith without works is dead, and that pious talk masking brutal action does not effect reconciliation.

Yours in Christ,

Some in the Episcopal hierarchy were astounded by Cheek's resolve. A priest and canon in the Diocese of Massachusetts responded after he had read a copy of her letter. He spent the first part of his own letter listing his many liberal activities (including having delivered a sermon in which he had spoken in favor of women's ordination) and allowing that he himself had received his fair share of hate mail, "some of it blathering and some of it vicious." Then he made the point that her letter to the Presiding Bishop had been *both* blathering and vicious: "in expression inept, in content inappropriate, in spirit uncharitable." He continued,

> The only thing that saves it from outright vicious-ness is that every paragraph exudes the same kind of outraged and slightly ridiculous virtue of the kind exhibited by the heroines in turn-of-the-century drawing-room romances by Ouida or Mrs. Grace Livingston Hill. Inadvertently, and I'm sure, mistakenly, your letter to Bishop Allin reflects you as a person of a small sense of personal dignity and a smaller sense of personal worth. If you truly are interested in communicating with Bishop Allin, and equally interested in his response to you—then by all means communicate, but without having copies of your correspondence fluttering to the four winds like feathers of some demoralized hen. If you are not interested in communicating with Bishop Allin, but are only interested in getting the message of your discontent broadcast as widely as possible—then by all means continue to do what you have done, but acknowledge it for what it is—a tired ploy in a game at whose relevance the world at large looks askance.

Bishop John Burt of Ohio, a supporter of women's ordination, also responded to Cheek's letter. He began by reaffirming his support and acknowledging the "depth of disappointment" she and the other women must have felt at the convention in Louisville. Then he argued that her claims about the bishops treating the women as non persons in Chicago was unfair, and that in fact, if it had been eleven male deacons who had been ordained without authority, the bishops would not have gone to so much trouble to meet. Perhaps Burt was unaware of just how true his point was. The Chicago meeting would never have occurred if the ordinands had been men. He wrote,

> Had eleven male deacons been ordained by bishops acting without authority and without the consent of the Church through local Standing Committee approval (which in turn affirms that academic, moral, medical, psychiatric, etc. standards have been met), we would not have called a special meeting

of the House of Bishops to determine that "The necessary conditions for a valid ordination to priesthood in the Episcopal Church were not fulfilled on the occasion in question." It was because the July 29 ordination involved women and because we wanted to give special collegial thought to the implications for the role of women in the Church that we gave up vacation time, expended large amounts of money and went to Chicago. Our very being there on that mission was a gesture of concern for you and the other ten ordinands.

He ended his letter:

The House of Bishops is not a deceitful community, Alison. Those of us who supported the Chicago action yet who favor women's ordination want the ordination of women to be affirmed by the whole Church and not sneaked in by the back door through the hands of unauthorized bishops in defiance of the canons by a rite everyone acknowledges was irregular at best.

Burt wrote that it was important for those who favored women's ordination to "not be set one against the other," though by the end of the year, an event would occur in Ohio that would set Burt and Cheek on opposing sides in an ecclesiastical trial, a case a reporter from *The Cleveland Plain Dealer* wrote "belong[ed] more in the Middle Ages than in 1975."

Chapter 10

THE TRIALS, PART I: "ADJECTIVES ARE ALWAYS DANGEROUS"

As it turned out, it wasn't all that easy to rattle a World War II fighter pilot who had flown eighty missions, had marched in Selma, and had his coffin delivered to his office, where he turned it on its end, added a few shelves, and used it as a bookcase until he would need it for its intended purpose. In truth, he never quite recovered from his time in Selma. He had talked his friend James Reeb—a minister in the Unitarian Church—into going with him to the march. A group of whites attacked Reeb, beat him with a baseball bat, and he died two days later. "It is my agony that I talked him into going," he later admitted.

A small, slightly pigeon-toed man with coarse features, William Wendt was born in Mitchell, South Dakota, in 1920. After his service in the war, he entered General Theological Seminary in New York City and joined the Urban Priest Group, composed of seminary students and graduates—including Paul Moore and C. Kilmer Myers—who worked with the city's poor. He married Mary Malmborg and lived in inner-city housing where he served as a pastor. He was arrested in New York for attempting to desegregate a Woolworth's drug store. In fact, he was arrested four more times over issues of civil rights and spent seven days in jail in Jackson, Mississippi, after working to desegregate the bus lines. In 1960, he accepted a call to St. Stephen and the Incarnation in Washington, D.C., where he focused on desegregating the parish by opening the church doors to the African-American community.

In 1973, Paul Moore's wife Jenny, who was dying of cancer, added another component to Wendt's vocation. Wendt ministered to her during the illness, but during that time she told him, "Bill, don't pray for me. Just rub my feet." And she told him she wanted to be buried in a plain pine coffin. Wendt wasn't able to find one, so he had hers built. As it turned out, these two acts—rubbing a dying woman's feet and building her a pine coffin—were the beginning of the St. Francis Burial and Counseling Center, which he opened with the Reverend Robert D. Herzog in 1975. The center offered counseling to the grieved and low-cost burial alternatives, including coffins that could be made into wine racks and, as Wendt illustrated, bookshelves. Today, that project lives on in the Wendt Center for Loss and Healing.

In a talk at St. Stephen's in 1977, Paul Moore described Wendt as a pastor who "always brought the kingdom into the church, and brought the church out to the kingdom." And, he was, as Moore pointed out, always more concerned with the kingdom. "I suppose," he added, "his formula for the life of the church is to bring the church out, bring the world in, mix them all up, apply a little danger, and a little bit of mud, and lots of tears and laughter."

Like their pastor, the members of the congregation of St. Stephen's were not easily shaken by the politics of the day or by the weight of church tradition. They were open to the ordination of women and wanted to invite one of the eleven to officiate at their church as soon as they became aware that the Philadelphia ordinations were going to occur. In fact, on August 4, not even a week after the Philadelphia service, Alison Cheek found herself preaching from the pulpit of St. Stephen's. Wendt, however, had told the vestry that he wanted the church to inhibit itself from celebrating the Eucharist during Cheek's visit. He wanted to give the bishops a chance to speak at Chicago and then at their annual meeting in Mexico. "I was convinced," he said, "that something good would come of these meetings, in favor of the women . . . [that the] ordinations would be recognized." Also, Bishop William Creighton of Washington had sent Wendt a letter asking him to withdraw the invitation to Cheek.

The service was nevertheless a momentous one, celebrating Cheek's new priesthood and making the cover of *The Washington Post.* Next to the story was an accompanying photo of Cheek being lifted into the air by Wendt and the Reverend Lauren Mead. The move by the two priests took her completely off guard. "I told them to put me down," she said, "you'll get a hernia, but then I threw my head back and laughed, and that's when the photo was taken. People either love that photo or are deeply offended by it."

But then the Chicago meeting disappointed the hopes of supporters of women's ordination. The October meeting in Mexico, while seemingly less provocative, nevertheless gave the bishops a chance to strengthen their pact of collegiality. The Standing Committee of the Diocese of Washington sent a letter to the bishops asking for them to call a special convention to settle the ordination issue, but when it became clear that the bishops had agreed to wait until the 1976 convention, the congregation at St. Stephen's decided not only that it wanted to celebrate the priesthood of Cheek, but that it wanted to give her a chance to exercise it. She would preside over the Eucharist, the first time that one of the eleven had presided over the Eucharist in a service held in an Episcopal Church. The date was set for November 10.

Bishop Creighton began sending letters and issuing statements about the service and inhibited Wendt and Cheek from taking part. Creighton was an avid supporter of the ordination of women to the priesthood, even publically announcing that he would begin ordaining women himself if the General Convention didn't approve it in 1976. But on hearing about Cheek's invitation to St. Stephen's, he sent out a statement to the parishes reaffirming his position on the issue and confirming that he had no intention of proceeding with disciplinary action:

> While we should not be surprised if some actions are taken in defiance of present canonical and traditional structures neither should we forget that within the order of our Church there is more room than exists in most societies for honest disagreement and for the strong expression of sincerely held convictions. A good working principle in a mixed context of order and ardor is that no actions be taken with the intent of injuring others or that may damage for others the ministries we seek for ourselves. . . . I have found it necessary to request Fr. Wendt not to proceed with this celebration of Communion. As an act of conscience he is disobeying my request. I do not intend to take any action of a disciplinary nature because I do not believe any such action would make a positive contribution to the solution of our present dilemma.

The decision about whether to proceed with disciplinary action would, however, be taken out of his hands.

In the meantime, Wendt had determined that there were "two kinds of laws; the laws of man and the laws of God." He acknowledged that there was meaning and purpose in the former, but that as a priest, he was to "give conscience to the highest authority." And so the service went forward, again making the pages of *The Washington Post* where Marjorie Hyer referred to it as one of "solemn prayer, joyous hugs and bursts of spontaneous applause." Four hundred people were there to take part in the ceremony. In his sermon, Wendt spoke forcefully and to the point, telling his parishioners, "I have searched the Gospels and I do not hear [Jesus] say, 'Wait for the General Convention.' I don't hear him say, 'We must have collegiality.'" He continued to press his point about the bishops, echoing the warning of Jesus to be wary of religious leaders who don't live up to their positions. "Beware of bishops," he said, "who sit in motel lobbies and meet in long sessions in places like Mexico." This statement drew long applause. He continued, taking a swipe at the rules of the General Convention: "Beware of the General Convention where two votes yes and two votes no means one vote no."

Cheek wasn't preaching that day. She was there to serve the Eucharist. When the gold and purple vestments were placed over her head, the congregation again burst into applause.

And while Creighton was willing to let this day pass without prosecution, eighteen priests of the diocese were not so forgiving, and they took the unusual move—against the stated wishes of their bishop—of bringing a priest to trial for not following the wishes of his bishop. And bringing a priest to trial was no small undertaking. The Diocese of Washington had not even conducted a trial in the twentieth century, and besides, many people—like the reporter from *The Cleveland Plain-Dealer*, were finding the whole notion of ecclesiastical trials medieval and otherworldly. Other commentators struggled for the right analogy to describe them. Columnist Carl Rowan of *The Chicago Sun-Times* employed a wide variety of historical and contemporary references to denigrate the trials, including the Salem witch hunts, the comic strip Beetle Bailey, the Nazis, the Prussian command system, and Watergate. If those were not enough, he raised the disparaging comments by Samuel Johnson: "Sir, a woman preaching is like a dog's walking on his hind legs. It's not done well; but you are surprised to find it done at all." In the midst of his reproach of the church, Rowan recreated the image problem the bishops were having: "It comes out looking like a bunch of old men manifesting their cruel enslavement to prejudices that antedate the Dark Ages."

Bad press and all, the trial date for The Board of Presenters vs. the Reverend William Wendt was set for April 30, 1975. Initially, the trial was to be held in a school, but defense attorney William Stringfellow wanted as many people as possible to witness the proceedings. He knew that no matter the outcome of the verdict, a trial would serve to promote the cause of women's ordination and would make the opposition look like institutional bullies. He also knew he had the court of public opinion on his side and friendly allies in the media, including Rowan and the cartoonists, and also Betty Medsger, Marjorie Hyer in Washington, and Eleanor Blau in New York. Of course, he had opponents in the press corps, but many of the nation's major newspapers had, to that point, been supportive of the women.

William Stringfellow was an impressive force for the church advocate's lawyer E. Tillman Stirling to face. Stringfellow was a Harvard Law School graduate, but what made him particularly daunting in this case was that he was both an activist and a theologian who had written extensively about theological issues and about the Episcopal Church. He had a long history of helping those oppressed by racism, by poverty, and by the military complex. He housed Father Daniel Berrigan, an FBI fugitive convicted of burning draft records in Maryland. Knowing his phone was being tapped by the FBI, Stringfellow read lengthy passages of the Bible into the receiver, believing the agents needed to hear them. With Anthony Towne, Stringfellow lived what he called a monastic life at Eschaton, his home at Block Island, Rhode Island, where the two of them "railed against death's triumphal procession and its 'collateral casualties'—the poor, the outcast, and the marginalized." Stringfellow was a small man and not often in good health. He spoke quietly. He loved his dogs, and he was fascinated with the circus. He kept a "Question Authority" sticker on his car and a "Go Away" mat at his door, but few, said his friend R. Scott Kennedy, "took [the mat] seriously."

When Swiss theologian Karl Barth traveled to the United States and met Stringfellow, Barth said, "This is the man America should be listening to." Sue Hiatt wrote that Stringfellow knew more about the bishops "than anyone else in the church, including the bishops themselves." And though it was this man, William Stringfellow, who was defending Wendt against the church, both men realized they were up against a powerful institution with years of tradition behind it and a bureaucratic system holding it in place. Still, Stringfellow was well aware that it would be possible to lose the battle of the trial but use it to ultimately win the war against the church's long-held beliefs.

Of the five judges chosen to preside, three were priests in the Episcopal Church and two were lawyers. Only one, Janet McCaa, was a woman. About a month after closing arguments for the trial, McCaa would be on the front page of *The Washington Post* for another reason. The paper did an anniversary story about her as one of three survivors of the June 7, 1971, plane crash of Allegheny Flight 485 that went down on a foggy morning in New Haven, Connecticut.

Two passengers survived as well as the co-pilot, but twenty-eight were killed. McCaa followed the other surviving passenger through a hole in the side of the plane, to a burning wing, and then to the ground. "I just remember stumbling barefooted," she told Timothy S. Robinson of *The Post*, "stumbling across the field and seeing this man sort of vaguely ahead of me." The two of them made their way to a nearby clubhouse where people had gathered to watch. "They didn't realize we were survivors," McCaa said, "until they looked at us and saw the burns." Every year, around the anniversary, she struggled with a haunting sense that she was about to die. As she sat in her black robe at the judges' bench, that anniversary was quickly approaching.

The previous November, a friend had invited McCaa to attend Cheek's service at St. Stephen's. McCaa wasn't eager to go and suggested that they take two cars in case she wanted to leave. And she did leave. "I was offended," she said, "because they [the Philadelphia Eleven] hadn't followed the rules." When she was offered the chance to sit as a judge at the trial, she didn't jump at it. In fact, it wasn't an easy seat for the church to fill. Even so, McCaa thought that listening to the evidence would help her determine what she actually believed about the ordinations. She decided not to let the opportunity pass.

It fell to McCaa to open the trial with a prayer. At opening and closing moments throughout the proceedings, whether breaking for lunch or adjourning for the day, prayer and sometimes devotionals were offered. With a crowd of about a hundred and fifty people and a large contingency of the press listening, McCaa prayed, asking that those participating be equal to the task before them. Judge Thomas, the Chief Judge, issued a few preliminary statements, and then directed Stirling to begin the Board of Presenter's case. "But just before we begin," Thomas interrupted, "I want to ask one question." It was a pointed question and one he most likely knew the answer to. "Has there been any word from the witness who was summoned?"

"The Presiding Bishop?" the lay assessor of the court responded.

"Yes," Thomas said. John Allin had refused to appear in court, even after being issued a subpoena.

The assessor answered that he had talked with the Presiding Bishop's counsel and that he wasn't certain the Presiding Bishop could "rearrange his schedule so as to appear."

Stringfellow replied, "The subpoena is out so we expect him to appear." Throughout the proceedings, Stringfellow kept the issue of the Presiding Bishop's absence in the thoughts of the judges and of the members of the press by occasionally calling Allin as a witness. Allin's refusal to appear became as large as the trial itself, prompting another front page story for *The Washington Post*. Stringfellow insisted that Allin's testimony was a necessary part of the defense because Allin was best suited to interpret the bishops' action in Chicago. At the beginning, Allin sent notice that he was declining the "invitation" to appear, to which the court responded by sending a memorandum intended to correct "his impression that the subpoena was only an 'invitation.'" Then Allin sent word that he had too many other obligations that could not be cancelled—including a meeting with the Archbishop of Canterbury—but that he was willing to give a deposition. The court noted that the deadline had passed for giving depositions. The trial could have been postponed, but Stringfellow decided to let it go forward and watched as the press printed charges that Allin had become entangled "in a process he himself set in motion eight months ago," referring to the meeting in Chicago. He was in danger of coming across as a leader who saw himself as above the law and one who had intentionally skipped town during the Church's moment of crisis. *The Post* noted that "the unprecedented citation against the Presiding Bishop John Maury Allin, holder of the highest office in the 3-million-member Protestant denomination, lays the groundwork for separate disciplinary charges against him."

Meanwhile, the trial moved forward, with the Clerk of Court reading the charge against Wendt: that he had violated "his ordination vow to reverently obey his Bishop and follow his godly admonition." Stirling argued that the trial was about that one point and that one point only and not about whether women should be ordained in the Episcopal Church. He called Creighton to the stand and offered into evidence a series of letters between Wendt and Creighton and from Creighton to Cheek showing that Creighton had inhibited both parties.

Then Stringfellow began his cross examination. He asked Creighton, "What in the world is a 'godly admonition?'" Creighton's answer brought laughter from those attending and was quoted by the press: "I'm not sure, sir," he said. Creighton was in an odd position because there is no evidence in the court records that he ever used the term in his correspondence with Wendt. Creighton had inhibited Wendt and he had referred to a godly admonition that Bishop Robert Hall, Cheek's bishop, had issued to Cheek, but he had not used the term himself. But because the Board of Presenters had charged that Wendt had failed to obey the bishop and follow his godly admonition, Creighton found himself on a witness stand attempting to define the term. In fact, much of the trial was dedicated to defining this term that had not even been used in the original documents.

Creighton did attempt to answer the question, saying that he thought a godly admonition was distinct from a purely advisory relationship bishops had with priests. Stringfellow pursued the question, asking if a godly admonition was like a physician's counsel or if it was more like a general's order in the military. Creighton responded, "I can't believe that it would . . . I think military analogies don't fit the life of the Church." Stringfellow then asked if he believed that the canons of the church prohibited the ordination of women to the priesthood. "No, sir," he replied, "my position is that there is nothing in the present canons that prohibits the ordination of women to the priesthood of the Episcopate but that it would be desirable and much better for the Church in general if the Church, together in General Convention, did express itself affirmatively."

Stringfellow ended his cross examination, but Stirling redirected, asking a question that had been put forward by opponents of women's ordination: "Do you feel there's anything in the canons which *allows* the ordination of women?" The point was that even if the canons did not expressly forbid the ordination of women, it did not necessarily stand to reason that they allowed it. One wonders, though, where this line of reason would have taken the court. For instance, even if the canons allowed men to be priests, did they necessarily allow *white* men to be priests or *black* men or men who had blonde hair or men without blonde hair or men who had children. . . . It was also an odd question in the context of the trial because Stirling was asking the question of his own witness, who clearly believed that the canons did allow for the ordination of women. Creighton said so on the stand, after which Stirling ended his redirect.

The judges were allowed to question each witness after the lawyers had completed their examinations. McCaa asked Creighton if a godly admonition should be obeyed at all costs. Creighton didn't answer directly, but said that he thought there was some understanding that a penalty would be attached if the admonition were not obeyed. Judge Martin asked Creighton how often he had issued godly admonitions. "Very seldom," Creighton answered. Judge Ferrell asked him a series of questions about the validity of ordinations, including whether he would ordain a woman unilaterally without the approval of the General Convention or his Standing Committee. On the stand, Creighton said, "I hesitate to commit my future actions to that extent." When Creighton was excused, it was evident that Stirling's request that the case be narrowly defined by a question of obedience would not win the day and that, in fact, the validity of the ordinations would be—if not on trial—at least argued in a very public setting.

In the afternoon, Stringfellow opened for the defense and argued that Wendt, when he asked Cheek to celebrate at St. Stephen's, had been authorized by the people and vestry of that church and that he had acted in good faith according to his ordination vows and according to the word of God as he perceived it. Stringfellow said that he did not think of the trial as an opportunity for a discussion on the ordination of women, but one that would examine two "intertwined" and "inextricable" events: one, the celebration of the Eucharist by Cheek on November 10 and, two, the ordination of Cheek on July 29, 1974. "There is no way," he argued, "the first event can be considered without consideration of the second event." And he went further, stating that Wendt was "a kind of accessory after the fact in the Philadelphia ordination." Stringfellow ended by discussing the irony, or anomaly as he called it, of the presentment issued against Wendt when the bishops in Philadelphia and the eleven women had not been charged.

Stringfellow then spent the next several days calling a long list of witnesses, including among them, John Hines, the previous Presiding Bishop; Ed Harris, the co-dean of Episcopal Divinity School; Robert DeWitt; Alison Cheek; Sue Hiatt; Paul Washington; Roman Catholic theologian Rosemary Reuther; Henry Rightor, professor from Virginia Theological Seminary; Charles Willie, and William Wendt. The court heard from several lay leaders in St. Stephen's, but after a short break, Stringfellow's assistant, Edward Bou, once again called John Allin to the stand. The court recorder noted: No response. Bou said, "May the record show the witness is not here." Judge Thomas responded, "The entire file is noted."

Hines, who had been thought of as a fairly liberal Presiding Bishop, ended his term on June 1, 1974, less than two months before the ordinations had occurred. On the stand, he said that he believed the ordinations were valid, but irregular, and that the General Convention was not of clear mind in relation to the canons and had failed to clarify particular sections of them. When Judge Farrell asked him what he understood a godly admonition to be, Hines replied,

> I don't want to be flip, but I was hoping you wouldn't get around to this. It is a very difficult question to answer precisely because it lies primarily not in the juridical area, but in the pastoral area. And I always felt that it was a last resort and a failure of pastoral relationship if one had to exercise even a godly admonition, that it represented a breakdown in a relationship within the household of God.

He went on to say that when he issued one, he expected it to be obeyed, but that if a priest had refused out of a duty to conscience, then he would have given "it very serious rethinking."

Ed Harris took the stand and discussed the article he, Harvey Guthrie, and Hays H. Rockwell had written in response to the outcome of the Chicago meeting in which they had argued that the bishops had come to a hasty and ill-informed decision about the validity of the ordinations. At the end of Harris' testimony, Judge Draper asked him if a bishop could deny permission to an irregularly ordained person to officiate within the diocese. Harris answered *yes*, and within a few minutes, the court adjourned for the day.

The next morning Robert DeWitt took the stand. In his cross examination, Stirling chose a direct approach, asking DeWitt why he didn't ordain the women before he resigned and questioning his claim to have been moved by the spirit:

> **S:** "When you were an active Bishop with the diocese, how many women did you ordain?"
>
> **D:** "None."
>
> **S:** "Why not?"
>
> **D:** "Because I was about to resign, and was afraid it would look as though I had done this and then resigned."
>
> **S:** "How long had you been a Bishop?"
>
> **D:** "In 1960, I was ordained—consecrated a Bishop."
>
> **S:** "And when did you resign?"
>
> **D:** "January, 1974."
>
> **S:** "So you were a bishop 14 years. Did the Spirit move you any of those years to ordain women?"
>
> **D:** "No."
>
> **S:** "When did the Spirit first move you?"
>
> **D:** "July 29, 1974."
>
> **S:** "It must have moved you before that, didn't it? Some of the statements apparently—you were thinking about it before that."
>
> **D:** "Oh, yes, yes. I have been thinking about it for some time."
>
> **S:** "But the Spirit didn't actually move you until the day of the 29?"
>
> **D:** "The Spirit had been moving, and I did not move until July 29."

His response elicited laughter from the crowd. DeWitt apologized, saying, "I'm sorry, I didn't know how better [to answer] the question." Under cross examination, DeWitt also discussed a position paper, "Christian Obedience," that had been published by the House of Bishops in 1967 and had argued that though laws were meant to be obeyed, it was possible, as an act of Christian obedience, to violate the law.

Stirling questioned DeWitt on the belief that a bishop, by the mere laying on of hands, could properly ordain a person. "So a ten-year-old child," he pursued, "could be ordained if three Bishops could be persuaded to put their hands on that child and say the proper words?"

DeWitt answered, "I would think so."

S: "There is some magic to it, then?"

D: "There is some precedent for it."

S: "There is some magic to the ordination service?"

D: "I would resist that word."

The judges, at their time of questioning, wanted DeWitt to define *godly admonition*. DeWitt answered that "adjectives are always dangerous" and that he didn't remember ever issuing one. "I've given a lot of advice quite freely, but I don't think that I have ever designated such advice or counsel or admonitions as godly."

In the afternoon, Alison Cheek took the stand. Her testimony proved to be powerful. When, on the night before, she and Stringfellow had discussed how she should present herself as a witness, he had given her only one piece of advice: just be honest. McCaa said that it was Cheek's testimony that changed her position on the actions of the eleven in Philadelphia.

Stringfellow asked Cheek about her call to the priesthood, and Cheek responded that she found it difficult to speak about because it involved her whole self. She pointed out that a psychiatrist at the seminary had told her he had no doubt that she had been given a call to the priesthood. What Cheek didn't tell the court was the reply a previous therapist had given her, an Episcopal priest who had gone into the field of analysis. She had confided in him about the moment of her call, about how she had been visiting an Episcopal convent and was lying on the bed, relaxed, when she heard a voice saying, "I want you to be my priest." He told her he thought she had misunderstood and that what she had actually heard was her mother's voice saying, "I want you to be my penis." But for the courtroom, Cheek said that her classmates had helped her to realize her call. Stringfellow asked her if the service at St. Stephen's was one of the ways she could "affirm the integrity" of her call, and Cheek answered, "Yes. I feel that sun shines, rain falls, wind blows, and priests preside at Eucharists."

Soon after, Stirling began his cross examination and moved quickly to the issue of obedience:

S: Having been inhibited by your Bishop and having had your Standing Committee refuse to approve your ordination, do you feel you were obeying the Bishop?

C: I did not feel that I had been technically inhibited by my Bishop. My Bishop wrote me a letter saying that he requested me not to present myself for ordination in Philadelphia, but I did not take that as a technical inhibition.

S: What did you take it as?

C: A request.

S: From your Bishop

C: From my Bishop.

S: Then, you did not obey that request, did you?

C: No. I respectfully declined to accede to that request.

When the judges began questioning her, they again returned to the definition of a godly admonition. Judge Martin asked, "How do you determine the godly admonitions that you will obey and those that you won't?" Cheek replied:

I don't feel that I have ever disobeyed a godly admonition. My Bishop has given me some admonitions which in no way can I interpret as godly, believe me. There is nothing godly in treating women . . . in systematically inferiorizing women. There is nothing godly in squelching their vocations. There is nothing godly in that at all.

And with Cheek's testimony, the morning session ended after prayers and devotion.

But for McCaa, the implications of Cheek's testimony would prove life-altering. She believed that Cheek's words were coming "from a different place" than those of the other witnesses and she found them particularly meaningful. She looked out across the women priests sitting in the front pews and began to believe that their situation was not so very different from her own. They, too, had acquired advanced training and education. They, too, had worked hard to follow their vocation. She came to believe that the only reason they were not allowed to follow their calling "was because they didn't have a penis." At that moment, McCaa said, she "got radicalized."

Many of Stringfellow's next witnesses were called to speak to the validity of the ordinations and to serve as character witnesses for Wendt. Paul Washington testified to the numbers that attended the Advocate at the Philadelphia services. Rosemary Reuther, a professor at Howard University, addressed the issue of Catholicism in relation to the ordinations and said that in the context of apostolic succession, the ordinations were valid. She was about to speak to the approval of the ordinations by other Roman Catholic scholars when Stirling objected: "Your Honor, I certainly am going to object if this lady is going to tell us what other Roman Catholics said about the ordination. That certainly is hearsay." The bench agreed.

Henry Rightor addressed the issue of validity. He had been a professor of Cheek's at Virginia Theological Seminary. She remembered walking into class one day to see a stack of papers that was taller than the table next to them. Rightor was making a point. The papers were copies of all the studies that had been conducted about women's ordination to the priesthood that had concluded there were no theological reasons women could not be ordained. In fact, Rightor believed that there was nothing in the canons that argued against women's ordination. At the trial, he also made the point that he had never known anyone who had kept all of the canons and rubrics, nor who had even claimed such a feat. After Rightor's testimony and a point of clarification from another witness, the court adjourned for the day.

That night, DeWitt wrote a letter to the three other bishops in Philadelphia—Corrigan, Welles, and Ramos—giving them an overview of what had happened thus far at the trial. He pointed to the absurd news value that trial was generating, noting that Wendt was being tried for an offense no one seemed to be able define; Corrigan had said he would begin ordaining women if the General Convention didn't vote in favor, thereby potentially placing him in the same situation as Wendt; and Allin had failed to honor a subpoena, had violated the canons, and had left himself open to a presentment. He added that a man in Washington had set up a code-a-phone message system. People could call in and find out the latest information about the trial. "Two mornings ago," DeWitt wrote, "the code-a-phone regaled the caller first with a brilliant passage from Gilbert and Sullivan's *Trial by Jury*. It was not inappropriate!" Gilbert and Sullivan's comic opera mocked the levels of hypocrisy found among characters set in a courtroom scene.

On the morning of the last day of the trial, Charles Willie was the first to take the stand. Stringfellow asked him if there had been a canon change when the Episcopal Church began ordaining African-American men. Willie said that he wasn't familiar with the history. "I simply know that there are not many." Stringfellow persisted, "It didn't require a change in the canons, did it?" Willie responded *no*, that the church finally began to ordain black priests because they realized "that blacks were fully human."

When Stirling cross-examined Willie, his approach to the witness was more aggressive and sardonic than it had been with the others, with the possible exception of DeWitt. "You have a special insight," he asked, "into reading the canons and the Constitution that the House of Bishops doesn't have?"

Willie responded that he had "no special insight," just the "insight that an intelligent human being should have." After a few rounds of Stirling's questions, Bou for the defense became concerned that Willie was being both interrupted and badgered by the prosecution. He asked the bench to compel Stirling to give Willie a chance to complete his answers, but Stirling argued that Willie wasn't answering the questions with precision and Judge Thomas seemed to agree. He told Willie to make his "answers as brief as possible." The court transcript, however, does not seem to confirm Stirling's claim that Willie's responses lacked precision, particularly in relation to the responses of other witnesses.

Sterling then asked Willie a question that itself lacked precision: "And you say that if the canons or Constitution don't prohibit something, then it's alright to do it?" As so ordered, Willie answered briefly: "According to my understanding of the canons, yes." Stirling saw an opening and, in the tradition of earlier comparisons made between the ordination of women to the ordination of monkeys or jackasses, he raised the example of ordaining animals as one of those prohibitions not found in the canons:

> S: "I gather some far-out religions, they can even ordain or make saints out of animals."
>
> [*Bou objected*]
>
> W: "No religion that I know of does that. That's magic, not religion."
>
> S: "That's not prohibited by our canons, though, is it?"
>
> W: "I said no religion I know of makes saints out of animals."
>
> S: "It is prohibited, would you say, by our canons?"
>
> Bou: "Your Honor, I object. He is trying to ridicule the witness. I object. It is irrelevant and immaterial."

Judge Thomas: "I ask the witness to give a direct answer to the question. The question is quite clear."

W: "Our canons are silent on whether or not animals—nonhuman animals—can be made saints."

S: "Would you, therefore, say that they can be, since it's not prohibited?"

Bou: "I object, Your Honor. Would you rule on my objection?"

W: "I have no opinion on it."

Bou: "This isn't proper inquiry. It's making a farce out of the case. I think it's improper. It is undignified."

S: "Your Honor, it's not improper at all. They have paraded a bunch of witnesses up here who have said that there's nothing to prohibit it, they can do it. I'm trying to find out how far they can go."

Bou: "The question is irrelevant, Your Honor."

Judge Thomas: "Just a minute. The Court is ready to rule on this. We gave you a tremendous amount of latitude in examining this witness, and I think the cross-examination can proceed if the witness will give crisp, direct answers to what seem to me crisp questions."

W: "Yes, sir. May I reply to you, sir?"

S: "I beg your pardon?"

W: "May I reply to you?"

Judge Thomas: "Is there a pending question?"

W: "The question is whether or not—"

S: "Whether or not the canons prohibit—or whether, since they don't prohibit the ordination of animals, would you say it could be done if three Bishops did it?"

W: "My understanding of the canons, sir, is that they apply to human beings."

Still, the answer was neither crisp nor precise enough:

S: "Where do you find that [in the canons]? Because of the words *he* and *she*?"

W: "As a conferring member of the Episcopal Church, I know that religion applies to human beings."

After a long question by Sterling about the position of the canons on issues of race and sex, Sterling followed, "Are you saying that they have no right, that the legislative body of the Episcopal Church has no right to exclude women if they want to?"

> **W:** "Oh, yes. I would say the legislative body of the Episcopal Church was in a state of sin. It had no right to exclude women as delegates, even when they were excluded."
>
> **Judge Thomas:** I think your answer could have been much shorter than that."

And so it went. But Willie did have the last word when the only African-American judge, Judge Farrell, asked him if Martin Luther King, Jr., thought a Christian and a human being had a duty to oppose unjust laws and to expose himself to the penalties. Willie replied in agreement and the court allowed him his full response:

> Of course, and if you would know the vilification that many of these women have experienced, the vilification I have experienced, the friendships I have lost, and the threats to depose me if I had not resigned. Certainly, we have willingly accepted the consequences of our actions. I'm not here to recite what has happened, because I know what one will suffer when one does this. I have lost many good friendships, many good people whom I would not wish to have lost their friendships, because of this. But even other things have happened, even beyond that. So when I said in the ordination ceremony that we stand ready to suffer the consequences, that is true. My only belief is that the Church, through bodies such as this, once it understands the difference between grace and sin, will not perpetuate sin further by punishing those who have really tried to enhance the whole Christian community.

"Whereupon," according to the record, "a short recess was taken."

Chapter 11

THE TRIALS, PART II: BUT CONJUNCTIONS?

Part of what makes the scene in the courtroom between Stirling, Willie, and Thomas both insulting and tragically reflective of a larger historical and cultural context is that a black man, the grandson of a slave, was sitting in a witness chair defending white women who were being compared to animals. This scene was occurring in a church that had been converted into a courtroom just below the Mason-Dixon line, close to the boundaries of a society where black men were labeled as beasts and lynched by whites in the name of protecting the virtue of white women. And in this courtroom, as in the larger culture, it was primarily white men holding the power.

On the final day of the trial, the defense once again called the most powerful man in the Episcopal Church, John Allin, to the stand. After the lunch recess, the judges came back into the room and issued a statement regarding Allin, Chief Judge Thomas reading it from the bench:

> Since he has disregarded this subpoena, and our explicit expectations, and is in violation of the canon . . . we do hereby . . . adjudge and declare that John M. Allin, Member and Presiding Bishop of the Protestant Episcopal Church of the United States of America . . . is in contempt of this Ecclesiastical Court.

Then each judge was given a chance to make an individual statement in order of their seniority. The first four spoke of the remorse and/or humility they felt in issuing the contempt citation. "For myself, I say that I read this order with humility and deep regret," Judge Thomas began. Judge Martin followed, "I made it with great regret and with full respect for the office of Presiding Bishop and with full respect for he who holds that office." Judge Draper added: "It is with the same feeling of regret that I signed this order. . . ." Judge Farrell concluded the statements from the four men: "I wish to express the same degree of great humility and regret that this action has become necessary." The four then went on to explain why they had signed the order. The final judge to speak, Janet McCaa, kept her comment to one sentence and did not issue an apology with it: "I took this action of signing my name to this document," she told those in the courtroom, "because I understand my life in this society; no man and, for that matter, no woman, is above the law." What she did not clarify at that point was the position she would take if she believed the law to be unjust.

The contempt citation issued, the final witness for the defense was called, William Wendt. Members of the St. Stephen's congregation stood as Wendt took the stand. Bou rather than Stringfellow examined him, and Bou directed his witness to lay out his work in the Civil Rights movement and at his parish. Wendt described his arrests and other calls to conscience and then discussed his relationship with Creighton, giving his bishop credit for informing his own conscience, not only about women's ordination, but about many issues. He spoke of the influence of the Gospels on his beliefs, telling the court that "the Gospels speak, to me, of liberation, they speak of freedom; they speak of great concern for people who are in need."

When Stirling cross-examined Wendt, he once again began with the strategy he had employed with DeWitt and with Willie, asking him why he had not felt moved to follow his conscience until that moment. Stirling pointed out that since Wendt had argued against having Cheek preside over the Eucharist in early August, his conscience must have been amenable to a change in plans: "When your conscience was speaking to you at the end of July," he said, "you were apparently able to convince your conscience to wait awhile, is that right, let's not do it early in August?" Wendt apparently ignored the tone and answered directly: "Yes, because I had seen hope within the institutional structure that excited me, and hope that the Bishops of this Church could, in meeting together, reason together, pray together and lift up, for the whole Church, as they have done." Wendt argued that the action in Chicago had left the "poor priests" in a state of confusion.

Stirling asked him if he really believed, given the 128–9 vote in Chicago, that there was confusion about the position of the bishops, to which Wendt replied, "I think it is so ambiguous that we are sitting here in trial today and trying to resolve something that we can't." In general, though, Stirling's examination of Wendt lacked the temerity evident in some of his other cross examinations and, after answering a few questions from the judges, Wendt was excused. Stirling called forth three other witnesses who spoke to the presenters' case. The second, Richard C. Martin, was actually one of the eighteen presenters who brought forth the charges. Martin testified that if given the chance, he would have voted for the ordination of women, but that he brought the presentment together with the others because of his own conscience: "the rest of us also have a conscience, and so many people—laypeople and other clergy—were terribly disturbed. . . ."

By late afternoon, the testimonies of the trial were winding down, but the closing statements were still to come. Throughout the trial, Stirling had not been successful in keeping the arguments confined to the issue of obedience. The members of the bench had either agreed with Stringfellow that the discussion about the validity of the ordinations was relevant or they were simply willing to give the defense a great deal of latitude to make their point. In his closing, Stirling began by arguing that the canons did not at that point allow for the ordination of women, but that the defense had spent so much time trying to prove the validity of Cheek's ordination that it had ignored the reason for the trial: whether Wendt had disobeyed his bishop. "I have spent substantial time," he said, "discussing the canons and the Philadelphia ordinations. But again, I must vigorously urge that the service in Philadelphia has no bearing on the question before this Court."

He then criticized the individual testimonies of most of the witnesses. He said that Bishop Hines' testimony gave a "magical, mystical quality to the act of three Bishops" and that he thought in the case of Charles Willie that it was "not a matter of conscience . . . but more of a matter of subjective view." In fact, in framing the defense's reference to conscience, Sterling referred to it as an argument based on the idea that "my conscience made me do it." Certainly, Sterling would have been aware that his audience would have replaced the word *conscience* with the original term *devil* in the wildly popular catchphrase of the time, made famous by Flip Wilson's character Geraldine in the show that ran from 1970–1974. Stirling said that Ed Harris' points "struck [him] as arrogant." He compared Paul Washington's testimony to one validating "mob rule" and said he wasn't certain "what Rosemary Reuther, a Roman Catholic, add[ed] to the trial."

In his own summation, Stringfellow for the most part decided on a softer touch, showing appreciation to the court for upholding due process and even thanking the presenters for giving him a chance to meet the members of St. Stephen's. Stringfellow argued that the testimonies were "simply overwhelming" in support of the validity of the ordinations, and he told the court that the testimonies "could have been multiplied by other witnesses that could [have kept them there] for the rest of the month." What Stringfellow wanted, and what he asked the court to do, was to find the ordination of Cheek valid, if irregular. He argued that the actions from the bishops were based on a "gentlemen's agreement" and were decided upon based on "a question affecting the etiquette of the fraternity of Bishops," not on a "question of validity."

He then turned to the question of whether Wendt had disobeyed his bishop and pointed to Bishop Creighton's own understanding of a godly admonition as being something other than a military order. Creighton was not, Stringfellow contended, "a figure in some kind of chain of command, uttering orders to which automatic and stupid obedience must be rendered by those lower on the chain of command."

The judges disagreed. In a 3–2 vote split between the priests and the lawyers, the court convicted Wendt of disobeying his bishop's godly admonition and recommended discipline. The three priests, in arguing the court's majority opinion, were nevertheless sympathetic to the dilemmas faced by both Wendt and Cheek. "It is greatly to be regretted and deplored that this situation exists," the majority held, adding, "We believe that the freedom of the individual to realize his or her full potential in God's service is not to be limited by the accident of sex." They wrote that they understood the dictates of conscience and believed that Wendt had followed his. Still, they argued that while he had informed his conscience, he had not informed it enough and thereby "declared his perception of the Will of God to be more valid than that of his Bishop."

The dissenting opinion, put forth by lawyers McCaa and Chief Judge Thomas, placed more emphasis on the question of the validity of the ordinations. Like so many other decisive moments in the women's ordination movement, the inspiration for the dissenting opinion came in the middle of the night. And it came to Chief Judge Thomas. "I've been given more credit for that opinion than I should," Janet McCaa said. According to McCaa, Thomas stayed up through the night writing it after his thoughts suddenly became clear on the issue. He showed her the opinion so that she could make changes. She told him she wouldn't change a word, but he insisted because he wanted both of their names on the dissent. "So I changed and added a few small things," she said.

What Thomas argued was that the ordination issue was central to the case because Creighton had said that a deacon (Cheek) could not preside at the Eucharist. But Thomas and McCaa disagreed with the assertion that Cheek was still a deacon, and they agreed with the defense that she had been validly ordained in Philadelphia. They acknowledged that the testimonies had done much to persuade them, as well as their reading of Hiatt's and Hewitt's *Women*

Priests: Yes or No? Thomas wrote that there were times when the good news had to break through the law and that this was one of those moments in history. He brought in C.S. Lewis's "Priestesses in the Church," a source often quoted by opponents of women's ordination, and said that Lewis's protest that women in the priesthood were destructive of the concept of God as father seemed "quaint and puzzling" by modern standards. "Today," the dissenting opinion argued, "we reach fulfillment when we reject as sinful, any limitation on opportunities for service based on sex, just as we reject such limitation based on race." They believed that the bishops had no authority, in the name of collegiality or otherwise, to remove Cheek's priesthood and that the only way that she could be denied her vocational calling was by deposing her in an ecclesiastical trial. They closed their opinion by cautioning their fellow judges against ignoring the magnitude of their decision: "A great moment in church history is before us," they wrote, "and the majority of this court is allowing it to pass by."

Stringfellow applied for an appeal, including a sixty-seven page brief to a panel of seven new judges, again losing in a close vote. This time, the vote was divided along lines of gender with four men voting to uphold the decision and three women voting to reverse it. Stringfellow voiced his disappointment in a piece he wrote for *The Witness*, arguing that the Appellate Court did not convene to deliberate the motions of the Defense. "We do not even know if they were read," Stringfellow lamented, and he opened the door for civil proceedings in his article.

All seven judges expressed support for women's ordination, but disagreed on the scope of their purpose and the meaning of Wendt's act of conscience. Judges Theodore Eastman and Almus Thorpe, Jr., believed that the trial court had focused on one priestly vow at the expense of seven others, most especially the vow that Wendt followed: "to banish and drive away from the church all erroneous and strange doctrines contrary to God's word." For Eastman and Thorpe, denying women the opportunity to be ordained fell into the category of erroneous and strange. Eastman believed, and Thorpe concurred, that while Wendt had disobeyed one vow, he had kept another and that the debate should have remained within the pastoral relationship to be worked out by Wendt and Creighton. Thorpe added that finding Wendt guilty was important, though, because to do otherwise would belittle his act of disobedience: "To find the appellant innocent of breaking a law which he knowingly violated as an act of conscience would be contemptuous and demeaning." Two of the other male judges, David Beers and Edgar Romig, argued more forcefully for the need for order within the church, noting and quoting the obedience vow as written in the year 1550 by Bishop Cranmer:

> *The Bisshoppe.* Will you reuerentlye obeye your Ordinarie, and other chiefe ministers unto whom the gouernment and charge is committed ouer you; folowing with a glad mynde and will, their godly adminicion, and submytting youreselues to theyr godlye judgementes?
>
> *Aunseere.* I wyll so doe, the Lorde being my helper."

"The church plainly intended," they wrote, "that a bishop's order to his clergy should be obeyed and that one disobeyed at his peril." They then went on to quote Richard Hooker, another sixteenth century theologian who wrote that one person's view of God cannot justify taking action against the ancient practices of the church.

The female judges took issue with these positions, most especially with the use of Hooker as an example. Quoting from *Women Priests: Yes or No?*, they pointed out that Hooker was perhaps not the most forward-thinking supporter of women, having defended the practice of "giving away" a bride during the ceremony of marriage on the grounds that "it putteth women in the mind of a duty whereunto the very imbecility of their nature and sex doth bind them; namely to be always directed, guided, and ordered by others."

In her opinion, with which Judges Catherine Coleman and Verna Dozier concurred, Judge Sally Bucklee wrote that "for me, this trial has had more to do with of the Gospel of our Lord Jesus Christ than with order and unity in the Church. . . ." The three argued that Beers and Romig had "tragically misinterpreted" the source of unity within the church. Coleman wrote that "our colleagues and those on the lower courts, who reject the arguments based on conscience and obedience . . . seem to have forgotten who Christ was or to have decided that such considerations have no place in the life of the Church."

Verna Dozier was the only African-American judge of the seven. She was a highly respected secondary English teacher and layperson from D.C. Years later, as a measure of the love and respect she had garnered, her home parish of St. Mark's in D.C. would place a stained glass window of her image in the church. In her written remark, Dozier argued that it was not "possible or even desirable" to come to a decision that would maintain the identity of the Church as it was then understood.

Dozier also confronted the point that Wendt's dignity would be compromised with a verdict of not guilty. This position as argued by those in power in the church seemed to ignore the purpose of civil disobedience, which was employed so that the powerful could see the need for change, not singly for the purpose of giving the powerful a chance to admire the courage of those they were persecuting. Dozier made clear that no one need worry about compromising Wendt's moment of suffering: "The ordeal of two trials, costs, awaiting verdicts, hostile opinions of fellow Christians . . . are consequences. There is no reason for the majority to feel that without its adverse action, Father Wendt's struggle will be demeaned."

To those who asked why the supporters of women's ordination remained in the Episcopal Church, Dozier wrote that it wasn't that they didn't want to be Episcopalians, but that they wanted "to be Episcopalians in a Church more responsive to the possibilities for complete ministries for all her people." They understood "radical action" as being the way "to bring that possibility into being." She accepted Wendt's plea of conscience because the House of Bishops had opened the possibility for a conscience clause in the 1960s, in the cases when other avenues of affecting change had failed:

> The General Convention by using "divided vote," diocesan bishops by refusing to act singly on their given authority, standing committees by being unable to muster effective strength to bring about a positive response to women's call to be ordained priests—all these means of legal recourse have proved demonstrably inadequate to solve the issue of ordination of women to the priesthood and precipitated a turning to irregular ordinations which in turn produced the rare circumstances of this trial.

On the morning of January 10, 1976, after the failure of the appeal, William Wendt went to the National Cathedral to accept his sentence, walking down into the "bowels"—as Stringfellow described it—of the Cathedral. It was a "tomblike" atmosphere, "grave and somber," according to Hyer of *The Washington Post*, even though about two hundred of Wendt's supporters crowded the steps and passageways. Both Stringfellow and Wendt read statements, Stringfellow calling the sentencing of Wendt "outrageous," particularly in the context of John Allin's own actions, and Wendt asking Bishop Creighton to help him open a place where the women priests would be welcome. Wendt stepped forward to receive his sentence with Alison Cheek and Lee McGee standing beside him. Creighton motioned for the women to move back, but they remained. Reading from a two-page statement, Creighton said, "I do, in all charity and brotherly love, as the ecclesiastical court did, admonish you

William A. Wendt, for disobeying the godly admonition of your bishop," and he warned him not to repeat the transgression. He then laid his hand on Wendt's shoulder and handed him a copy of the document. Cheek read a statement to the reporters, saying that "instead of sentencing Bill Wendt today it would have been more truthful for Bishop Creighton to have caused charges to be brought against me." And thus, the sentencing of good Father Wendt, as both the judges and Stringfellow referred to the moment, was concluded.

Then there was the matter of what to do with John Allin. A group of clergy and laypersons had met in Connecticut, where Allin lived at the time, to discuss whether to bring a presentment against the Presiding Bishop, which would have to originate from the current home domicile of Allin. The group decided against the action, releasing a statement announcing that although "reasonable grounds" existed for making a presentment against him, they found it "literally appalling . . . that the Episcopal Church [had] embarked on a self-destructive series of trials which demean the Church. . . ." They argued that no matter how much the presenters attempted to narrow the charge against Wendt, the issue in front of the church was larger than the allegation of disobedience. The church had to confront the question of whether it would allow women to serve as priests. They blamed the church for "the lack of resolute leadership," but believed that bringing another trial to the table "would add yet another chapter in the Episcopal Church's bid to becoming the theater of the absurd."

As the group's statement made clear, the trial of Wendt was not the only one on the church's docket. Not even two weeks after the closing arguments in Washington, the Standing Committee in Ohio took the Reverend Peter Beebe to court. The twenty-nine-year old Yale Divinity School graduate was on a fast track towards becoming one of the leaders in the Episcopal Church, having accepted the role of rector of Christ Church in Oberlin at the age of twenty-six, a desirable position for the young priest. His college buddies thought of him, according to Beebe, as a "rock-ribbed don't rock the boat conservative." He would grow into a man with a different set of goals, but in his early days in Oberlin, he had been "buying the male success bit." And he, his wife Judy, and the children were well loved at Christ Church.

Beebe had come from a broken home, the son of successful parents who were involved in a range of social issues. His mother Lorraine Beebe was a state senator, a Republican who had fought for penal reform, the ERA, sex education, the rights of the mentally disabled, and a woman's right to choose. In 1969, she stood on the state house floor and revealed that in 1948 she had undergone an abortion for medical reasons. She lost the next election; she received threats; her tires were slashed. When Beebe was a teenager, his parents divorced, but they had already had an impact on the type of priest he would become. "I just firmly believe in basic human rights," he told a reporter. "The right of a person to say, 'I feel my God has called me to serve the church' is a human right and it must be guarded carefully."

Beebe had, with several members of Christ Church, attended the Riverside service in October where Carter Heyward, Alison Cheek, and Jeannette Piccard had presided over the Eucharist. After the service, they all met in Heyward's apartment, along with others of the eleven, to discuss the possibility of at least a few of the women presiding at Christ Church. It was decided that Heyward and Cheek would come on December 8, if they were officially invited. In a close 6–5 decision, the vestry voted to issue the invitation.

Christ Church sits a few blocks from the square at Oberlin College, a school known for its history of progressive thinking on a range of issues. It was the first school in the United States to graduate women in a coeducational structure and as early as 1835, began admitting students of color. It was a stop on the Underground Railroad and the site of the Oberlin-Wellington Rescue, when an escaped slave was taken to Canada by a group of abolitionists from Oberlin, an act that some have argued led to the beginning of Civil War. An unusual school, Oberlin is historically proud of its commitment to social issues, if not so much its athletic programs. For many years, even the fight song lacked that certain bravado that could inspire a team to victory:

> We're the Oberlin Yeomen. We fought, fought, fought, fought, fought.
> We aced the test but on the field our efforts were for nought.
> We're Oberlin. We never win. We're Oberlin. We never win.
> Some things just can't be taught.

It is a small school of around three thousand students in a town with a population slightly over eight thousand. As Barbara Drebing recalled—Drebing was a student at Oberlin at the time of the ordinations—Christ Church opened it arms to the students and offered a variety of opportunities for them to become involved in church life. The students and other members of the community were "extremely proud" of the school's tradition, Drebing said, so that when women's ordination continued to be defeated, they came together, reminding themselves, "We are Oberlin, we will do this . . . we need to stand up."

After the bishops voted in Chicago to invalidate the ordinations, a prominent woman in Christ Church, Nona Thompson, resigned from the vestry in protest:

> Because of the events of the past weeks, I feel compelled to make a new and different kind of commitment. I must protest! And so, I do and will protest to God in my prayers. I do and will protest to the diocese through letters, conversations, and other ways as I am able. And I do protest to Christ Church by resigning from the Vestry and all commissions of which I am a member.

Thompson and other women—including Drebing, Edna Pittenger, Midge Brittingham, Phyllis Jones, Judy Harrelson and Cynthia Henderson—began meeting to discuss the issue. Potluck dinners were organized. The Beebes attended. Drebing said her impression was that Judy Beebe would come to the meetings feeling uneasy about pushing the bishop too far, but that by the end of the meeting, would be willing to go along with the group's plans. "She got nervous as a young mother," Drebing said. Judy's instincts were accurate; her family's welfare was in danger.

The Bishop of Ohio, John Burt, was in favor of women's ordination, though not of the Philadelphia Eleven serving as priests. He believed that the eleven had not proven that they were priests and, therefore, that their credentials were not impeccable. On December 3, he wrote Beebe, warning his young priest that, according to the canons, he had at least two requirements he was "solemnly obliged to heed," that of obeying a godly admonition from the bishop and of allowing only those who could show "sufficient evidence of his being duly licensed or ordained" to officiate at a service. As it would turn out, the fate of women's ordination may have rested on the use by Burt of that small word *or* between the words *licensed* and *ordained*. If, as DeWitt had pointed out in Wendt's trial, adjectives were dangerous words, then conjunctions were going to prove downright treacherous. Burt ended his letter to Beebe saying that he had confidence Beebe would obey the admonition even though it would cause him embarrassment. Then he argued for his own sense of morality as a reason for obedience: "My appeal in this letter is, therefore, entirely an attempt at moral suasion, calling on you to set aside your personal desires to employ the Eucharist as a means of prophetic witness in this instance and to respect the moral authority entrusted to me. . . ." In a move that illustrated that Burt placed as much emphasis on moral *authority* as moral *suasion*, he carbon copied the letter to the vestry of Christ Church, to the Standing Committee of the

Diocese, to Heyward and Cheek and their bishops, and to Sterling Newell, Jr. (who would serve as the lawyer for the church when the Standing Committee brought charges against Beebe).

From the outset, Heyward directly questioned Burt's claim to moral superiority. He had written to Heyward and Cheek telling them that he did not like invoking the canons, but would be forced to if, as he told Cheek, she couldn't "find it in her heart" to obey him voluntarily. He argued that he was concerned "for the distress of many fine parishioners in Christ Church" and that he found it "unseemly" for women who did not live in Ohio to be the first to preside in a church in the state. Heyward wrote back, once again asking why a liberal bishop on matters of race would not find the cause of the women compelling enough to risk offending others:

> That you and other bishops of our church whom I know (personally or by reputation) to be sensitive and courageous leaders can continue to uphold your present stand on our ordinations saddens me. . . . Would you have requested a member of the clergy not to preach a controversial sermon on racism in 1960 or not to participate in the March on Washington in 1963 out of your "concern for the distress of many fine parishioners?"

She took her criticism a step further by enclosing a Rog Bollen "Animal Crackers" cartoon in the letter. In Bollen's cartoon, a small animal is waiting for a large elephant to finish at the watering hole. The small animal asks the elephant if it were fair that he had to wait for hours just because the elephant was bigger. The elephant responds in an entirely sympathetic and understanding manner, bemoaning the injustice of it all. Then he goes back to washing himself in the water.

Burt was not amused, nor was Paul Moore when informed of the cartoon. In fact, according to Heyward, Moore expressed shock at her response to Burt. And Moore was also angry that she had not backed down from her plan to celebrate in Oberlin. Heyward tried to explain her position to him, and also confirmed her resolve that Oberlin would not be the last place she would celebrate.

Cheek was initially more cordial in her reply to Burt, writing that "I do trust that my visit to the Diocese of Ohio will in the end prove to be helpful and creative, and a witness to the primacy of the gospel, the wholeness of priesthood, and the full personhood of women." Burt wrote back arguing that her own bishop, Robert Hall of Virginia, had recognized her "only as a Deacon in Holy Orders" and that he himself was officially admonishing and inhibiting her from officiating as a priest in the Diocese of Ohio. Later, Cheek issued a more direct challenge to Burt's position on moral authority, saying that "the attempt of moral persuasion for a basically amoral stance is anomalous."

In spite of Burt's efforts, the service was held at Christ Church on December 8, 1974. And while Heyward and Cheek would later officiate at several services over the Easter season, the Standing Committee of Ohio brought charges against Beebe for the service in December. The trial was set for mid-May, a few weeks after Wendt's. In the meantime, most of the eleven women priests had met for a meeting in February in Alexandria, Virginia, where they discussed their relationships with the bishops. They were "becoming increasingly convinced" that the canons did not prohibit women in the priesthood and that their bishops, either in an attempt to "father them" or to "protect their own professional interests" had not recognized their dilemma: "Our bishops had failed to grant us the mature human dignity of even the ecclesiastical trial procedures, in which the validity of our ordinations might have been upheld, or if not that, at least our predicament acknowledged and dealt with openly and publicly."

Heyward met with her lawyer and discussed her situation, telling him that she wanted to exercise her priesthood in as many places as possible. They discussed her relationship with Moore and concluded that the pastoral component of it was offering her little relief and could, in fact, interfere with legal action she might choose to take against the church as she worked to be regularized. She sent Moore a letter explaining her position and asking him to contact her only through her attorney:

> Dear Paul,
>
> My attorney, Frank Patton, and I have discussed my ecclesiastical situation at some length. He and I are in agreement that my ecclesiastical standing and my priestly activities are not a matter of pastoral relations, but rather constitute a serious legal matter. Therefore, upon his counsel, I have made some decisions: (1) To request that any correspondence you would send me regarding my priesthood be sent to my attorney. . . . (2) To tell you that I will no longer report to you the specificities of my public ministry; but rather, that I like any member of the clergy, will submit to you an annual report of my ministerial functions. . . .

Along with Patton, yet one more lawyer would play a prominent role in the history of the women's ordination movement—Beebe's lawyer John Rea, who took the case pro bono. An Episcopalian, he was in the Christ Church congregation on December 8 when Heyward and Cheek celebrated. Beebe saw him, knew he was going to need a lawyer, and asked the fifty-two-year-old Rea to represent him. Rea had a favorite saying—"Always keep pushing. You never can tell when you are just a quarter of an inch from the other side of the wall." And he had a reason for accepting cases that involved justice issues. His sixteen-year-old daughter had died suddenly five years before. He and his wife Ruth had come to the understanding with their daughter's death that life was short and that "if there was anything worth doing for others, the time to do it was now." Fortunately for the supporters of women's ordination, Rea decided that representing Peter Beebe was worth doing.

Making the decision to obtain a lawyer did not come naturally to Beebe. Sue Hiatt was the first to suggest the option to him:

> I was really naïve in a lot of ways and we were fighting this battle and Sue kept saying, "You know, they're really going to go after you, they're really going to go after you." I said, "Come on, Sue, they're the church, they're not going to do that." And then one Saturday morning I was at my office at Christ Church working and Sterling Newell, who was the chair of the Standing Committee of the diocese and also partners of one of the largest law firms in Cleveland, called me, trying to talk me out of doing these celebrations coming up, and I was adamant. He said, "Well, we're going to put you from the frying pan into the fire." . . . I remember calling Sue Hiatt . . . and saying, "Oh my God, you're right. What do I do?" And she said, "You better find an attorney."

For Beebe's defense, Rea took a position similar to the one Cheek had argued in the Wendt trial, that though Beebe had, indeed, been admonished by Burt, the admonishment could not be called *godly*. But the second point he argued was in relation to the charge by the Standing Committee that Cheek and Heyward were not licensed or ordained. The official charge was that Beebe had violated Title III, Canon 24, which requires, "that ministers in charge of congregations not permit persons to officiate therein unless there be sufficient evidence that such persons be duly licensed or ordained to minister in this Church." Rea argued that though the women were not licensed, they had been ordained.

According to the memories of those who attended both trials, the atmosphere of the Beebe trial was more official, more authoritative and frightening than Wendt's. The press referred to the testy exchanges between Beebe and Newell. Heyward called the atmosphere "peculiar" and "terrifying." She described the thickness in the air, the "organic malevolence," the five judges in black robes framed by the pulpit and the cross of Jesus. "You have entered a place," she wrote, "in which the gavel and the Lord's Prayer will run concurrently along the same track—and where, if the spirit of one must get bumped off, it will be the latter." Beebe recalled that he was frightened. "They were doing increasingly frightening things, the church authority . . . What is little known is that I was about to be brought up on charges of heresy . . . I was a public enemy so to speak . . . They had the power, I didn't. The parish got splintered. I knew I was going to lose my job. I didn't know what I was going to do. I had two children to take care of."

At a pretrial hearing, several motions were filed by the defense, including one that would allow the defense to question the judges—five Episcopal priests—for bias, another that would allow the Christ Church parish to be included as a co-defendant, and a third that would allow the case to be tried as a criminal rather than civil one so that the burden of proof would fall on the church rather than on the defense. All of the motions were denied. In response to the charge of potential bias on the part of the judges, the judges said that they had questioned themselves for bias but had found none. The prosecution filed motions in an attempt to keep the issue of validity of the women's ordination out of the proceedings, but that motion also failed.

Much of the same ground was covered in the two trials including discussions about the definitions of godly admonitions and questions about the validity of the women's ordinations. One aspect of the second trial that Beebe's supporters found particularly insulting was that the judges did not require Bishop Burt to be sworn in.

The judges released their decision on June 20 and found Beebe guilty on the charges brought forth by the Standing Committee. They argued that the allegation of the admonition being less than godly was "entirely unpersuasive." Oddly, given the judges' willingness to rely on self-examination as a safeguard to their own bias, they argued that in a case where a bishop and a priest found themselves in disagreement, a third party should be consulted. They recognized that a Standing Committee was not such a party. After all, it was the Standing Committee in this case that brought the presentment against Beebe. The judges recommended an ecclesiastical court, presumably like the one they were currently overseeing.

After announcing their verdicts, the judges added a comment about the place of women's ordination within the context of their decisions. "In a strict sense," the court argued, "the issue of validity of those ordinations is not specifically relevant to the charges of the Standing Committee," but it addressed the current conditions that "could constitute some doubt" of the presence of equitability within the canons. "The first condition of which we take note is the essentially unjust, inequitable and unfair way the Ordination (and therefore the licensing) canons of this Church are at present administered by Bishops and Standing Committees." They then reproached the bishops, the standing committees, and indeed the entire church structure and upheld Beebe's disobedience as an act of concern and compassion:

> We have heard, though testimony and evidence, that the principals in the service of December 8 at Christ Church, Oberlin, Ohio were in all respects qualified to serve as priests of the Church, the sole reason for their rejection by their Bishops and Standing Committees being that they are women. We believe that this notorious inequity gravely affects and taints the entire system of canon law as pertaining to ordination and licensing. Having been denied, through this inequitable system, their legitimate aspirations and vocations, the two women involved sought and received Ordination to the Priesthood by irregular means. That persons should seek justice through irregular means when the regular means are corrupted by inequitable and discriminatory elements is both reasonable and fundamentally fair. That they should be required so to do by a Christian Church is a scandal not only to the faithful but also to all reasonable and fair people everywhere. Mr. Beebe, in response to these women and their predicament, took upon himself the responsibility of affording them an opportunity to exercise a ministry elsewhere denied them. . . . We have found him guilty as charged . . . but we must take notice, with deepest regret, that in the circumstances of his disobedience we find a sincere endeavor to extend a ministry of affirmation and compassion to persons suffering outrageously inequitable and humiliating treatment by the authorities of this Church.

The court followed this statement with a critique of the bishops' actions in Chicago, especially in relation to the concept of collegiality, and noted that they had "intruded" into the licensing system. Then they recommended a sentence for Beebe: that the bishop admonish him to refrain from violating canon law until the last day of the General Convention of 1976. If Beebe were to violate the canon again, they recommended suspension. In other words, Heyward and Cheek—or any of the eleven—were not to be invited back to serve as priests at Christ Church. Beebe, however, informed Burt that he would continue offering such invitations. "Just because someone threatens me with suspension," he told a staff writer at *The Washington Star*, "I will not compromise my conscience." Within forty-eight hours, Heyward and Cheek had returned as priests to Beebe's parish. And by mid-July, *The Plain Dealer* announced that Beebe had been asked by the vestry of Christ Church, in an 8–3 vote, to appoint one of the eleven as a priest associate.

If Beebe were not yet a thorn in the side of Burt, he then filed an appeal a week before his sentencing. On July 24, Burt wrote to him, saying that he viewed his appeal as a publicity stunt rather than an attempt at receiving due process, which in Burt's opinion, he had already been granted:

> Many people, Peter, are seeing your actions . . . as demonstrations of ridicule and/or contempt for the Church's law and judicial process. Members of that Court and scores of other people went to great lengths, and expended considerable time and money, to see to it that your case received a fair hearing. Some are now raising the question of whether you may be using the very process of appeal as a ploy to "buy time" before the final judgment or to stimulate publicity for your cause, rather than to engage in a serious search for truth and justice.

It was a disingenuous charge by Burt to argue that in filing for an appeal Beebe was ridiculing the judicial process, and seemingly unfair for the bishop to use an unidentified group of opponents to argue his own case. Of course, Burt was correct in his understanding that the publicity generated by the trials was almost always friendly to the movement for women's ordination; the bishops were looking like elite power brokers making decisions about people's lives on the back nine of a private club. In that same letter to Beebe, Burt informed him that he was inhibited from practicing his priesthood outside his parish and from making any hiring decisions without his permission. He wrote that the inhibitions would remain in effect until " 'after the judgment of the Trial Court becomes final' or until I may choose to modify them." There was obviously little doubt in Burt's mind that the appeal would go in favor of the Standing Committee. He carbon copied this letter to the vestry at Christ Church, to the Standing Committee, and to the clergy in Ohio.

Other members of the clergy in Ohio were also keeping the issue in the minds of the public, though they were not brought to trial. Still, they had other threats to confront. The Reverend Dalton D. Downs was an African-American priest who was the only member of the Standing Committee to vote *no* to filing charges against Beebe. He was also the rector of Emmanuel Episcopal Church in Cleveland. When his vestry voted to welcome the women as priests, seven of the eleven accepted the invitation and in September celebrated the Eucharist along with Downs, Beebe, and five other male priests. Of the eleven, Betty Bone Schiess, Merrill Bittner, Sue Hiatt, Carter Heyward, Alison Cheek, and Jeannette Piccard were there. The newly ordained Betty Powell Rosenberg (now Betty Powell) of the Washington Four also attended. Though Piccard had backed out of the December service at Christ Church (a decision she had regretted), she wrote Burt in August to say that it had been a "naïve cooperation" on her part and that she no longer believed, according to the canons, that he needed to "pass judgment" on her ordination in order for her to serve as a priest in the diocese. She would, she said, be one of the priests celebrating at Emmanuel. Burt wrote back to say that she needed his recognition and that he was admonishing her and inhibiting her from participating.

The service itself was another lively celebration, full of gospel music and songs from the Civil Rights Movement. Two of the women priests played the guitar. But once again, the bishop—a man who had spoken out for women's ordination, had protested the Vietnam War, had supported Cesar Chavez, and had been a friend of Martin Luther King (sitting on stage with him during rallies and preaching against racism)—could not find a way to overcome his conception of collegiality. In its article covering the service at Emmanuel, *The Plain Dealer* reported that Bishop Burt had sent a memorandum to a council of the Diocese suggesting that it might want to consider reevaluating an $11,000 grant given to Emmanuel Church for its inner city ministry. It seems unfathomable that a man with this track record on social issues would suggest such a strategy.

The previous February, the month that the Philadelphia Eleven had met in Alexandria to discuss the impasse with their bishops, Burt had attended the annual meeting of the Diocese of Ohio, that year held in Perrysburg. At the meeting, he made an announcement: "There is no issue confronting all of us in our Church today which is of greater importance to our ongoing corporate life in Christian fellowship than how we shall affirm the full personhood of women." Then he announced that if the General Convention did not approve the ordination of women to the priesthood, he would resign as bishop. "I shall resign as an act of conscience," he said, "against what I will then consider to be a determinative decision by our Church to continue sexual discrimination in our practice of ordination."

In the meantime, the ramifications from Beebe's own act of conscience were still reverberating. The majority of the vestry of Christ Church had been in support of Beebe from the beginning and remained with him throughout the process until they were forced out. And, initially the majority of the members of Christ Church seemed to support Beebe. But with pressure being applied from Burt and other diocesan officials, many members became increasingly concerned about division within the church. Four days before the December 8 service, the senior warden of the church wrote Heyward, Piccard, and Cheek praising Piccard's decision to follow Burt's inhibition and pleading with the other two to follow suit. He wrote that if Cheek and Heyward would back down, it would send a message that would appeal to opponents: "To submit to our chief pastor's appeal to refrain from celebration . . . is to say . . . 'I am a priest of this Church and your sister in God. Won't you please free me to exercise my priesthood by demanding and working for changes in the rules and inter- pretations of rules which now prevent it?'" The warden wrote the letter "after prayerful and thoughtful reflection upon parish concerns and the dialogue with Bishop Burt." That same day, the associate rector of Christ Church, the Rev- erend David L. Anderson, followed with his own letter backing the stance the warden had taken. The warden and associate rector were asking the women to beg for their priesthoods when the women felt called to claim them. Of course, the women and Beebe were extremely vulnerable in this power arrangement.

When the rest of the Philadelphia Eleven realized that Burt, Anderson, and the warden were attempting to divide the women in terms of how Heyward, Cheek, and Piccard had responded to Burt's inhibition, they quickly sent off a letter to the parishioners of Christ Church reaffirming their own sense of community:

Dear Friends:

We rejoice in your courage and witness as our sisters preside at your weekly Eucharists today. Another chapter has been added to Oberlin's long history of making "no peace with oppression." (BCP, p. 44).

We are surprised to learn that we have been represented as divided in our support of you and of our sister priests. We affirm and respect each other's judgement as to how and when our priesthood will be exercised.

We thank God for you, and for our sisters, Alison and Carter. We are with you in spirit and in prayer.

Shalom!

Merrill Bittner	Jeannette Piccard
Alla Bozarth-Campbell	Betty Schiess
Emily Hewitt	Katrina Martha Swanson
Suzanne Hiatt	Nancy Wittig
Marie Moorefield	

But after the December service, the trial, and the guilty verdict, Beebe decided not only to continue providing a place for the women to exercise their priesthood, but to hire one of the eleven for a part-time position. On July 10, 1975, vestry members voted 6–5 to approve the position and stipulated that they would call a parish meeting for September 9 to continue discussing the ramifications. On July 13, the position was offered to Cheek. The small stipend paid to Cheek would be taken from Beebe's salary. On the 24, Burt wrote to Cheek, "While it may be that you intend to honor no canons respecting issues involving the Philadelphia ordination rite, I do add a final plea, appealing to your sense of integrity and fair play." Nearly a week later, Cheek answered his letter and questioned his definition of fairness:

> In the church I haven't experienced a great deal of integrity and fair play. Consequently I've found it necessary simply to go about my business of answering my call as directly and faithfully as possible.

Beebe sent a letter to his parish on the twenty-fifth, the day after Burt had inhibited him from fulfilling any priestly duties outside of Christ Church or making any hiring decisions without his approval. The letter indicates that Beebe was feeling both sorrow and fear from the increasing pressure from Burt and what it would mean to him and his family in terms of his call to Christ Church and his broader call to the priesthood. Nonetheless, he remained committed and in this letter attempted to explain his decisions:

> I have been accused by members of this parish and by others of wanting to destroy the Episcopal Church, of never having wanted to be a priest. It is strange and painful how love can sometimes be interpreted, even by those who have experienced that love. I am "guilty," in my own eyes, of no more than a desire to see the church become itself, grow to a fuller stature . . . expand its vision so that those who turn to it for nurture, for strength might expand their own vision, their own hope. . . . The Gospel accounts compel me to believe that more is accepted by our Lord than is ever rejected, that our God wills the response of each person to his or her own sense, as unique as it may be, of calling, that that calling is intimately connected with every part of the body, soul, and mind of the person. And that my calling will not be stilled, will not be put away, will not be waited for. The call, the ultimate call is to follow . . . *now*, not once the nets have been put away, the boat stored, the father buried . . . but NOW.

The tensions in Christ Church continued to escalate, and a parish meeting held on January 12 would become the breaking point. Six people were running for four new vestry seats. Three of the four who won were against having the women celebrate and were for the removal of Beebe. The fourth was for the removal of Beebe, though he thought the women should be allowed to continue to celebrate. The other two, who had run and lost, were supportive both of Beebe and the continued celebrations by the women. One of the original vestry members, Midge Brittingham, described what happened next:

> In a political move designed to force the Vestry majority to resign, the voters were urged by Paul Donley and Koste Belcheff to vote down the parish budget. This was done by a margin of five votes. According to the outlined strategy, a parish budget will not be approved until the Vestry majority resigns.

The majority of eight did resign a week later and left Christ Church to form the Community for Christian Faith and Action. In their statement, they pointed to diocesan (or bishop) interference as a cause of the conflict: "With much pain and some anger about the persistent diocesan intervention that has inevitably led to this separation, we sadly turn away from this parish [and] place it in the hands of those who have exerted their control." Writing an individual statement of resignation, vestry member Josephine Gilbert noted that she had been in the Episcopal Church for seventy-five years, seventeen of them at Christ Church. She held "no bitter feelings toward anyone in the parish or diocese," but had been disappointed by the meeting of the bishops in Chicago and their "wounding words—'Invalid!' and 'Collegiality!'" She laid out why she felt intense anger, once again pointing to the abuses of the hierarchy:

> In looking back over the long history of the Church I have time and again come across the most shocking misdeeds on the part of its clergy, all the way up to popes and Archbishops of Canterbury. Yet they're OK, they're in apostolic succession, they're duly and validly ordained. Apparently the only unforgivable sin when it comes to ordination is that of being born female. It doesn't take a rampant women's libber to see the injustice of that. And it is this injustice that arouses deep wrath, even in a rather mild person like me.

Burt severed Beebe's relationship with Christ Church. And the only thing left to sweep up was the appeals court's, or Court of Review's, decision. The Court of Review had been established in 1904, but had never heard a case, not until it heard Beebe's on February 24, approximately a month after those leaving Christ Church had attended their last service. A decision was announced on April 3.

It should have been a slam dunk for the Standing Committee and the hierarchy of the Episcopal Church. The Chief Judge and President of the Court was Bishop Stanley Atkins of Eau Claire, who that year would be unanimously elected Chairman of The Coalition for the Apostolic Ministry (CAM), who had been one of the bishops to bring charges against the four ordaining bishops in Philadelphia, and who had published an essay the year before with the straightforward title "The Theological Case Against Women's Ordination" in which he argued that "what man is to woman is an emblem of what God is to us all." His point could have been a question from the Graduate Record Exam: Man is to *woman* as God is to *people*. More specifically, he called the ordinations in Philadelphia "illegal and a gross violation of the collegial basis on which the Episcopal Church is organized."

Things didn't turn out quite so predictably. In a surprise decision, the Court of Review reversed the decision of the trial court and sent the case back for a new trial. The Court held that the trial court had not been sufficiently examined for evidence of bias, that it had refused testimony on important materials, that it had misinterpreted one of the canon laws, and that it had not required the prosecution to establish its case beyond a reasonable doubt. And they agreed that the prosecution had never proved that the admonition given was actually godly. For the sake of clarity and because judges on the Court of Review could not find a definition of a godly admonition, they laid out the parameters of one, calling it "a solemn warning to a Presbyter or Deacon by the Bishop of the Diocese in question or other Bishop having canonical jurisdiction over the Presbyter or Deacon." They stipulated that, among other things, it had to be made in writing and that it not be arbitrary nor contrary to the Canons. In the case of disobedience, a presentment could only be issued with the consent of the bishop who gave the admonishment. This final point would have been useful to Bishop Creighton in the Wendt trial because the decision to bring a presentment would have ultimately belonged only to him and not to the eighteen priests who brought the case to trial.

After the decision was announced, Hyer from *The Washington Post* reported that Burt and the Standing Committee had spent the better part of a day behind closed doors. When they emerged, they had decided to refer the matter to their attorneys. Eventually the charges were dropped, though Beebe and others had hoped for another trial because it would have most likely forced the new court to rule on women's ordination. As Rea wrote, "It is just a matter of time before some Ecclesiastical Court, using the Beebe decision as authority, will hold that the canons as they now stand permit the ordination of women." Rea also pointed to the key word that the Court examined, that tiny overlooked word *or*. He wrote that the trial court had read *or* as *and* in the canon that stipulated that a person had to be "duly licensed or ordained to minister in this Church." The Court of Review argued that *or* meant just that: "In our view, the words 'duly licensed *or* ordained' . . . cannot be construed as meaning 'duly licensed *and* ordained.'" All agreed that the women had not been licensed, but the issue of ordination was at the crux of the debate. Given the ruling of the court, with the burden of proof now on the church, it would be "extremely difficult for any prosecutor to convict a priest" who had invited a woman to serve as a priest in his parish.

Hyer wrote that "what makes the Ohio situation so sticky is that a month ago Bishop Burt, without waiting for the review court decision, fired Mr. Beebe from the rectorship of Christ Church, which has split as a result of the controversy." She quoted Beebe who reflected on the irony of the situation: "I've lost my employment as the result of the trial which the appellate court said wasn't fair." Unfortunately, the unfairness of the moment had multiple layers. For instance, during the time of the trials, Beebe's confidential psychiatric profile, required of those entering the priesthood, was leaked. Even today, Beebe doesn't know who leaked it, only that the claim that he had difficulty with authority was meant to undermine his stance on women's ordination. Within the next few years, Beebe's marriage came to an end. He entered Kent State, earned a Ph.D in Psychology, and left for the West Coast, opening a practice in Seattle. About ten years ago, a friend wanted him to officiate at a wedding. To do so, Beebe needed to have verification of his affiliation with the church, so he called the Diocese of Ohio and talked to the new bishop, who praised him and his work, but said that someone was supposed to have told him years ago that he had to renounce his orders. The bishop said that the only way he would approve the wedding was if Beebe would agree to renounce his orders first. "They finally got me," Beebe said. It was not that the diocese could force him into renouncing his orders, but that the leadership could effectively keep him from practicing as a priest. By that point in time, it was a battle he had little interest in fighting.

• • •

In the midst of the trials of William Wendt and Peter Beebe and the media attention around them, something else was stirring, an event that would raise the stakes for both supporters and opponents of women's ordination to the priesthood. It took the shape of further disobedience. Once again, we return to St. Stephens in Washington, D.C., and once again enter a world where people who were celebrating the Eucharist in an Episcopal church were also frightened for their lives.

Chapter 12

THE WASHINGTON FOUR

On her twenty-eighth birthday in November of 1960, in the Congo of Africa, Alison Palmer found herself crawling off a terrace with a colleague and through his apartment, trying to dodge bullets being fired between the Congolese Army and forces from the United Nations. The two made it inside to relative safety, but the event capped a forty-eight hour period in which Palmer, in her job as vice-counsel for the U.S. embassy, saved the lives of three journalists who were about to be executed—a writer for *Time*, another for United Press International, and a freelancer—and then rescued future U.S. Secretary of Defense Frank Carlucci and his traveling companions from an angry mob intent on killing them. While transporting top secret documents in her blue sports car, Palmer had driven up on the Carlucci party whose car was tilted in a ditch after they had hit and killed a young Congolese man on a bicycle. Palmer led the blood-soaked driver of the car to her own, raced him to medical care, and made certain the others in the party had been removed from the scene.

Palmer had entered the foreign service with the hope of working in London, Paris, or even Rome, but her first assignment took her to the Congo just as it was achieving its independence from Belgium. By the time her tour was over and she had arrived home to Long Island, stories of her heroism had made newspapers across the nation, many of them sounding like a scene from a Nancy Drew book. Writers referred to her "girlish gusto," to the "pert and bouncy blonde," to the girl with the "quick smile and blonde ponytail bobbing behind the wheel of her blue convertible." They quoted her saying things like, "I'm afraid anywhere else they send me after this will be kind of dull" and "I'm having too much fun to think about marriage." One reporter noted that "whenever there was trouble in the streets sooner or later 'Miss Palmer' would turn up—generally alone, stand up to her full five feet and one quarter inch and sternly reproach offending troops or hoodlums in her schoolgirl French." Her nickname was Tally, for Tally-ho, given to her because of the equestrian skills she displayed in Africa on a horse named Houdini.

Her father met her at the airport on the day of her return to the United States, telling her that their home phone had been ringing off the hook. One of the calls was from the producer of the game show *To Tell the Truth*, a CBS show from the Fifties and Sixties in which four celebrities were presented with a panel of three people all claiming to be the same person, normally someone with an unusual job or some other claim to fame. The celebrities were allowed to ask a series of questions in order to correctly identify the "real"—in this case—Alison Palmer, heroine of the Congo. Palmer and her two imposters ran through a rehearsal before the show, with substitutes filling in for the celebrities. It became quickly evident in the rehearsals that the real celebrities were going to have an easy time of it when one of the imposter Alisons was asked to name the Secretary of State and couldn't come up with an answer. She just froze, as Palmer remembered. "I turned to her and I said, 'just make up a name, give them the name of your uncle . . . or your dentist, just say something.'"

By 1965, Palmer was with the U.S. consulate general in Georgetown, British Guiana, when a bomb destroyed her office. She had left her office only ten minutes before the bomb exploded. She returned to the United States and at the State Department's request entered a year-long African Studies program at Boston University. She had fallen in love with Africa and looked forward to returning to the continent, but her plans were ended when in a period of a few months three different U.S. ambassadors objected to her appointments. They did not want a woman in the positions she would fill. These rejections served as a turning point for Palmer in her relationship with the State Department, which she had previously thought of as "family." She decided to fight back, filing the first discrimination suit the department had ever faced.

With the suit pending, she volunteered in 1968 to serve in Vietnam, wanting to find out for herself what was actually happening in the war. In the Congo, she had become friends with David Halberstam, who would win a Pulitzer for his work on Vietnam. Palmer was concerned by his reports that both the military and the American Embassy were lying about the war. Though Palmer trusted Halberstam implicitly, she found it difficult to believe his stories were accurate. What she discovered while analyzing and compiling field reports was that areas of Vietnam that had supposedly been "pacified" (secured), had remained, in fact, dangerous and unstable war zones. On her first day of work in a province reported to have been one hundred percent pacified, Palmer felt her office building begin to shake and watched as black clouds moved across the horizon. "Oh, don't worry about that, Alison," one of her colleagues said,

"we're just dropping napalm on the Viet Cong . . . nobody is getting hurt."
The Viet Cong, according to the colleague, were hiding in the mountains.
"That confirmed," Palmer said, "what I had been hearing from David Halberstam and others that this whole thing [was] a charade."

When a civilian refugee officer reported that the village of Khiem Can had
been destroyed by friendly fire, killing many civilians—including children—she
forwarded the report to Saigon, angering commanding general Major General
William R. Peers. He made his own report arguing that the deaths had been
caused by the Viet Cong, and he prohibited her from releasing other reports
without his prior approval. When Palmer left Vietnam and arrived back in
Washington, she employed a technique that she would use often in the next
years: she made contact with a member of the press and told her story. In the
article, she described writing the judge advocate general of the Army, emphasizing that "such incidents may or may not be considered inevitable during a war,"
but "failure to investigate and correct mistakes is not inevitable." The editors of
The Washington Evening Star titled the article, "A Pint-Sized Crusader."

In the end, the military did not change its position on Khiem Can, but
Palmer changed her perspective on the State Department and the U.S. government, not only in relation to foreign policy but also regarding the Department's
labor and management practices. As she later wrote in her unpublished memoir:

> When I first began working for the State Department I thought that our foreign policies were right and I never wanted to do anything but work hard to
> help carry them out. Now I have submitted more dissent papers than any other
> officer in the foreign service. I used to be so proud of being a foreign service
> officer that I gladly worked long hours, volunteered for "hardship posts" in
> Africa, Latin America, and Vietnam, faced dangers which I thought my duty
> required—now I file a complaint if I am denied overtime pay, I am unwilling
> to risk my life, and I am ashamed of being a foreign service officer. . . . Now
> I stand on the sidewalk outside the State Department handing out leaflets
> accusing top officials of mismanagement, prejudice, injustice. . . . For years I
> considered myself part of a white-collar elite, a part of a managerial class making foreign policy; now I see myself as a trained union "shop steward."

With monies she won from her first sexual discrimination suit against the
department, she filed and eventually won a much larger class action suit against
it. She told the members of the press to end the blue-eyed, blonde shtick when
writing about her. When one reporter asked her exactly how tall she was, she

said she would tell him if he put his height next to his byline. In 1976, Mike Causey of *The Washington Post* wrote a piece about Palmer, recommending that the State Department focus on something other than fighting her, that it spend its energies on issues like worldwide disarmament and peace in the Middle East. "You know," he wrote, "the kind of thing where it has a chance."

The leadership within the Episcopal Church would have been wise to have listened to Causey's advice because at some point in her time in Vietnam, Palmer had heard a call from God. "Get ordained," was the message. At first, Palmer thought that either she or God had gone crazy, but when the sense of that call continued to haunt her, she took it seriously and organized with three other women to become the Washington Four, a group that continued applying pressure on the Church (as begun by the Philadelphia Eleven) by becoming irregularly ordained themselves. Palmer met two of the other four, Lee McGee and Betty Powell, in Washington, but would come to know the fourth, Diane Tickell, when she flew in from Alaska to participate in the ordination.

The ordinations of the Washington Four proved to be important to the success of the women's ordination movement because they indicated to the church that the issue was not likely to fade away over time. And this second round of ordinations showed that even if all of the Philadelphia Eleven were eliminated, taken down one by one like—in a metaphor used by an opponent of the ordinations—ten little Indians, there would be others to follow behind them. Palmer and McGee had perfected a particular strategy for the fight. As McGee said, "The person I was known to be in the diocese . . . was not a troublemaker, as Alison Palmer was—which she was very proud of. We were a perfect combination . . . like the good cop/bad cop combination."

Born in Baltimore, Maryland, in 1943, McGee graduated *Magna Cum Laude* from Maryland State College in 1965 and entered Yale Divinity School in the fall of that year. Two years later, at the age of twenty four, in what was assumed to be her final year at Yale, she began having trouble reading traffic signs. She went to a doctor at the university who tested her vision. His news was devastating. "I dropped," McGee said, ". . . from September until November of that year . . . from correctable 20/40 vision to 20/200, legal blindness. It was shattering." She had developed a rare and genetic eye disease, and the doctors couldn't tell her whether she'd be completely without vision by the age of thirty or if the level of damage had peaked. She attended a six-week program at the Columbia Lighthouse for the Blind in Washington, D.C., an organization that provides various forms of skills training to the blind or visually impaired. McGee told one of the women at the Lighthouse that she was planning to be married, and the woman asked if she would be open to talking to the seamstresses at the workshop. When McGee spoke with them, one of their leaders asked if they could make her wedding dress. She agreed. Modeling the dress for them was an experience she never forgot. "It fit perfectly," she said. "I was so excited. And they were excited. And they said, 'May we come feel it because that's how we see?' And their hands just went all over. Nearly fifty years later, she tells this story with tears streaming down her face. "The woman who had arranged all of that said, 'You know, this means all of the world to them because most of them will probably never marry.' That was how it was," McGee added, "to be blind back then."

A year after her marriage and, in spite of her diagnosis, McGee finished her degree at Yale and spent a year at the University of Edinburgh. Then she and husband Kyle, an Episcopal priest, moved to Washington, D.C., where he had been hired as an assistant priest at St. Stephen and the Incarnation, in the parish of William Wendt. She was hired as a chaplain at American University in D.C., but when students and staff began asking her to perform baptisms and weddings, she was unable to complete the ceremonies without the assistance of a priest to sign the documents. Students wondered why she didn't have the same authority as other ordained ministers on staff. "I've always taken this as really important," she later reflected, "because what that means is that my call came from the community as opposed to from top down." The experience shaped her theology. "God calls you through the community and the church then . . . ratifies that."

She discussed her calling with Bishop Creighton who sent her to a one-day conference to talk with members of a committee composed of people from the dioceses of Washington and Maryland who were to give feedback to the bishop. With that step completed, he asked her to have a psychology exam. McGee remembered that the examiner gave her "a very positive" recommendation, but at the end wrote to Creighton that though he believed McGee to be gentle and caring, she had a firm resolve. He warned the bishop to watch out for her. "I always thought that was very funny," McGee remembered with a laugh. Many in the church, though, would find it less than amusing a few years later when she, Palmer, Betty Powell, and Diane Tickell would decide to continue the process begun in Philadelphia by the eleven.

Betty Powell was born in Delaware in 1945 to "a southern lady" from Virginia and to a German immigrant escaping Hitler. She admired her father's pioneering spirit both in his willingness to begin life again in a new country and in his work as an organic chemist, but she recalled that he could be reclusive and distant. "He was a scientist," she said. "He lived in his mind." Her mother, Powell believed, probably suffered from depression and alcoholism, but had found purpose in her work for the Junior League, though not as a mother or as a homemaker. When angered, her mother's temper could explode, Powell said, "Like a volcano."

As a girl, Powell found refuge in one of the local parishes, Trinity Episcopal Church in Wilmington. Her parents rarely attended, so she would ride with the neighbors. "I got a lot of support in the church—I felt like I belonged there." The church, she said, "had been Mother Church for me." She was supported by a loving confirmation teacher and was given leadership roles in the youth groups and parts to play in church productions. She assumed the role of Mary in the Christmas pageant and then later, donned black tights and a silver tunic, marched down the church aisle carrying a sword designed from wood and aluminum foil, and made an entrance as Joan of Arc. Well before her portrayal of the saint, Powell had already absorbed her story, taking it "very seriously" and greatly admiring the woman who had followed her understanding of divine guidance.

Powell also found mentors and role models outside the church. She adored her pediatrician Margaret Handy, who would achieve fame for several reasons, including the fact that she was the first pediatrician in Delaware and the first female native-born doctor in the state. She also became known in the art world for serving as a subject in Andrew Wyeth's *The Children's Doctor*. Wyeth had painted Handy's portrait after she had treated his children, a work intended to be an "expression of affection" for the family friend. Handy inspired affection from her young patient as well, who described her doctor as "amazingly kind, compassionate, and knowledgeable," a woman who displayed "a healing presence." As a child, Powell said of herself, I "wanted to be just like her" and planned for a career in medicine. In later years, while remembering Handy's impact on her, Powell noted, "I realized it's exactly what I've tried to become."

After receiving an undergraduate degree in biology, Powell entered graduate school at the University of North Carolina in Chapel Hill to study physiology. It was there one night that she had "Samuel's Dream," what she understood to be a spiritual calling. She woke from a dream having heard her name called. She went back to sleep and heard it again, at which point she said, "God, if it really is you it's got to happen a third time before I am a believer":

> The third time I was awakened hearing my voice I just rolled out of bed onto my knees. It was one of those "here I am, what do you want me to do" kind of moments. I knew there was some special path I was supposed to take.

She completed her studies in Chapel Hill and left for Virginia Theological Seminary. In fact, both she and Nancy Wittig earned degrees from Chapel Hill and entered seminary together and both would assist in bringing the introductory meeting of the Episcopal Women's Caucus to campus, the one Sue Hiatt had organized in the fall of 1971. Seminary was, for Powell, a "huge swirl of the good, the bad, and the ugly." Founding the Caucus was part of the good, part of the "wonderful," as she remembered. And she enjoyed her academic work. Also, in the summer before her senior year in seminary, she worked for the diocese, spending her time on a project designed to examine the connection between the Episcopal Church and the women's movement, which led her to interviewing women leaders within the Church and to attending NOW meetings and consciousness-raising groups for the first time. "I had my consciousness raised tremendously," she said.

But to a large extent, seminary was also an experience in exclusion and alienation, a place where women were "not good enough." When it was her turn to practice celebrating communion in her liturgics class, only two students attended class. Then, during a small group meeting, a fellow seminarian handed her a cartoon he had drawn of a nearly naked woman wearing a stole in the fashion of a priest (deacons and priests wear their stoles differently). The cartoon was accompanied by the question, "Would you like to commune with her?" Powell remembered that she was mortified by the sexual overtones, for at that point in her life she believed that being a good girl meant refraining from having sex before marriage. On another night, she returned to her room to find on her door a "Playboy-like" picture of a naked woman priest on a pedestal with three naked men bowing down to her. "It was incredibly upsetting to me," Powell remembered. At the end of her seminary years, she was ordained, along with four men, as a deacon. During the sermon, the priest told them that some of the five would go on to be priests. Powell understood that because of her gender, she was not included among the *some*. "It was like a sword through my heart," she remembered. "I knew I was called to be a priest."

And so she tightened her resolve to become one. With Palmer and McGee, she began to organize, meeting monthly at McGee's home with a group of thirty or so women in the Washington area dedicated to bringing women's ordination to the diocese. They were attempting to create an atmosphere in the diocese, McGee remembered, that was friendly to women's ordination. Between these meetings, Palmer, McGee, and Powell met every two weeks, McGee explained, to "talk about what we were experiencing and how to be supportive of each other." They developed a plan to present themselves for ordination whenever men were to be ordained and to place the bishops, who were in favor of women's ordination, in the position of having to reject them. McGee believed that this strategy led to Creighton placing a moratorium on all ordinations in the diocese, though he did allow bishops from other dioceses to ordain men in the Washington area. The women were successful, by and large, in creating a favorable atmosphere for women's ordination within the diocese and were able to secure the approval of the diocese's Standing Committee, a feat the Philadelphia Eleven had not been able to accomplish at the time of their ordinations. The only missing link, the women understood, was Creighton's refusal to ordain them. Creighton still wished to wait until the General Convention had been given another chance to vote. McGee voiced her disagreement, stating that it was wrong to vote on "a category of people," that it was "sanctioning prejudice."

In January of 1975, Palmer wrote Creighton a five-page letter attacking the logic of his and the other bishops' preference for waiting for General Convention approval. She examined three parts of the bishops' argument: (1) waiting would create a more clean-cut decision, (2) the entire church could celebrate a favorable vote at the Convention, and (3) ordinations were intended to be accepted by the whole church. Palmer wrote that when fundamental change had occurred in the church, it had "very seldom come in a neat and tidy manner" and that "neatness and orderliness have never been a characteristic of the Gospel." Secondly, she pointed out that the Convention would not be a joyous event in any case if, beforehand, at least one of the bishops had not ordained a woman from his own diocese. "There will be so much pain, frustration, anger, hostility, bitterness, and disappointment," she wrote, "that a favorable decision in 1976 will be like signing a peace treaty after a war had dragged on unnecessarily for months and years." And on the third point, she wrote that when men were scheduled to be ordained in the Diocese of Washington, they were not denied simply because some other diocese somewhere in the future might choose to reject them.

Palmer addressed one more comment Creighton made concerning the Diocese of Washington and other dioceses on the East Coast, those that were "seen by some as part of the liberal Eastern Establishment and therefore not part of the 'real' Episcopal Church":

> I must say honestly that if this Diocese, and you in particular, are moved in good conscience to take some action, such as ordaining me, then I hope you will proceed. I see no reason to pretend to anyone that this Diocese

is on the same wavelength as the Diocese of Wisconsin, just to present a façade of church unity. Our church is not unified on ordination of women and may never be; some Dioceses inevitably will move faster than others, and be criticized for so doing. Let us not delay in the vain hope that the conservative wing of the church will catch up.

Creighton responded a few days later, thanking her for her "thoughtful and persuasive letter." He pointed out that as a deacon, she was an ordained minister and that he did not want her "to be obsessed with the single issue [of ordination to the priesthood]," though it be an important one. He praised her tenacity, but ended his letter, "I can only believe that I have a broader and longer experience of the Church's life and ministry than you have and that considering all the factors, it would not be wise nor helpful for me to act unilaterally in the ordination of women."

Even with her expression of tenacity on the issue, Palmer recalled that at the time she was having issues of her own with the idea of women priests. She writes of going to McGee's home in April for a service in which Alison Cheek was presiding over the Eucharist. It was to become one of the most important spiritual experiences in her life. The woman who had rescued journalists from executioners, saved the life of the Secretary of Defense, served in Vietnam, sued the State Department, and was currently looking to upend years of tradition within the Episcopal Church, admitted to being frightened of receiving communion from a woman priest:

> I had had opportunities earlier but had hesitated because I was not sure I was ready for this. I fully understood the feelings of many people who were doubtful about women priests. Even though I myself expected to be ordained to the priesthood I still felt afraid of the experience, because it was totally new.

That night, after participating in the service, she went home and thought about what had happened to her, surprised by how quickly something that had felt so alien began to feel "natural and true."

The next month, in May of 1975, McGee, Powell, and Palmer met with Robert DeWitt, who was in Washington to give testimony in the William Wendt trial and to attend a fundraising event that the parish of St. Stephen was holding for its rector. At the fundraiser, the three women found a quiet place on the steps of the church and discussed with DeWitt their hopes for another irregular ordination. DeWitt did not believe that he was the right bishop for a second irregular ordination. He would have been aware, of course, that his own position within the House of Bishops had remained fragile and tenuous since Philadelphia, and he told the women that he hoped they could convince a bishop currently serving in a diocese to preside and thereby deflect concerns over irregular procedures.

At Powell's suggestion, the three women began what Palmer referred to as "a massive phone campaign," calling any female deacon they believed might be interested in participating in an irregular ordination. They found some who wished to be ordained, but could not afford to lose their jobs as deacons in the church. One deacon answered that she would be seeking employment in an oil company, where she believed she would not be "subject to financial blackmail." As a result of the calls, seven more women agreed to become ordained, though only one would be able to follow through on the commitment.

Diane Tickell was born in Massachusetts in 1918, the daughter of an advertising executive and, as she later told an interviewer, "a socialite type." She graduated from Smith College and then worked for the Red Cross in Boston. After marrying Army Sergeant Albert Tickell, she moved with him to Alaska, where he developed tuberculosis. She had four children, losing a daughter in infancy. Her first son was born developmentally disabled. "For the first time in my life," she said about being the mother of a disabled child, "I knew what a true minority was." In the late 1960s, after the death of her husband, she temporarily returned East to attend Episcopal Divinity School (then ETS). It proved to be a transformative time for her. She had not been one of those children, as in the case of some of the other women priests, who had wondered why only boys were allowed to serve at the altar. And she had not initially shared the level of anger some of the other women had felt over being denied what they believed to be their calling in the Church. "It took me awhile to get tuned in," she said. "I think the pain and anger that I felt was more as I got into the ordination issue. I mean you meet some people who treat you like dirt. . . . My own experience was terribly painful and really terrific, both."

She was in seminary during the 1970 invasion of Cambodia and was arrested for her participation in one of the student protests sparked across the nation. "If you want to radicalize somebody," she observed, "put them in jail for the night." She found role models in the older women she was surrounded by in Cambridge and Boston, "remarkable old gals," as she called the women. After she graduated, she bought an old car with the few dollars she had left and in June of 1974 drove with her son back to Alaska. Leaving the East again, and the close friends she had made in seminary, proved to be a "painful break" for her. When she arrived back in Alaska, she received a phone call from one of the eleven asking her if she wanted to be irregularly ordained the next month in Philadelphia (it is unclear which of the eleven phoned). Tickell immediately answered yes. As in the other cases of calls made to the women deacons, she was given a few days to reconsider. With no one to talk it over with in Alaska, those few days were to be "a hellish time" for her. She decided against participating in the Philadelphia ordinations, later reflecting, "I have known all along that I lacked the courage and vision that it would have taken. . . . I always appreciated the risks they took. Sometimes I hurt so bad that I wasn't sharing the experience of ordination with them."

When the call came again, a year later and this time from the women in Washington, she did not hesitate. And for the record, Tickell is not remembered as someone who lacked either courage or vision. McGee says that she flew both the Eucharist and medical supplies to remote places in Alaska. "She was a calming influence," McGee continued, "a real voice of conviction . . . this woman was tough in the right way to be a real leader in the Church." A case in point concerning the clarity of her convictions: nearly ten months after the Washington ordinations, Tickell wrote a letter addressed to "Sisters" (apparently all or some combination of the eleven and three in Washington) to bring them up to date on her status in Alaska. She voiced her concerns about her home parish whose members had contributed only sixty-one dollars for the hungry, but were raising sixty-one thousand dollars for a new parking lot. And they seemed, she wrote, more concerned about their own self development than about the plight of prisoners or the recent Chinese earthquake victims.

Tickell would become the fourth of the Washington Four. And while there were four willing deacons, there was still not a single willing bishop ready to ordain them. Palmer remembered that DeWitt would provide her with a name to call, then she would call it and be rejected for any number of well-meaning reasons. She came to the conclusion, she later wrote, that "all of the bishops I had spoken to . . . were waiting for the 'risk-free' time to take a risk, the 'safe' time to do something dangerous." Finally, DeWitt gave her one more option: Bishop George Barrett. He told her that Barrett had once been the Bishop of Rochester, but had resigned after leaving his own wife for the wife of a priest. He had resettled in California and had assumed the Executive Director position of the Planned Parenthood in Santa Barbara. Barrett had been a strong advocate for women's issues within the Episcopal Church and, in fact, for peace and justice issues in general. In the 1960s, he served on the House of Bishops

Committee on the place of women in ministry. To the women's relief, Barrett agreed to preside over the ordinations. He told *The Washington Star* that he had asked the women if they were concerned about his marital situation:

> I realized my own divorce and remarriage and my resignation as bishop of Rochester—all of these things, personal issues which would have no place in any discussion of the ordination question—might be used in an attempt to discredit what these women wanted to do, and I raised the question with them. They each replied in effect, that they felt my private life, or anyone else's for that matter, had no bearing on their desire to seek ordination by me.

The ordinations were on. On August 25, the women announced their plans publicly. *The Washington Post* ran a front page story quoting from the letter McGee had written on behalf of the women to the bishops of the Church. She spoke of the "grave injustice" that was "not only harming women deacons but crippling the church." By the twenty-seventh, the women began receiving letters in response to the coming ordinations. Palmer recalled one she received from Edward Welles, who wrote, "When God calls and commands obedient disciples to act, they do not procrastinate or make excuses for delay." Betty Ford wrote to express thanks for receiving an invitation and to send her regrets at not being able to attend. On the twenty-ninth, they received a letter from Creighton asking them to come to a meeting on September 3. "My purpose," he wrote, "is to make very sure that you all understand the canonical situation and the implications of it." Palmer remembers that the three of them arrived early and met in the women's restroom, "the only place we were sure no man was going to suddenly walk in on us." They agreed to avoid any arguments on their positions at that point because they had already made their decisions. They thought they would be meeting, as they did usually, in Creighton's comfortable office, complete with "overstuffed armchairs" and a coffee table. Instead, they were led into a conference room and asked to sit at a long table. Creighton walked in followed by what seemed, to Palmer, to be "a small army of staff members." Creighton gave the women each a letter informing them that he had not given Barrett permission to ordain them and that the Standing Committee of the diocese had given only Creighton (and no other bishop) consent to perform the ordinations. After resolving a few points of clarification, the women left. Later that day, Palmer and McGee picked up the Barretts who had just arrived. Powell collected Diane Tickell.

The next day, Creighton called Powell back to his office to speak with her alone. At the age of thirty, she was the youngest of the three (Palmer was forty-four and McGee, thirty-three) and possibly the most vulnerable because she did not yet have firm employment. Powell reported that Creighton went over his primary arguments to no avail. He resorted to another argument, telling her, "I am your Father in God." Powell discussed with him what she believed to be the value of each person's individual relationship with God.

On September 6, a morning rehearsal for the service was held at St. Stephen's. Palmer remembers it being a time of laughing and joking and goodwill. The women were to return to Palmer's apartment for a time of retreat, but a reporter from *The New York Times* called for an interview. The women believed that it was imperative that they take advantage of every opportunity to tell their version of the story and so they gave the rest of the afternoon over to public relations.

Someone else had plans for Palmer's overnight hours. She received a series of anonymous calls throughout the night. At 4:00 a.m., the caller finally spoke, but only four words: "My name is Legion," the words said to Jesus in the Gospel of Mark by a person possessed by demons. Palmer thought about the recent letter she had received from a priest from Arlington, Virginia, a ten-page rant that concluded if she were made a priest, she "would form a coven and charge money for people to see [her] administer the Eucharist in the nude." She was glad she had asked her mother to stay away from the ordinations.

As in the case of the Philadelphia ordinations, security was tight at St. Stephen's. McGee wanted to arrive especially early to the church to gather her thoughts, but Wendt would not allow her to enter. He said that the church was receiving bomb threats and that the security staff was bringing in dogs to do a complete sweep of the building before sealing it off. At that point in the day, it still would not have been clear how many people would actually come to the service since Creighton had issued a letter asking priests and laity not to attend. But by the time Palmer attempted to pull up to the building in her car a few hours before the 4:00 p.m. service, it had become evident that the church would be overflowing. Even at 2:00, she was having difficulty finding a parking space or even maneuvering through the traffic jam of cars and church buses. The women had decided to park at the side door and to carry their keys with them in their clergy shirts. If something happened to disrupt the service, they would drive to American University to complete the ordinations. The four women, Barrett, and DeWitt gathered in a church office before the service, again laying out plans and again discussing the risks.

• • •

McGee sat in the pew, terrified. She thought that her anxiety might have been heightened by her blindness, though she remembered that she was not disoriented. She was in a familiar space, surrounded by her sisters, by the congregation that she loved, and by her family and friends. But she was concerned about the threats. Her husband Kyle, an Episcopal priest, was giving the sermon. "I was sitting with my four-year-old," McGee said. "I thought, 'I could die and my child could die.' I was trembling." She felt shattered, but she also felt a deep sense of conviction. "As so often happened," she remembered, "I had to say, 'God, we are in your hands.'" What looked like a gun barrel appeared through a window. Security pounced on it. It turned out to be a camera lens. The photographer was sent to the balcony where members of the press had been relegated. She heard someone yell, "There are impediments to this ordination," and she listened as the protestors stood to speak. James Wattley (the priest Hiatt would refuse to appear with in Olympia, Washington) said, "My presence here witnesses to the anguish which this situation so aggravates." Barrett responded to the Wattley and the other protesters: "It seems," he said, "that God is willing to remove the offense of sexist discrimination."

McGee heard her husband speak of the prophet Isaiah's faithfulness to God even in the midst of doubt: "He had no more assurance he was doing God's will than what we are doing today." She began to relax into the moment, hearing Peter Beebe read from the Gospel. She heard Alison Cheek deliver the charge. While all of these participants received long and sustained applause, *Washington Star* reporter William Willoughby noted that Cheek's charge received the "loudest." Cheek said,

> My sisters—my very loved sisters—your ordinations here today make visible the very heart of the law. . . . In our church at the present moment there are those who confuse the good order of the church with the corrupt use of power. Be very clear about the distinction, for in your hands, too, lies the good order of the church. Where it is present you will find love and justice and shared power—mutuality, and respect for each other, under God. Where there is corrupt use of power, you will find arbitrary control and emotional manipulation—prejudice and exclusion. . . . Go forth clothed in [Jesus'] divine humanity—that the universality of his priesthood may be proclaimed.

Palmer recalled later that even with the bursts of applause throughout the service, when the women said their vows, the congregation grew absolutely quiet. When the bishops and priests (estimates were that thirty to fifty attended against the wishes of Creighton) began the laying on of hands, Palmer felt a sense of being "outside of time and space, a moment of infinity and eternity":

> I felt that everything that had ever happened to me, good and bad, and every-thing that I had ever said, thought or done, right or wrong, was present in that moment, and also everything that would ever happen to me and every-thing I would ever do for the rest of my life, was present.

Barrett gave a gift of a Bible to all four women and as the church exchanged the moment of peace, the congregation erupted in joy. "People surged forward to greet us," Palmer said. The Eucharist followed. And soon after, the new priests followed Barrett down the center aisle of the church. Reporters gathered to ask questions. A reception was held in a nearby house, a time to relax for a moment. But as Palmer recalled, "already people were starting to scatter back across the country." The ordination was over. Its effects, of course, were not.

The next day, Palmer, Powell, and McGee were to meet with Barrett in Palmer's State Department office over lunch. Around 10:00 a.m. Palmer received a phone call from Bishop Creighton's administrative assistant inform-ing her that Creighton had written letters to the women. They should, she said, be picked up immediately. Powell agreed to retrieve them and brought them to the meeting in Palmer's office. The women decided to open them together, "We did a simultaneous one-two-three open and read," Palmer wrote.

Creighton, who had said earlier that year during Wendt's trial that he did not know the definition of a *godly admonition*, nevertheless thought the time was now appropriate to employ a few in relation to the women. He admon-ished the three to refrain from performing their priestly functions. The women discussed their options, including the possibility of risking an ecclesiastical trial. Powell suggested that if they were charged, that they simply ignore it. "What if," she asked, "they held a trial and nobody came?"

Perhaps it is too optimistic to assume that Powell's strategy was one the Presiding Bishop was using all along in relation to the trial of William Wendt. Though, in Allin's case, the issue was complicated by the fact that everyone else had shown up, a point certainly not lost on lawyer William Stringfellow.

Chapter 13

FAREWELLS: THE GENERAL CONVENTION OF 1976

"It's time for Christian women to climb down off our crosses. . . ."

Alla Bozarth, *Womanpriest*

A coffin would have cost you ten dollars. The cardboard one, that is. The real thing, the one made from pine, sold for a hundred and eighty-five, though for an even two hundred, you could have added the four wine shelves and, like William Wendt, used the coffin for other purposes until the arrival of that inevitable day. St. Stephen and the Incarnation had brought its spun-off ministry of the St. Francis Burial Society to the Convention. They were located in the basement of the convention hall, along with one hundred and fifteen other exhibitors selling everything from Amish fudge to crucifixes. St. Stephen's was also selling homemade bread for a dollar, apparently a public relations move from a parish that had stirred up all sorts of trouble for the national Church: "We're here," a representative from St. Stephen's told *The Daily*'s Paula Bernstein, "because we're trying to spread the spirit of joy of our congregation." He then spun the dough around on his finger.

Other organizations . . . many other organizations . . . had established a presence at the convention as well. "For the first time at an Episcopal convention, gays are here," wrote Bernstein. A spokesperson for Integrity, the national Episcopal LGBT advocacy group, reported that they "had been very well received." In fact, the Church would pass several important resolutions concerning gay rights, including the resolution that homosexual persons were "entitled to equal protection of the laws with all other citizens." The Recovered Alcoholic Clergy Association—a group of one hundred and forty bishops, priests, and seminarians—had set up a booth at the Convention, one so popular that its spokesperson, the Reverend H. Gordon MacDonald, was concerned about running out of pamphlets. As MacDonald explained,

> We're here to confront the church and say, "Hey, your priests are human beings, too. When are you going to stop shoving this problem under the rug and start dealing with it creatively . . . ?" A priest can be a lonely person. You can't get friendly with your parishioners.

RACA and Integrity were joined by many other groups, representing the needs of neglected children, Native Americans, farm workers, service men and women, and married couples.

A Check-It-Out table had been set up in the convention hall, a place where attendees could go during the ten days to test the veracity of rumors floating around the convention. The table, along with a program called Talk-It-Out, was the brainchild of a meeting at Seabury in the weeks prior to the convention between the Presiding Bishop and selected groups both opposed to women's ordination (CAM, ACU) and supportive of it (the National Coalition and the EWC).

The meeting fueled suspicion among the women priests and their supporters in Women's Ordination Now (WON) that the Coalition could not be trusted in relation to protecting the ordinations of the Philadelphia Eleven or the Washington Four. WON had thrown its allegiance behind the ordained women and the male priests (William Wendt and Peter Beebe) who had been brought before ecclesiastical courts. In fact, WON had developed out of Oberlin in response to Beebe's trial before going national and had remained a steady support for the women's public celebrations of the Eucharist. The Coalition had evolved from the Episcopal Women's Caucus and was co-chaired by Patricia Park (who had participated in the Philadelphia service) and by George Regas. Regas explained the Coalition's "three-pronged agenda":

> First, to prepare the environment of the whole Episcopal Church to say yes to women in the priesthood. Second, to secure the necessary votes in the House of Bishops and the House of Deputies to pass the canonical change. Third, to respect in grace those who disagreed with us, but to fight hard to win the vote in Minneapolis.

None of those three prongs necessarily guaranteed support for the women who had already been ordained. In fact, some members of the Coalition vehemently disapproved of the irregular ordinations. In her memoir, Bozarth discussed the concerns about the Seabury meeting and the position of the women priests in relation to the Coalition:

> It appeared to others of us, particularly those of us involved in WON, that the political compromise achieved behind the scenes was to involve the sacrifice

of the fifteen women who were already priests. Clearly, we were troublesome to both the opposition and the "pro" side, for we represented a radical position that didn't mesh well with the Coalition's intent to work through the existing political and legal structures. Some of the "pro" people were as eager as the "con" people to have us out of the way during the tense sessions of the General Convention.

In her journal from the 1976 convention, Alison Cheek commented on the reception she received from the Coalition on the day of her arrival, when she attended a party hosted by the group. At the event, she felt "attacked" by a Coalition member who wanted to know why she was attending the convention.

Cheek had arrived in Minneapolis by plane, being welcomed at the airport by Carter Heyward, Sue Hiatt, and a friend from Australia. After dinner, they left for the home of Hiatt's parents, where Cheek and Heyward shared the same room. "We talk a lot," Cheek wrote in her journal, adding, "I am very mixed up about this church, I find, but feel pretty clear and united about myself." It is perhaps both ironic and fitting that Minneapolis would be the city where the vote for women's ordination to the priesthood would be decided. As it was from here that Hiatt, as a young girl, went in search of friends for her siblings, had met the local rector's family, and had established a long lasting relationship with the rector of the local church. It was here where that same rector had told her that he believed she had work to do in the church and where she told him that she agreed, but could not commit herself to a church that treated its women with disdain.

Hiatt was not the only one of the eleven with roots in Minneapolis. Jeanette Piccard had lived in the area for years, and Alla Bozarth moved there as an adult and was living in the city at the time of the convention. She had, however, planned to be out of town with her husband Phil on the day of "The Vote" because she found herself becoming ill from the stress of the convention. The vote Bozarth made reference to was the one to be taken in the House of Deputies on September 16. It had been no surprise that the day before the House of Bishops had given approval to women's ordination to the priesthood, even though two hours of intense debate had preceded the vote. The Suffragan Bishop of Dallas once again raised the issue of the "unbroken line of maleness" and added his belief—one he said was shared by many of his colleagues—that the ordination of a woman could not and "would not take." From the pro position, Paul Moore stood and said, "No one will take my word about the place of the poor in New York City or other cities if our church has turned inward in fear today." After the bishops' votes had been tallied, the count ran 95–61 in favor of changing Title III, Canon 9, to read, "The provisions of these canons for the admission of Candidates, and for the Ordination to the three Orders: Bishops, Priests and Deacons shall be equally applicable to men and women." Immediately after the vote, Stanley Atkins—president of the American Church Union and the Chief Judge over Peter Beebe's appeal—read a statement of protest signed by thirty-seven of the bishops, arguing that to accept the action of the house would be to violate their ordination vows and would be giving the General Convention power it did not possess. The convention could not, in their eyes, make a unilateral decision without the "ecumenical consensus" of the Roman Catholic and Orthodox Churches. In some ways, their argument would have made sense to the six women priests listening in the front rows. They, too, believed (and had been arguing for over two years) that the General Convention was not the correct forum for the issue to be decided, that their own diocesan bishops should be the ones to recognize their priesthoods by simply signing a document and regularizing their ordinations. Also, the opposing bishops' statement made clear once again that "ecumenical consensus" did not include some of the other Protestant churches that had been ordaining women for years, that the term was, in fact, a euphemism for Vatican approval, but one that ignored the support of Roman Catholic groups attending the convention. This presence was so visible that a group opposed to the ordination of women—Episcopalians United—sent a letter to Pope Paul VI "expressing dismay over the 'unconscionable intrusion' of certain Catholic groups into the debate on the issue of women's ordination."

Even with the controversy, most people were fairly confident in predicting how the House of Bishops would vote. The House of Deputies' vote, however, was anyone's guess. The August edition of *The Witness* revealed that the Coalition was being circumspect concerning the number of deputies willing to support women's ordination, quoting Patricia Park that the Coalition had counted in their corner "something less than fifty-eight domestic dioceses." Fifty-eight was the number of dioceses needed to pass the measure.

It was the discussion over women's ordination in the House of Deputies that Bozarth had hoped to avoid, but at which she found herself on the afternoon of September 16. She believed that it had been a cosmic joke that had landed her in the midst of the debates. When she and her husband Phil had left their home, they thought they were going to a "clergy couples" lunch at the Holiday Inn. Katrina Swanson had called her at the last minute to invite them, but when they arrived at the hotel, they were informed that lunch had been cancelled because the vote had been moved to an earlier time. Bozarth decided to attend the meeting, partly out of allegiance to her supporters from WON and to the female deacons at the convention. But she and Phil agreed they would stay for only a short while. "I really didn't want to be there," she wrote, "when the bad news came." Many did want to be there and were captivated by the debates in both Houses. A photograph from *The Daily*, one of the convention's newspapers, showed a large room full of people gathered and watching the proceedings on two standard televisions sitting on pedestals, the caption estimating the crowd to be in the hundreds. House President John Coburn began the discussions by inviting to the microphone those who wished to comment. When fifty to seventy deputies stepped forward, Coburn joked, "And if any deputies are left seated they may be excused."

Each of the deputies who had come forward to speak—*The Daily* confirmed the following day that the number had been fifty-eight—had been given two minutes to address the House. Bozarth reported that at 2:00 p.m. she was giving back rubs to nervous supporters while attempting to raise the spirits of others. By 3:30, she had heard nothing that, to her mind, had added anything to the debate and she decided it was time to leave. Besides, she had planned to serve dinner to the women priests, members of WON, and to their families, and she still had groceries to buy. On her way out of the convention hall, however, she received word that a reporter from the local television station wanted to interview her. She reluctantly decided to stay.

At 5:50, debate ended. David Collins, the dean from an Atlanta cathedral and head of the Committee on Ministry that had put the resolution before the House of Deputies, returned to the microphone and spoke to the crowd about his understanding of the distinction between reconciliation and agreement. Reconciliation, he said, "means loving and caring across the deepest divisions we have." He asked that the last five minutes prior to the vote be given over to silent prayer, and he pleaded with those in the room that "there be no winners and no losers." After the silence, the deputies and gallery gave the Committee on Ministry a standing ovation, then stood once more to applaud the President and Secretary of the House. The gallery applauded the deputies; then the deputies applauded the gallery, moving John Coburn to comment, "This is a real love-feast." And the voting began.

The reporter from *The Daily* observed the movements of those in the crowd as they waited the thirty minutes for the results, noting that they "milled aimlessly around the floor," "stood quietly in hunches, sagging under the emotional load," and "exchanged nervous smiles and touches." The reporter interviewing Bozarth asked her on live television what she thought would happen. Even she was surprised by her answer: "The power of prayer we shared together in this room just now can lead to only one thing. The Holy Spirit is among us. The outcome will be positive."

Coburn asked the House to come to order. "There was absolute silence in the room," Bozarth wrote. "No one was breathing in my section of the gallery." Coburn quickly read the results. In the clerical order, fifty-eight votes were needed for passage. The resolution received sixty (with thirty-eight against and sixteen divided). In the lay order, fifty-seven were needed for passage, and the resolution received sixty-four, with thirty-six against and twelve divided. The resolution affirming women's ordination to the priesthood had been passed. "No one spoke," Bozarth said. They were crying, reaching out to one another, but there was silence in the hall. "Phil and I reached for each other's hands. . . . Phil was weeping." Even with the sense of peace that had come over her while the votes were being counted, she felt at that moment "thoroughly stunned."

A press conference was set up for 7:00 p.m. for the women priests (six were present) and organizers of WON and of the Coalition. Park gave credit for the vote both to the efforts of the Coalition and to those of the fifteen women. The women priests were subdued. Some of the members of the media seemed taken aback by their lack of enthusiasm, but after enduring two years of accusations, oppressive theology, suspensions, and admonitions . . . after receiving death threats and materials with which to hang themselves . . . after being called fat and bucktoothed, mother fuckers, whores, and sluts . . . and after being denied employment after years of education in schools such as Radcliffe, Union, Smith, Duke, Northwestern, the University of Chicago, and Yale all because they were perceived not to be proper matter, closer to jackasses and monkeys than to the priests they were . . . after those two years, they saw their lives within the church through a different lens than they had in the summer of 1974. In fact, they saw the church through a different lens as well. It was no longer enough for them to be allowed access to the church. They wanted a drastic change within the institution regarding its sexist treatment of all women, whether those women wanted to be priests or not. Many wanted changes in liturgy to reflect a much broader image of God. And some voiced deep concern over a group, particularly a predominantly male group, voting on their validity to their calling. Alison Cheek told the reporters that she had come to the conclusion that it was "an arrogant and shameful thing" for the convention to have voted on whether women could be called to the priesthood.

Though Bozarth had believed that the church had restored some of its "own integrity" with the vote, she, too, was concerned about the General Convention's validation of their priesthoods as being indicative of tokenism rather than substantive change:

> A positive response from the Convention could easily lead to co-optation, the easy pacification of women by a Church that was still male-dominated, allowing a few token women into the sacred male ranks of priesthood and episcopacy, but maintaining its misogynist posture toward lay women at the grass roots level.

So when asked their opinions about the vote at the press conference, the women agreed: "This is just the bare beginning."

The opposition was talking, too, urging a boycott of women priests and calling the General Convention's actions "null and void." The Fellowship of Concerned Churchmen (an umbrella group for fifteen organizations) charged:

> No so-called ordinations which may occur as a result of this action can possibly be valid, nor can any sacramental acts performed by women claiming such "ordination" be valid or effective.

In spite of the questions being raised, Bozarth still had the meal to prepare. She, Phil, and Diane Tickell raced to the grocery store, grabbed three different shopping carts, and in ten minutes were back at the house cooking. Tickell was put in charge of the noodles; Phil, the hamburgers; and Bozarth the cheese dish. Five minutes later Robert DeWitt arrived and then the Corrigans and then the others. A WON member vacuumed, Elizabeth Corrigan served wine, and Phil sat down with DeWitt, grabbed a guitar, and the two sang "Jamaica Farewell" together. Then the group gathered and took stock of where they had found themselves both emotionally and professionally. "We spent the rest of the evening talking about the future, and sharing our confused feelings of shock, exhaustion, fear and hope," Bozarth wrote. "It was another beginning. It was also an end."

Yet as all who came together at the meeting knew, nothing had been decided in relation to the fifteen women who had already been ordained. The canon change would not go into effect until January 1, 1977. In terms of having their vocations recognized, the fifteen were perhaps never more vulnerable than at that moment. For one, the bishops were not to address their situation until the last few days of the convention after many people had already returned home, including Patricia Park of the Coalition. And in relation to the media, the Episcopal Church was now on record as voting for women priests and was reaping some much needed positive press, appearing to be, for the most part, a more unified church. Eleanor Blau of *The New York Times*, who had followed the women's cause throughout the two years, wrote a story under the headline "Ordination of Women as Priests Authorized by Episcopal Church" with the subtitle "House of Deputies Decides to Concur with Resolution Passed by Bishops." *The Christian Science Monitor* wrote that "it is fitting that the Episcopal Church, which has contributed so vigorously to the American civil-rights movement, should remove the barriers to women in its own priesthood." The opposition kept its own position in front of readers. On the day the bishops began debates about the fifteen, a Minneapolis paper ran a two-page advertisement bought by members of the Anglican Orthodox Church, who described themselves as Episcopalian, but who stated they would not accept women priests. And in their newsletter, Episcopalians United ran an article warning those churches opposed to women's ordination to begin taking steps towards protecting their real estate. Still, the mainstream media had, by and large, reported favorably on the vote and since much of the women's power had come through the support of the media, this small group of women could have potentially been facing the church without the powerful and influential voice of one of their most consistent allies.

What developed with the fifteen during the next week surprised almost everyone. Some called it a miracle. Paul Moore gave credit for the development to the Holy Spirit. Bishop Donald Davis referred to it as a movement "from death to resurrection."

To back up for a moment: The bishops had given themselves three options (reordination, conditional ordination, and completion) in relation to the fifteen. From the perspective of the women, the first two were off the table. They saw both as insults, direct assaults on the validity of their ordinations in Philadelphia and Washington. They argued that reordination was unnecessary—they had already been ordained. It would be equivalent to remarrying her husband, one of the eleven argued, a mockery of the sacrament another said. The conditional ordinations, which would also require another laying on of hands, would be modeled after conditional baptisms, employed in cases where it was unclear whether a person had been baptized earlier in life. The women pointed out that two thousand people had been in Philadelphia to witness the ordinations. There was no doubt that they had been ordained. In fact, conditional ordination, in this light, was just another name for reordination.

Nonetheless, on Sept 21, the bishops voted 87–45 to conditionally ordain the fifteen. John Raeside wrote tongue-in-cheek that the "scenario" would be played out as such: The House would admit that "something of extraordinary significance took place in Washington and Philadelphia"; the women would consent to reordination; and conservative bishops would be convinced that there was to be no coddling of outlaw women. Result: unity.

The women presented a solid and adamant position in their response to the bishops' vote: they absolutely refused to submit to conditional ordination. They met with William Stringfellow that night, confirming their position with him and discussing their willingness to continue presiding over the Eucharist and to continue forcing the church into ecclesiastical trials and/or civil suits. The next day, things began to get interesting. Suddenly, as Raeside observed, "reconciled bishops who had been feuding all week left the room arm in arm." As the House of Bishops gathered for their session, Arthur Vogel (Katrina Swanson's bishop) suggested that the House do a "rehash" of the previous day. And after rehashing the issue, the bishops not only changed their decision— replacing conditional ordination with a completion ceremony that would avoid a laying on of hands—but they voted *unanimously* for the completion option. People were confounded, not only by the change, but by the unanimous nature of it. No one seemed able to explain it, at least not in procedural terms. One reporter wrote,

> To the Church at large, *what* they did was most important, but to many
> who participated and watched, the *how* was more dramatic. Some who saw
> it called it the work of the Holy Spirit and hoped—or wished—it could be
> repeated at home.

Of course, the women's refusal to participate in the conditional ordinations was the major contributor to the miracle experienced in the house that day. And why not? What is more miraculous than a small band of dedicated women standing up to longstanding, institutionalized misogyny—made all the more insidious by its appearing to have the stamp of a male God? Perhaps in this case, Hiatt's earlier thought—the one she voiced about taking proper security measures in Philadelphia—also held true: "in this world God's work must truly be our own."

The fifteen were not alone. They had other supporters. While reporters had initially responded favorably to the church's decision to ordain women, they did not let the fate of the fifteen go unnoticed. *The New York Times* ran a story by Eleanor Blau quoting Stringfellow, who said that conditional ordination was a "substitute punishment," designed as a means of humiliating the women. Marjorie Hyer published a piece in *The Post* with the headline: "For 15 Ordained Women, Issue Still Not Resolved." She wrote:

> For the fifteen women who brought the issue of women priests in the Episcopal Church to its most poignant focus, Thursday's historic decision to admit women to the church's higher orders is almost irrelevant. A cloud of disapproval still hangs over the women who bent church laws to get themselves ordained.

Additionally, Betty Bone Schiess' civil suit against the church would have kept the media interested in the women's fight, particularly since her suit raised issues that affected not only the Episcopal Church, but questions about the separation of church and state.

If the media weren't abandoning ship, neither was WON. After the vote for conditional ordination, members of the group stayed up through the night making "Conditional Ordination Is Not Reconciliation" signs and posting them in the Convention Hall. The slogan referred to Allin's emphasis throughout the convention on the theme of reconciliation. These signs stood in contrast to the American Church Union's signs: "No Surrender, No Desertion, No Priestesses."

Many members of WON did not trust the Coalition to show leadership in support of the fifteen. Historian Heather Huyck, a founding member of the Minnesota branch of WON, later wrote that while the women's ordination movement needed the efforts of both groups, WON felt that the Coalition was more than willing to sacrifice the fifteen to the cause:

> The National Coalition believed that its work was now done. Friday night, a day after the vote had passed, it hosted a large and very lively dance complete with reggae band, to celebrate its victory. The hotel room was crowded with people as the music blared out. Organizers, women deacons, friends of the Coalition were everywhere. One bishop, standing to the side of the dancers and noticing the numerous women deacons, remarked to another bishop, "There's the future church." For the many women who had not chosen

irregular ordination, the vote made their professional careers possible. Having waited for the 1976 convention, they would not have to decide whether to postpone again their priestly vocations or to seek irregular ordination. By the weekend, most of the Coalition and organizers who were not deputies had left. Their goal—the vote—had been achieved. Action on the 15 irregularly ordained priests was not their responsibility. As Carter Heyward had written in January 1976, the "National Coalition does not consider the Philadelphia 11 and the Washington 4 to be its business." The battle over conditional ordination was to be waged wholly by the women priests, their W.O.N. supporters, and their diocesan bishops. The Coalition . . . had gone home.

Nonetheless, a member of the Coalition interceded at a critical moment. Patricia Park had read about the bishops' decision to conditionally ordain the women, and she sent a quick telegram to the House of Bishops which Robert Hall (Cheek's bishop) read publicly when the bishops next convened. Park wrote:

> I have read the action you have taken with regard to the women priests, and my heart has broken. . . . You are making one group of women pay the price for other groups' liberation. . . . You have known that my sister priests would not accept re-ordination. If they must be punished, then I must consider not pursuing ordination to the priesthood.

Withdrawal by Park at this point could have potentially brought the powerful Coalition back into the debate.

Another source of pressure came from the diocesan bishops of the eleven who (except for Vogel) presented a statement denouncing conditional ordination:

> To accept it as amended would submit many faithful and devoted people, lay and ordained, in our diocese to a cruel extension of the agony they have already experienced because they desired a good and just thing earlier than some of their fellow communicants in the Episcopal Church.

And finally there was the influence of William Stringfellow. According to Hiatt, Stringfellow was acutely aware of the mind of the House of Bishops and was a "master strategist and lobbyist of [its] meetings." When he died in 1985, Hiatt wrote that "when bishops engaged in racist, sexist, or homophobic behavior, Bill seemed especially hurt and offended as though they, of all people, should know better and act in a more exemplary way," and Hiatt argued that in relation to the conditional ordination debate, "Bill's quiet but effective lobby-ing behind the scenes made the difference":

> Because Bill has died, I'll never know exactly what sort of hardball he played, but, as an observer of the situation, I certainly know Bill Stringfellow's influ-ence made an enormous difference on both issues.

Recently, one of the eleven said privately that she believed Stringfellow had been holding a card at the convention, that he had gathered enough signatures to bring charges against the Presiding Bishop in an ecclesiastical court.

Whatever combination of forces shifted the mind of the House of Bish-ops, the women left the convention knowing they had helped push open the doors for women to enter the priesthood of the Episcopal Church. The con-vention, though, had not solved all the issues. Arthur Vogel would continue to deny orders to Katrina Swanson. Some bishops refused to ordain women at all. And not until 2010 did the last diocese holdout—Quincy, Illinois—ordain a woman priest. Some parishes did leave the church, though not as many as had been feared. Most of the women went on to practice their ministries directly or indirectly in seminaries, churches, hospitals, hospice centers, private prac-tice, and in ecumenical centers and retreats, though a majority of them have said that their actions in Philadelphia permanently damaged their ability to acquire parish positions. For at least one of the women, the loss of parish ministry is one she continues to mourn today. Eleven of the fifteen are still living . . . and still keeping an eye on justice issues in the world. Most have remained involved, at least in a small way, with the Episcopal Church, though one has left it entirely. And many have raised deep concerns about the use of male-centered language in liturgy, particularly as that use inevitably serves as a justification for misogyny and limits how the church imagines and chooses to conceptualize its vision of God.

On that last point, in 1975, a year before the Minneapolis Convention, the Bishop of Lexington in Kentucky was quoted in *Time* on the topic of wom-en's ordination. He said that if there were to be more "illegal" ordinations, he would ask permission to ordain the horse Secretariat. A newspaper from Illinois reported that the bishop had explained that at least Secretariat had followed the Biblical command, "Be fruitful and multiply." Yet again, a leader in the church had found a way to compare ordaining a woman to ordaining an animal.

Fast forward to 2001. Carter Heyward published an essay titled "The Horse as Priest," followed in 2005 by the book *Flying Changes: Horses as*

Spiritual Teachers. In the book, she introduces her horse Feather, a new foal on her farm in the mountains of North Carolina. Feather, she envisions, has the power, as does all of life, to introduce her to spiritual knowledge, to connect her to Spirit, to "struggles for justice," to "the earth's soil," to "intimate relationships," to compassion, and to peace. To serve, in other words, as her priest. Heyward explores the implications of her theology:

> What does this mean—God actively trying to reach us through other creatures? It means that other creatures, like humans, are infused with a sacred Spirit that is active—stirring, calling, moving through their bodyselves, as she is also moving through humans. It means the God whom Jesus loved is not inactive or silent in trees or stones. It means that we humans share a vocation to learn how to communicate with other creatures, especially how to listen to what is being said to us. That is what the images in these pages are meant to convey—the Spirit's reaching toward us through other creatures in an effort to save us humans from our fear-based, seemingly hell-bent compulsion to destroy the world, ourselves, and other creatures with us.

. . .

So we will leave this story here with the memory of a chestnut racehorse running through the bluegrass of Kentucky and with Feather, who still lives and breathes in the Blue Ridge of Appalachia and, for that matter, with all the animals and rocks and trees brought forth in comparison to the women priests, knowing that a group of fifteen gutsy, gritty, intelligent women have pushed the church well beyond that "bare beginning" they identified back in 1976, to a place where representatives of the infinite are not limited to the powerful few within the elitist structures of religious institutions, but are found wildly abundant throughout all of creation.

Epilogue

The Philadelphia Eleven:

Merrill Bittner eventually married the old college friend who traveled with her across the country. They lived for twenty-five years in a log cabin they built together deep in the woods of New England. Today, she rarely discusses the Philadelphia ordinations. "I think," she said, "I became the mourner for the group."

Alla Renée Bozarth opened Wisdom House, an "ecumenical feminist retreat center," in Minneapolis soon after her ordination to the priesthood. When her husband Phil died unexpectedly in 1985, she returned to her home state of Oregon and continued her ministry in Wisdom House West.

Alison Cheek moved to Maine after closing her private practice in psychotherapy and retiring from her teaching position at Episcopal Divinity School. In Maine, she helped found the spiritual center Greenfire. She recently moved to the mountains of North Carolina, not far from the home of her friend Carter Heyward.

Emily Hewitt graduated with honors from Harvard Law in 1978 and recently retired as Chief Judge of the United States Court of Federal Claims. She is an avid long distance race walker and in 1987 won the U.S. National Race Walking medal.

Carter Heyward began teaching at Episcopal Divinity School the year after her ordination until her retirement in 2006. In the scope of her career, she has published groundbreaking books and articles on theology. As a lasting tribute to her ordaining bishop, Heyward wrote a book titled *Keep Your Courage*, a phrase Robert DeWitt used as a signature line in his letters to the eleven.

Sue Hiatt, who was also a professor at EDS, continued to work for justice throughout the remainder of her life. In the year before her death, during an interview at her hospice care, Hiatt discussed her work in placing people into the ministry: "I was a faculty member at EDS who would go to bat for people having a hard time getting ordained; people in hopeless situations. I'd try to get them into churches or ministries they'd fit in. Every one but one I've worked for has now been ordained and I'm still working on that." Hiatt died in 2002 from an aggressive cancer.

Marie Moorefield (Fleischer) was recognized as an Episcopal priest on December 2, 1985, more than ten years after her ordination. She served as a canon in the Diocese of North Carolina and has recently retired.

Jeannette Piccard continued to serve as an unpaid assistant in her home parish of St. Philip's in Minnesota and was a popular speaker throughout the area. In the early 1980s, she developed ovarian cancer and responded poorly to chemotherapy. When Alla Bozarth visited her friend for the last time, they talked about the wonderful life Piccard had lived. As she was preparing to leave, Bozarth asked her if she had words of wisdom for her. "She just twinkled," Bozarth recalled, "and said, 'Don't believe everything you hear or read.'" Piccard died in May 1981.

Betty Bone Schiess still lives in the state of New York. She recently wrote a letter to her local paper on the topic of the United States' failed immigration policy, suggesting that the U.S. give the Statue of Liberty back to France. She said that she received more hate mail over that one letter than she had during the days surrounding the Philadelphia ordinations.

Katrina Swanson died of cancer in 2005 as Hurricane Katrina was about to hit the Gulf Coast. The website dedicated to her memory noted that the hurricane brought home to America the plight of the poor in New Orleans and the rest of the nation, a problem she had fought for years.

Nancy Wittig served for twenty years as rector of the Church of St. Andrew in the Fields in Philadelphia. After retiring, she moved to Ohio. She currently holds a position as assistant priest at St. Peter's Episcopal Church in Lakewood.

The Washington Four:

Lee McGee (Street) taught at Yale Divinity School from 1987–1997. After retiring to Colorado, she customarily rode her horse Calibra on her ranch with her guide dog Winsome leading the way, the three of them becoming a team,

McGee recalled. In 2000, she married the Reverend Parke Street and they currently live in Connecticut.

Alison Palmer initiated and won a suit against the State Department for sexual discrimination, then used her settlement to win a class action suit that changed the hiring policies and promotional practices of the department. She retired to Massachusetts where she passionately follows the Boston Red Sox and continues to work on her memoirs.

Betty Powell received her doctorate from Colgate Rochester/Bexley Hall/Crozer Seminary and has spent much of her professional life serving as a psychotherapist, teacher, and writer. She is currently working on two books about healing misogyny and "raising human consciousness of the Feminine Divine." She has found her church family once again, this time in a Unitarian Universalist Congregation in Virginia.

Diane Tickell served as a parish priest for St. George's Episcopal Church in the small fishing village of Cordova, Alaska. She was remembered for having a remarkable sense of humor, taking joy from the fact that she lived in a building called The Red Dragon, once a recreation and pool hall in which a church altar was lowered from the ceiling once a week for service. Tickell died in April 2002.

The Bishops

George Barrett was temporarily banned from practicing his ministry after the Washington ordinations. He later served as Bishop in Residence at St. Alban's Episcopal Church in Los Angeles and Trinity Church in Santa Barbara. He died in 2000 of renal failure after removing himself from dialysis treatments.

Daniel Corrigan died at the age of ninety-three from internal bleeding after a fall. Ten years after the ordinations, someone walked up to him and said, "God bless you, sir." For the first time, he answered, "She always has."

Robert DeWitt served as an editor for *The Witness*, a progressive journal for "Gospel justice," and then retired permanently to Maine where he could be found playing the saxophone and other instruments in barn dances on one of the state's coastal islands. When his wife developed Alzheimer's, DeWitt wrote about the experience, commenting, "I had no preparation for the language my wife has come to speak." Robert DeWitt died in 2003 at the age of eighty-seven.

Tony Ramos, in his book, *The Suffering Marias: Memories and Reflection*, wrote, "I believe that since 1974 . . . I have lived in exile. . . . I have had to fend for myself, which I do not regret and which makes me feel proud." He resigned as the Bishop of Costa Rica in 1978.

Edward Welles eventually came to the point where he was able to write, "Fewer and fewer of my brother bishops treat me like a leper." In the 1980s, photographed wearing a tee-shirt that said, "A woman's place is in the House . . . of Bishops," he told a reporter that one of his greatest regrets was that a woman had not yet been elected a bishop. He died in 1991, peacefully during a nap, having lived long enough to see Barbara Harris consecrated as bishop in 1989.

The Episcopal Church

Since 1977, nearly thirty-eight percent of ordained Episcopal priests have been women. And since 1989, women have constituted just over eight percent of those consecrated as bishops. The threat of schism raised by the issue of women's ordination has intensified over the church's policy of ordaining and consecrating LGBT persons.

Notes

Chapter 1: July 29, 1974

1 "Father _____": _____ to Heyward, July 23, 1974, AWTS, Box 4, F14, Heyward Papers.

1 "women into submission": Editorial, *The Witness*, special issue 1984, 2–3.

2 monkey in a tree: Heyward, *Priest Forever*, p. 48; "There Shall Be a General Convention of this Church," Louisville, 1973, p. 24, AWTS, Box 29, Hiatt Papers; Montgomery to Piccard, January 11, 1976, AWTS, Box 23, F17, Hiatt Papers.

2 "highly irregular and potentially dangerous": "Invitation to Ordination," AWTS, Box 1, F4, Heyward Papers.

2 a defensive position: "View from the Press Agent's Pew," *The Witness*, special issue 1984, 2–3.

2 "was unbelievable": Ibid.

3 "institutional injustice": Editorial, *The Witness*, September, 1975, 2.

3 Alla Bozarth-Campbell remembered: Bozarth, *Womanpriest*, 102.

3 witches, don't they?: Editorial, *The Witness*, special issue 1984, 2–3.

3 "at the stake": Washington, *Other Sheep I Have*, 167; Hiatt, "July 29, 1974—*Kairos* as Paradigm Shift," 131.

3 "sight of perversion": Episcopal Digital Archives 74200, July 31, 1974.

3 in the air: Washington, *Other Sheep I Have*, 170.

4 "carefully set": Ibid., 1.

4 "cannot cross": Ibid., 19–20.

4 "else to go": Harris, Afterword, Editorial, *Other Sheep I Have*, 232.

4 "I'll do it": Washington, *Other Sheep I Have*, x.

6 "the black person": Cannon, Harrison, Heyward, Isasi-Diaz, Johnson, Pellauer, Richardson, *God's Fierce Whimsy*, 98.

6 "of my life": Washington, *Other Sheep I Have*, 171.

7 "Catholicity a fraud": *Commentary*, January 1973, 2.

7 "Apostolic Body": see Darling, *New Wine*, 138.

7 "canon of scripture": Atkins, "The Theological Case Against Women's Ordination," 26.

7 "on this score": van Beeck: "Ordination of Women?" 97.

7 "to the Holy Spirit": Hogan, "Women in the Church: Our Problem, Too!" *Courier-Journal*, September 11, 1974, 3.

7 of the eleven: "News Release on Eucharist to be Celebrated by Newly Ordained Episcopal Women Priests," AWTS, Box 1, F20, Smith Papers.

7 body of Christ: Sisters of St. Mary's Convent to Heyward, December 8, 1974, AWTS, Box 4, F12, Heyward Papers.

8 "a masculine conception": Myers, *The Episcopalian*, February 1972, 8–9.

8 "enlightens the Cosmos": Ibid.

9 "male is God": Daly, *Beyond God the Father*, 9.

9 "whole image of God": *Newsweek*, September 1, 1975, 72.

9 "is assured": Donovan, "Women as Priests and Bishops," 1.

9 "itself seems sexist": Moore, *Take a Bishop Like Me*, 35.

9 "in-the-closet homosexuals": Episcopal Digital Archives 77153, May 12, 1977.

10 "a polite note": Console, *The Episcopalian*, November 1974, 17.

10 "an Episcopal woman": *The Voice of Women's Ordination Now*, February 1975, 12.

10 "not left out": Ibid.

10 "holy moment of history": *Christianity and Crisis*, September 16, 1974, 194.

10 "Spirit's wings": Int. Barbara Schlachter, October 24, 2012.

10 into the future: Int. Linda Clark, November 20, 2012.

10 "around the wall": *The Witness*, special issue, 1984, 10–11.

11 "packed full": Int. Alison Cheek, June 2, 2013.

11 "nuns and Catholic priests": O'Connor, "11 Women Ordained as Priests," *Philadelphia Daily News*, July 30, 1974, 4.

11 "unattractive female": Allen to Bittner, February 18, 1975, Bittner private collection.

11 "accustomed to seeing": Pierce to Bittner, n.d., Bittner private collection.

12 "and saint": Int. Barbara Schlachter, October 24, 2012

Chapter 2: The Deacon's Tale, Part I

13 "about my sister": Int. Jean Hiatt Kramer, September 4, 2012.

13 "make her sick": Ibid.

14 "to act on": Hiatt, "Why I Believe I Am Called to the Priesthood," 36.

14 "a feminist": Int. Kramer, June 2013.

15 "fear of ridicule": Hiatt, "Outline, The Domestic Animal," Heyward private collection.

15 "Episcopal Church does": Hiatt, "Why I Believe I Am Called to the Priesthood," 36.

15 Minnesota by Monday: Biography, AWTS, Hiatt Papers, 1963–1998, Finding Aid, 2.

15 "to other denominations": Hiatt, "Why I Believe I Am Called to the Priesthood," 38.

16 "reshape the diocese": Burkhart, *The Sunday Bulletin*, March 4, 1973, 5.

17 "by Christian people": Ibid., 6.

17 "if it were yesterday": Heyward, *Keep Your Courage*, 230.

17 "but gentle New Englander": Sims, *The Philadelphia Inquirer*, November 26, 2003, obit.

17 "bottle of beer": Burkhart, *The Sunday Bulletin*, March 4, 1973, 5.

17 "loved to hate": Stickgold, *The Boston Globe*, December, 2, 2003, online.

17 "so we shared": Burkhart, *The Sunday Bulletin*, March 4, 1973, 6.

18 "to a status quo": *Benevolent Subversion*, film, RAPPORT, 1993

18 "had no opinions": Ibid.

18 "bishops to thurifers": Hiatt, "How We Brought the Good News from Graymoor to Minneapolis," 577.

18 "in the Episcopal Church": Hiatt, "Why I Believe I Am Called to the Priesthood," p. 40.

19 "around to convening it": Hiatt, "How We Brought the Good News from Graymoor to Minneapolis," 578.

19 "could still be defeated": Rightor, "The Existing Canonical Authority for Women's Ordination," 101–110.

20 "but turned hostile": Hiatt, "How We Brought the Good News from Graymoor to Minneapolis," 578.

20 proposed budget that year: Young, *Thankfulness Unites*, 85.

20 "left the Episcopal Church": Schiess, *Why Me, Lord?*, 55.

21 in the movement: Int. Carter Heyward, July 11, 2013.

22 "of the same name!": Episcopal Digital Archives 96-9, October 29, 1971.

22 "priesthood women deacons": Episcopal Women's Caucus to John Hines, October 30, 1971, quoted in Huyck, "To Celebrate a Whole Priesthood," 100.

23 "which sex should do what": Hewitt and Hiatt, *Women Priests: Yes or No?*, 17.

23 "farms north of Baltimore": Int. Emily Hewitt, July 24, 2013.

23 "Miss Faissler's model": Hewitt, "St. Mary Mead," 148.

24 "later that summer": Int. Emily Hewitt, July 24, 2013.

25 and Malcolm X: Copage, "C. Eric Lincoln, Race Scholar, Is Dead at 75," *NYT*, May 17, 2000, online.

25 "wanted," she said: Int. Carter Heyward, July 23, 2013.

25 "the Philadelphia ordinations": Ibid.

26 "people would talk": Int. Linda Clark, November 20, 2012.

26 "Sunday school teachers": Ibid.

26 "we were doing": Ibid.

27 "at these meetings?": Ibid.

27 "bankrupt overnight": Moore to Heyward, February 15, 1973, AWTS, Box 1, F2, Heyward Papers.

27 "Bishops after that": Int. Barbara Schlachter, October 24, 2012.

28 "what is your problem?": Int. Carter Heyward, November 21, 2012.

28 priests and bishops: Episcopal Digital Archives 72161, November 3, 1972.

28 either divided or against: Darling, *New Wine*, 119.

28 "to share [their power]": Int. Barbara Schlachter, October 24, 2012.

28 "various conservative factions": Darling, *New Wine*, 120.

29 "on our best behavior": Heyward, *Priest Forever*, 46–47.

29 "so to win ordination": Ibid., 47.

29 "already a priest": Huyck, "To Celebrate a Whole Priesthood," 80.

29 "anguish and despair": Ann Robb Smith to Hiatt, February 2, 1994, qtd. in *The Rev'd Suzanne R. Hiatt*, Heyward private collection.

29 "to an end": Darling, *New Wine*, 120.

30 "desire to delay": Hiatt, "Why I Believe I Am Called to the Priesthood," 42.

30 "the foreseeable future": Hiatt, "Kairos as Paradigm Shift," 124.

30 "Go out and organize": Huyck, "To Celebrate the Whole Priesthood," 83.

30 "ordination to the priesthood": Int. Barbara Schlachter, October 24, 2012.

31 "quite the same again"" Darling, *New Wine*, 125.

32 "if black people were excluded": Heyward, "Statement from the Women Deacons," 6.

33 able to laugh about it: Boyd, "Who's Afraid of Women Priests?" 49.

33 "will of the Lord": Willie, "The Everyday Work of Christian People," 4.

34 "access to power": Harris, June 15, 1974.

34 "words were like thunder": Washington, *Other Sheep I Have*, 163.

Chapter 3: The Deacon's Tale, Part II

35 post-traumatic stress syndrome: Kelly, "Jeannette Piccard, SM '19 (1895–1981)," online.

35 of an inch thick: *Piccard Balloon Flights: From Gondola to Manned Spacecraft*, film, NASA.

35 "to tell the tale": Ibid.

35 "White House lawn": "Stunts Aloft," *Time*, November 5, 1934, 54.

35 "part of eternity": Kelly, "Jeannette Piccard, SM '19 (1895–1981)," online.

36 uncommon in its time: Int. Kathryn Piccard, August 30, 2013; Hill, "Until I Have Won," 24–25.

36 fields of Nebraska: DeVorkin, *Race to the Stratosphere*, 165–167.

36 "to their death": "Stunts Aloft," *Time*, November 5, 1934, 54.

36 will be enough: Kelly, "Jeannette Piccard, SM '19 (1895–1981)," online.

37 crossing the street: Hill, "Until I Have Won," pp. 155, 163.

37 "Goodbye, Mother": *Piccard Balloon Flights: From Gondola to Manned Spacecraft*, film, NASA.

37 closed the hatch: Hill, "Until I Have Won," 164.

38 to the ground: Piccard, "Mrs. Piccard Tells of Flight Thrills," *NYT*, October 24, 1934.

38 "to the Anglican Church": Piccard, "Should Women Be Admitted to the Priesthood?" Library of Congress, Box II:85, F1, Piccard Family Papers.

38 from the college: Hill, "Until I Have Won," 34.

38 not her sons: Ibid., 40.

38 of family responsibilities: Ibid., 111.

39 "canons and traditions": Ibid., 288.

39 "the most glamorous": Bozarth, *Womanpriest*, 16.

40 "attack of adolescence": Ibid., 26–27.

40 1950s American teenager: Ibid., 37.

40 "of Thomas Merton": Ibid., 34.

40 "teased me forever": Ibid., 34.

40 inch of her throat: Ibid., p. 13; Int. Alla Renée Bozarth, July 25, 2013.

41 "to her exotic mystic": Bozarth, *Womanpriest*, 15.

41 "moment for me": Int. Alla Renée Bozarth, July 25, 2013.

41 case of fibromyalgia: Ibid.

41 "both of them": Ibid.

42 "two degrees at once": Bozarth, *Womanpriest*, 70.

42 "ordeal by fire": Ibid., 71.

43 "dance of death": Ibid., 79.

43 "up the line": Welles, *The Happy Disciple*, 1.

43 "an Episcopal convention": "The Welles Express," *The Episcopalian*, September 1974, 13.

43 *The Welles Fargo Express*: Ibid.

43 "the final few yards. . . .": Welles, *The Happy Disciple*, 19.

44 "too Romish": Ibid., 2.

44 "'abusive' and 'alcoholic'": Katrina's Dream, online; Hacker, *The Philadelphia Inquirer*, August 1, 1982, 24-A.

44 "stole[n] the show": Welles, *The Happy Disciple*, 68.

45 "on my birthday": Katrina's Dream, online.

45 "with the chicken pox!": Welles, *The Happy Disciple*, 68.

46 "sisters very much.": Schiess, *Why Me, Lord?*, 9.

46 "responsibility of parenthood": Ibid., 10.

46 "are all equal": Ibid., 12.

46 "of the women": Ibid., 18.

46 "was absolutely correct": Ibid., 22.

46 "the Episcopal Church": Ibid., 23.

46 "to abandon motherhood": Ibid., 50–51.

47 "was, is, my call": Ibid., 34.

47 "as my family": Int. Merrill Bittner, September 11, 2013.

48 "celebration of life": Ibid., Longstreth, *de-liberation*, August, September, October 1976, 8.

48 women like Phyllis: Int. Merrill Bittner, May 25, 2013.

49 "piece of bread,": Petraske, *Courier-Journal*, December 19, 1973.

49 "I rejoice!": Spears to Bittner, July 17, 1972, Bittner private collection.

49 "fear and suspicion": Cheek, "Autobiography," January 1976, p. 2, Cheek private collection.

49 "come the spring": Ibid., 1.

50 "to the muzzle": Int. Alison Cheek, May 18, 2013.

50 "with crepe serviettes": Western to Western, "Letter 3," December 16, 1943, Cheek private collection.

50 "breakdown over it": Int. Alison Cheek, September 8, 2013.

51 Cheek replied quietly: Cheek, "The Decision," p. 1, Cheek private collection.

51 "utterly unexpected": Ibid., 2.

51 would be deposed: Ibid., 2–3.

51 "inevitability of it": Ibid., 3.

52 Bruce said simply: Ibid., 4.

52 "I knew you would": Ibid., unnumbered page.

52 "part of," she said: Int. Nancy Wittig, August 2, 2013.

52 could help her: Kessler, *People*, September 16, 1974, 23.

52 "ceaseless cigarette-smoking": Ibid.

53 "no longer do that": Campbell, *The Free Lance-Star*, January 29, 1975, 23.

53 was "throwing rocks": Int. Nancy Wittig, August 2, 2013.

Chapter 4: The Gathering

54 they be irregular: "Informal Notes of Meeting," March 3, 1974, AWTS, Box 45, F—Ordination of Women, Hiatt Papers.

55 "ahead of time!": Ibid.

55 "if truly called!" Welles, *The Happy Disciple*, 187.

56 the week before: Ibid., 185–187.

56 "as an affront": Ibid., 186.

56 "by risking deposition": DeWitt, "Why the Other Bishops Balked," *The Witness*, 15–16.

57 for the church: "Home Provided Episcopal Bishop," *The Evening Independent*, August 30, 1947, 8.

57 "insensitive" and "insulting": Hiatt, "Kairos as Paradigm Shift," 123.

57 "Miss Bott's dancing school": Schiess, *Why Me, Lord?*, 64.

57 "of my miscarriage": Int. Carter Heyward, July, 26, 2013; October 7, 2013; Heyward, *Speaking of Christ: A Lesbian Feminist Voice*, 84.

58 "to this wholeness": Ibid., 82.

58 "to the quiet waiting": Ibid., 82.

58 "absolutely as one": Int. Alla Renée Bozarth, July 25, 2013.

59 "of St. Mary's": E. Allen Mellen to Moore, April 29, 1974, AWTS, Box 45, F—Ordination of Women, Hiatt Papers.

59 "it's all about": Heyward to DeWitt, May 1, 1974, AWTS, Box 45, F—Ordination of Women, Hiatt Papers.

59 "Tell me": Heyward to Moore, May 2, 1974, AWTS, Box 1, F 2, Heyward Papers.

59 "their own priesthoods": Heyward, "Ordination to the Priesthood of Doug Clark," AWTS, Box 1, F5, Smith Papers.

60 "will happen there": Corrigan to DeWitt, June 13, 1974.

60 "around a Western campfire": O'Connor, "11 Women Ordained as Priests," *The Philadelphia Daily News*, July 30, 1974. 4.

60 "for a generation": Corrigan, "Why I Ordained a Woman in Philadelphia," 59.

60 topic of discussion: Ibid.

61 "all other deliberations": Episcopal Digital Archives 72161, November 3, 1972.

62 at a later date: Smith, Notebook with Minutes of July 10, 1974 Meeting, AWTS, Box 1, F7, Smith Papers.

63 "Nancy Wittig": Merrill Bittner . . . to Dear Friends, July 20, 1974, AWTS, Box 1, F8, Smith Papers.

64 "The Rt. Rev. Edward Welles, II": Corrigan, DeWitt, Welles, "An Open Letter," *Christianity and Crisis*, September 16, 1974, p. cover, 188.

64 "my God. *How?*": Bozarth, *Womanpriest*, 95.

65 inform his clergy: Hiatt, "Kairos as Paradigm Shift," 129.

65 valid but irregular: Ogilby to the Members of the Diocese of Pennsylvania, July 1974, AWTS, Box 1, F10, Smith Papers.

65 "very far away": Moore, *Take a Bishop Like Me*, 16.

65 "down the middle": Moore to Heyward, July 22, 1974, AWTS, Box 1, F2, Heyward Papers.

65 not yet seen it: Bozarth, *Womanpriest*, 96.

65 he later said: Michal, "Battle Barely Begun for Women Priests," *The Virginia Churchman*, December 1979, 9.

66 "church as a whole": Allin telegram, July 23, 1974, AWTS, Box 1, F2, Heyward Papers.

66 "no gospel to preach": Cheek to Allin, July 26, 1974, Cheek private collection.

66 "at this point": *The Happy Disciple*, 188.

67 "certainly disappointed them": Ibid., 190.

67 "held these days": Ibid., p. 195.

67 he told the reporter: Flaherty, "She'll Become Priest Despite Church Rule—At Least for Awhile," *The Times-Union*, July 25, 1974, p. 15A.

68 "but as vagabonds": Shatzman, "Ordination of 11 Women Set Despite Pressure," *The Evening Bulletin*, July 26, 1974, 6B.

68 "at its disposal": Wallace, "Women Priests: A Court Case?" *The Philadelphia Inquirer*, July 26, 1974, p. 2A.

68 "heresy, and schism": Wallace, "Episcopal Clergy Get Warning," *The Philadelphia Inquirer*, July 27, 1974, 1B.

68 "and Apostolic Church": The American Church Union, "Bill of Particulars," AWTS, Box 1, F10, Smith Papers.

68 the Dewitt farm: Heyward to Dear Brothers and Sisters, July 15, 1974, Box 1, F8, Smith Papers.

68 Schiess wrote: Schiess, *Why Me, Lord?*, 70.

69 "to take notice": Heyward, *Priest Forever*, 83.

69 to do so: Bozarth, *Womanpriest*, 97.

69 "and follow Jesus": Welles, *The Happy Disciple*, 197.

69 his parish members: Schiess, *Why Me, Lord?*, 70.

69 a deposed priest: Hiatt, "Kairos as Paradigm Shift," 130.

69 "to speaking in church": Int. Alison Cheek, June 10, 2013.

70 "helped move him": Ibid.

70 grin on his face: Heyward, *Priest Forever*, 83–85.

70 convention in Houston: Hiatt, "Kairos as Paradigm Shift," 133.

70 "quietly to bed—to sleep": Corrigan, "Why I Ordained a Woman in Philadelphia," 67.

Chapter 5: "That Great Gittin' Up Morning"

72 "you choosing it": "Why They Did What They Did," *The Episcopalian*, September 1974, 8.

72 "having this service": Harris, "Pentecost Revisited," *The Witness*, special edition, 1984, 10.

72 "of the Episcopal Church": The Book of Common Prayer, 1977, 526.

73 "your common sense": Heyward, *Keep Your Courage*, 231.

73 "the Spirit of Christ": Bozarth, *Womanpriest*, 103.

73 "integrity intact": Heyward, *A Priest Forever*, p. 85; Hacker, "The Price of Priesthood," *The Philadelphia Inquirer*, August 1, 1982, p. A1.

73 about to occur: Hiatt, "Kairos as Paradigm Shift," 132.

74 clear vision in one eye: Int. Emily Hewitt, July 23, 2013.

74 "ruptured?" he asked: Washington, *Other Sheep I Have*, 168.

75 "this possibly was": Hacker, "The Price of Priesthood," August 1, 1982, 1A.

75 "share of crazies": Harris, "Pentecost Revisited," 11.

75 "be our own": Hiatt, "Kairos as Paradigm Shift," 131.

75 "steely determination": Ibid.

76 "actually going to do it!": Ibid., 132.

76 "not remain silent": Willie, "The Priesthood of All Believers," AWTS, Box 1, F11, Smith Papers.

77 "or impediment is": Episcopal Digital Archives 74200, July 31, 1974.

77 "eloquent if insulting": Hiatt, "Kairos as Paradigm Shift," 133.

77 "he thought Rutler": Schiess, *Why Me, Lord?*, 76.

77 "had just witnessed": Bozarth, *Womanpriest*, 140.

77 wasn't a priest himself: Int. Charles Willie, August 6, 2013.

78 one of them: Int. Alla Renée Bozarth, July 25, 2013.

78 "Victorian mother run": Waggoner, *NYT*, May 19, 1981, C12.

78 down his face: Washington, *Other Sheep I Have*, 169.

78 his daughter Swanson: Hiatt, "Kairos as Paradigm Shift," 133.

78 "lifeblood or holy water": Heyward, *A Priest Forever*, 90.

78 "it meant her": Schiess, *Why Me, Lord?*, 76.

79 "or truth whatsoever": Bozarth, *Womanpriest*, 105.

79 "sense of pull": Int. Barbara Schlachter, October 24, 2012.

79 "some of my fears": Murray, *The Autobiography of a Black Activist, Feminist, Lawyer, Priest, and Poet*, 430.

79 "taken that day": Ibid., 431.

80 permeated the building: "Memories Are Not Enough," *The Witness*, 1984, special edition, 24.

80 more cheering and applause: Hiatt, "Kairos as Paradigm Shift," 133.

80 "he'd ever done": Panero, "Father Figure," March/April 2012, DAM Online.

81 "on their own timetable": Darling, *New Wine*, 130.

81 "Thank you": Washington, *Other Sheep I Have*, 172.

81 in a diocesan court: "Why They Did What They Did," *The Episcopalian*, September 1974, 8.

81 "persona non grata in this Diocese": Turner to Moorefield, July 31, 1974, AWTS, Box 23, F13, Sue Hiatt Papers.

81 had been clarified: Ogilby, "A Pastoral Letter," August 1, 1974, AWTS, Box 1, F11, Smith Papers.

81 acting as a priest: Day, "U.S. Bishops to Meet on Women Priests," *The Philadelphia Inquirer*, August 1974.

82 "Theological Education were used": "Statement of Clarification and Concern from the Steering Committee of the Episcopal Women's Caucus," August 2, 1974, AWTS, Box 1, F11, Smith Papers.

82 "this is my time": "Why They Did What They Did," *The Episcopalian*, September 1974, 8.

82 "sake of a full ministry": Ibid.

83 "grown and independent person": Bozarth to author, August 11, 2013.

83 "finest hour," he wrote: "Chronology," *The Episcopalian*, September 1974, 6.

Chapter 6: The Bishop's Tale, Chicago

85 and busy wallpaper: Moore, *Take a Bishop Like Me*, 17.

85 "where the boys were": Int. Emily Hewitt, July 24, 2013.

85 when they had arrived: Moore, *Take a Bishop Like Me*, 26–27.

85 "to function calmly": Welles, *The Happy Disciple*, 202.

85 "completely and forever": Ibid., 199.

86 "at what happened in Chicago": Guthrie, Harris, and Rockwell, "A Personal Report on the Meeting of the House of Bishops of the Episcopal Church in Chicago on August 14 and 15, 1974, and Some Reflections on Process and Theology," p. 1, Cheek private collection.

88 done "was right": "Special Meetings of the House of Bishops," August 14 and 15, 1974, B-182–184.

88 "concern for this fellowship": "Special Meetings of the House of Bishops," August 14 and 15, 1974, B-185–186.

89 "had been voted down": Moore, *Take a Bishop Like Me*, 23.

89 "shooing them away": Int. Alison Cheek, March 18, 2013.

89 in case the problem persisted: Int. Betty Bone Schiess, July 16, 2013; Schiess, *Why Me, Lord?*, 80–81.

89 "They can't do that": Bozarth, *Womanpriest*, 108.

89 "They actually meant men": Int. Nancy Wittig, August 2, 2013.

90 "uttered under his breath": Moore, *Take a Bishop Like Me*, 25.

90 "for renewal among us": Hyer, *The Washington Post*, August 16, 1974, A3.

90 "may go far enough": "In Chicago: The Bishops Hold an Emergency Meeting," *The Virginia Churchman*, September 1974, 8.

91 "move in this stream": Ogilby, "Statement Presented by the Rt. Rev. Lyman Ogilby to the Special House of Bishops Meeting in Chicago," August 14–15, 1974, p. 2, AWTS, Box 1, F11, Smith Papers.

91 valid, but irregular: van Beeck, *The Journal of Ecumenical Studies*, 381–399.

92 "on July 29, 1974": "Special Meetings of the House of Bishops," August 14 and 15, 1974, B-194.

92 "cheap cop-out": *The Virginia Churchman,* September 1974, 9.

92 opportunity to speak: Int. Charles Willie, August 6, 2013.

92 "of *each other*": Heyward to Allin, August 29, 1974, AWTS, Box 1, F4, Heyward Papers.

93 "of van Beeck's theology": Welles, *The Happy Disciple*, 202.

93 "in this regard": "Special Meetings of the House of Bishops," August 14 and 15, 1974, B-198.

94 "I was stunned": Cheek, Journal entry, 2000, Cheek private collection.

94 "depth of her feelings": Ibid.

94 just voted on: Guthrie, Harris, and Rockwell, "A Personal Report on the Meeting of the House of Bishops of the Episcopal Church in Chicago on August 14 and 15, 1974, and Some Reflections on Process and Theology," Cheek private collection.

95 "a declaration of invalidity": Blau, "House of Bishops Disputes Validity of Ordination of 11 Women as Priests," *NYT*, August 16, 1974, 34.

95 "reconciliation of the Gospel": "Special Meetings of the House of Bishops," August 14 and 15, 1974, B-202.

95 "household of faith": "For Immediate Release," August 15, 1974, Cheek private collection.

95 "I've ever seen": Int. Charles Willie, August 6, 2013.

96 "stormy invective": Episcopal Digital Archives 74215, August 15, 1974.

96 "judgment of God Almighty": *The Virginia Churchman,* September 1974, 9.

96 "less than academic": Moore, *Take a Bishop Like Me*, 27.

96 "and I'd tell them": Int. Charles Willie, August 6, 2013.

96 "and said, 'Okay' ": Ibid.

96 " 'going to get' him": Ibid.

97 "half of the human race": Wolf, "Statement of Resignation," August 16, 1974, AWTS, Box 1, F11, Smith Papers.

97 "both sexes to holy orders": Guthrie, Harris, and Rockwell, "A Personal Report on the Meeting of the House of Bishops of the Episcopal Church in Chicago on August 14 and 15, 1974, and Some Reflections on Process and Theology," pp. 10–13, Cheek private collection.

97 "and a little legalism": Heyward, *A Priest Forever*, 94.

97 "exercise priestly functions": Ibid., 100.

97 into disciplining her: Ibid., 100.

97 to be reconciled?: Washington to Allin, August 23, 1974, AWTS, Box 25, F4, Hiatt Papers.

98 "constitutions and canons": Stringfellow, "Mischief and a Mighty Curse," *Christianity and Crisis*, September 14, 1974, 195–196.

Chapter 7: The Priests' Tale

99 approximately twenty churches: Darling, *New Wine*, 136.

99 "symbolic/sacramental power": "Statement Sent to the Presiding Bishop of the Episcopal Church," September 30, 1974, p. 2, AWTS, Box 1, F20, Smith Papers.

100 "action than this": Miller, "A Newsletter for the Diocese of Missouri," Association of Clergy, September 5, 1974.

100 "bitterness" upon herself: Heyward, *A Priest Forever*, 103.

100 Chicago had been: Day, "The Times Are Changing: Women Priests Gain Favor," *The Philadelphia Inquirer*, October, 1974, 1A–2A.

100 "Is that a promise?": Ibid.

100 "to the priesthood": "Special Meetings of the House of Bishops," October 14–18, 1974, p. B-258.

101 "but a reality": "News Release on Eucharist to be Celebrated by Newly Ordained Episcopal Women Priests," p. 4, Box 1, F20, Smith Papers.

101 "within its processes": Ibid., 1.

101 "not so cheap": Heyward to Moore, October 16, 1974, AWTS, Box 1, F2, Heyward Papers.

101 the other women: Ibid.

101 an uncanonical act: Moore, "Statement by the Right Reverend Rev. Paul Moore, Jr., Bishop of New York . . . ," Oct 22, 1974, AWTS, Box 4, F11, Heyward Papers.

101 "great deal of harm": Moore to Heyward, October 24, 1974, AWTS, Box 1, F2, Heyward Papers.

102 "care of yourself:" Ibid.

102 support of the service: "We the undersigned students . . . ," AWTS, Box 4, Folder 11, Heyward Papers.

102 Jeanne Audrey Powers remembered: Myer, "What Progress for Women Clergy?" *The Witness*, special issue 1984, 26.

102 "do while I waited": Piccard to DeWitt, November 1, 1974, AWTS, Box 23, F17, Hiatt Papers.

102 at the service: Int. Merrill Bittner, May 25, 2013.

102 ordained as a priest: Piccard to Bittner, June 10, 1976, Bittner private collection.

102 no "counter-demonstrations": DeWitt to Corrigan, Ramos, Welles, October 28, 1974, AWTS, Box 20, F11, Hiatt Papers.

103 "This is the goal": Ibid.

103 "our being Episcopalians": Heyward to Varian, November 7, 1974, AWTS, Box 4, Folder 11, Heyward Papers.

103 was not "tainted": Heyward to Moore, November 4, 1974, AWTS, Box 4, Folder 11, Heyward Papers.

103 "publicity on this, however": Moore to Heyward, November 7, 1974, AWTS, Box 4, Folder 11, Heyward Papers.

103 "fuss in the first place": Heyward to Moore, November 12, 1974, AWTS, Box 4, Folder 11, Heyward Papers.

104 "demands a response": Moore to Friends, October 30, 1974, AWTS, Box 4, Folder 11, Heyward Papers.

104 "intending it for none": The Reverend and Mrs. Jorge Gutierrez to Moore, February 12, 1973, AWTS, Box 1, F2, Heyward Papers.

104 "an unholy alliance": Ibid.

104 "not to be underestimated": DeWitt to Bozarth, November 13, 1975, AWTS, Box 20, F7, Hiatt Papers.

105 "a female Anglican priest": Bozarth, "Digging Down into the Dusty Past," Originally published in *Purgatory Papers*, online copy, 6.

105 of her efforts: DeWitt to Bozarth, November 13, 1975, AWTS, Box 20, F7, Hiatt Papers.

105 "two Roman Catholic Archbishops": Bozarth, "Digging Down into the Dusty Past," Originally published in *Purgatory Papers*, online copy, 5.

105 "be checking into it": Winiarski, "Celebration in Wisconsin," *NCR*, p. 14.

105 "sense of that word": Ibid.

105 "apologized for in advance": Bozarth, "Digging Down into the Dusty Past," originally published in *Purgatory Papers*, online copy, 6.

105 "devil here tonight": Bozarth, "Digging Down into the Dusty Past," Originally published in *Purgatory Papers*, online copy, 6.

105 "icy air of malice": Ibid.

105 "more colorful language": Bozarth, "The Philadelphia Ordinations," *http://allabozarthwords andimages.blogspot.com*.

106 "unbecoming a clergyman": qtd. in *The Episcopalian*, October 1974, p. 21.

106 "from an Ecclesiastical Court": Vogel to Swanson, July 31, 1974, AWTS, Box 24, F13, Hiatt Papers.

106 "and I buckled": Hacker, "The Price of Priesthood," August 1, 1982, 24-A.

106 the General Convention voted: "Significant Happenings at the Diocese of West Missouri Annual Convention in Springfield on November 14–16, 1975, the Rt. Rev. Arthur Vogel Presiding," AWTS, Box 24, F14, Hiatt Papers.

106 with Reye's Syndrome: Hacker, "The Price of Priesthood," *The Philadelphia Inquirer*, August 1, 1982, p. 24-A; Int. Kathryn Piccard, August 30, 2013.

106 "from an ecclesiastical court": Vogel to Swanson, July 31, 1974, AWTS, Box 24, F13, Hiatt Papers.

107 to a deacon: Welles, *The Happy Disciple*, 103–104.

107 "perhaps in vain": Moorefield to Moore, January 8, 1975, AWTS, Box 23, F13, Hiatt Papers.

107 "growing pastoral identity": Ibid.

107 "and/or deposed": Ibid.

108 "full ministry of women": Bittner . . . to Ernest T. Dixon, May 30, 1975, AWTS, Box 23, F13, Hiatt Papers.

108 she had imagined: Moorefield to Moore, January 8, 1975, AWTS, Box 23, F13, Hiatt Papers.

108 concerning ordination: "A Sermon Preached by the Rev. Nancy H. Wittig, at St. Peter's Church, Morristown, N.J., on August 25, 1974, the Twelfth Sunday after Pentecost, 'Obedience to God Comes before Obedience to Man,'" Cheek private collection.

108 "can't be hurt anymore": Burkhart, "The Reverend Nancy Hatch Wittig: The Female Priest Who Left Her Church Rather Than Bow to Sexist Pressure," *VIVA*, May 1975, 28.

108 "for other people": Ibid.

109 "toll on my health": Wittig to the Rector, Wardens, Vestry, and People of St. Peter's, October 25, 1974, Cheek private collection.

109 than that of a priest: Blau, "A Woman Priest Quits as Curate," *NYT*, November, 3, 1974, 56.

109 "couldn't promise such a thing": Burkhart, "The Reverend Nancy Hatch Wittig: The Female Priest Who Left Her Church Rather Than Bow to Sexist Pressure," *VIVA*, May 1975.

109 "contrary to doctrine": Schiess to Cheek, October 17, 1974, Cheek private collection.

110 occurred on July 29: Schiess, *Why Me, Lord?*, 88.

110 that she was female: "United States District Court, Northern District Court of New York, The Reverend Betty Bone Schiess against The Diocese of Central New York of the Protestant Episcopal Church of the United States of America and the Right Reverend Ned Cole, Bishop," Cheek private collection.

110 "she is a female. . . .": Ibid.

111 the General Convention of 1976: Hyer, "Woman Priest Sues Bishop," *The Washington Post*, July 13, 1976.

111 invited to preside: Stringfellow to DeWitt, December 11, 1974, Cheek private collection.

111 to "failed" leadership: Stringfellow, "The Church in Exile," *The Witness*, March 9, 1975, 6.

Chapter 8: Wind Shear

112 from opposing forces: Belcher to DeWitt, Hiatt, Ritchie, Smith, January 13, 1975, AWTS, Box 2, F1, Smith Papers.

112 "seems uselessly slim": Hiatt to Welles, February 4, 1976, AWTS, Box 25, F6, Hiatt Papers.

113 "can only speculate when": Ibid.

113 "vocation perfectly clear": Ibid.

113 of ordination of men: Episcopal Digital Archives, 75140, April 11, 1975.

114 "boldest of the bishops" of the eleven: Hiatt to Spears, August 5, 1976, AWTS, Box 20, F5, Hiatt Papers.

114 released from prison: Petraske, "Jail Project Lessens Women's Punishments," *Courier-Journal*, December 19, 1973.

115 "within the Monroe County Jail": Ibid.

115 "forbade her participation": Spears to the Standing Committee, July 30, 1974, Diocese of Rochester Archives.

115 had been valid: "Report to the Committee from the Standing Committee," November 8, 1974, 1, Diocese of Rochester.

115 "both male and female": Spears, "Statement," January 17, 1975, Bittner private collection.

116 "will not call me sister": Bittner, "Statement to the Clergy," January 17, 1975, Bittner private collection.

116 "equals to men": Mick Morgan, Editorial, WHAM Radio, January 17, 1975, Bittner private collection.

116 "glorious but horrible": Conley, qtd in "Change Comes to the Church," Box 20, F6, Hiatt Papers.

118 "Faithfully, +Fred Wolf": Wolf to Dear Friends in Christ, July 2, 1975, Box 25, F12, Hiatt Papers.

118 "may have been": Piccard to Wolf, July 10, 1975, Box 25, F12, Hiatt Papers.

118 not "take it seriously": Casey, "Maine Bishop Wolf Rebukes Women Priests for 'Disobedience,'" *Portland Press Herald*, July 24, 1975, 1, 6.

118 "on the Wright Brothers": Lamb to Wolf, July 29, 1975, p. 1, Box 25, F12, Hiatt Papers.

118 "many centuries anyhow": Ibid.

118 "received his letter": DeWitt to Washington, August 28, 1975, AWTS, Box 25, F12, Hiatt Papers.

119 "didn't murder that guy": Int. Emily Hewitt, September 5, 2013.

119 "feel the same way": Anonymous to Bittner, n.d., Bittner private collection.

119 "life of the Church": "Statement to the Diocese," October 28, 1975, Bittner private collection.

119 by the General Convention: Ibid.

119 "to the Church of God": Bittner to Brothers and Sisters, March 29, 1976, Bittner private collection.

120 "priests in the Episcopal Church": Press Release, April 2, 1976, Bittner private collection.

120 abandoned the Church: Buckley to Spears, May 3, 1976, AWTS, Box 20, F5, Hiatt Papers.

120 deposed from the ministry: Spears to Bittner, May 12, 1976, AWTS, Box 20, F5, Hiatt Papers.

120 "whenever you feel like it": Spears to Bittner, AWTS, Box 20, F5, Hiatt Papers.

120 "certainly news to me": Merrill to Everybody, June 1, 1976, AWTS, Box 20, F5, Hiatt Papers.

120 "major part of [her] life": Ibid.

120 "maybe I'll go with you!," Piccard to Bittner, June 10, 1976, Bittner private collection.

121 "I was saying . . . except me": Keaton, "Telling Secrets," October 18, 2010, blog post.

Chapter 9: Letters, Scarlet and Otherwise

123 communion at the ordination: "Abuse of Power," *Philadelphia Daily News*, July 30, 1974, cover.

124 three to one in favor: Welles, *The Happy Disciple*, 195, 199.

124 chaplain in a brothel: Bozarth, "Digging Down into the Dusty Past," originally published in *Purgatory Papers*, online copy, 10.

124 "pretenders on the prowl": Anonymous letter to Cheek, November 14, 1974, Cheek private collection.

124 "and divide the church": McNairy to Heyward, November 5, 1974, AWTS, Box 4, F11, Heyward Papers.

125 "gave the rights of priesthood?": _____ to Heyward, August 3, 1974, AWTS, Box 6, F1, Heyward Papers.

125 "what would be nice": *The Episcopalian*, "Switchboard," September 1974.

125 "I shall pray for you": Smith to Heyward, October 21, 1974, AWTS, Box 1, F2, Heyward Papers.

126 "SHAME!": _____ to Cheek, August 8, 1974, Cheek private collection.

126 "all of us to be": _____ to Cheek, Heyward, and Piccard, October 31, 1974, AWTS, Box 1, F2, Heyward Papers.

127 "it cuts very deeply": _____ to Heyward, October 28, 1974, AWTS, Box 6, F2, Heyward Papers.

128 "applying it to ourselves?": Schiess, *Why Me, Lord?*, 29.

128 "vindictive, and resentful": _____ to My dear sisters-in-Christ, August 19, 1974, AWTS, Box 6, F2, Heyward Papers.

128 "and for your bishops": Sims to Heyward, October 26, 1974, AWTS, Box 4, F11, Heyward Papers.

129 "with mistaken conscience": Nolan to Cheek, August 5, 1974, Cheek private collection.

129 *discredit* to our church": _____ to Cheek, Heyward, and Piccard, October 28, 1974, AWTS, Box 1, F2, Heyward Papers.

129 "wouldn't join as oppressors": _____ to Heyward, October 28, 1974, AWTS, Box 6, F2, Heyward Papers.

130 "and Apostolic Church stand": _____ to Heyward, July 26, 1974, AWTS, Box 4, F14, Heyward Papers.

130 "lines of authority": *The Episcopalian*, "Switchboard," September 1974.

130 "be lawfully changed": *The Episcopalian*, "Switchboard," November 1974.

130 "Homemaker for Equal Rights": _____ to Heyward, n.d., AWTS, Box 6, F3, Heyward Papers.

131 "an irregular consecration?": *The Episcopalian*, "Switchboard," November 1974.

131 "With unbounding admiration": Olgebee to Cheek, July 30, 1974, Cheek private collection.

132 "our church may, too": Hurmence to Heyward, August 15, 1974, AWTS, Box 1, F2, Heyward Papers.

132 "the good fight of faith": Demarest to Heyward, October 12, 1974, AWTS, Box 6, F2, Heyward Papers.

132 your "illegal" ordination: _____ to Heyward, January 11, 1975, AWTS, Box 4, F12, Heyward Papers.

132 "oneness with God": _____ to Heyward, February 17, 1975, AWTS, Box 4, F12, Heyward Papers.

133 "and best of luck": _____ to Heyward, September 14, 1974, AWTS, Box 6, F2, Heyward Papers.

133 "of life—new—life": _____ to Heyward, August 23, 1974, AWTS, Box 6, F2, Heyward Papers.

133 "gone fray-ward": The Bard to Heyward, n.d., AWTS, Box 6, F2, Heyward Papers.

133 "3 Folks for the Equal Rights Amendment": _____ to Heyward, Nov 4, 1974, Box 6, F2, Heyward Papers.

134 "hatred I'll evoke": Cheek to Allin, July 27, 1974, Cheek private collection.

134 during the conversation: Int. Alison Cheek, August 11, 2013.

134 "Yours in Christ": Cheek to Allin, September 6, 1974, Cheek private collection.

135 "the world at large looks askance": Jones to Cheek, September 30, 1974, Cheek private collection.

136 "irregular at best": Burt to Cheek, October 1, 1974, Cheek private collection.

136 "Middle Ages than in 1975": Holland, "Priest's Trial Throwback to Middle Ages," *The Cleveland Plain Dealer*. Reprinted in *WON*, February 1975. 12–14.

Chapter 10: The Trials, Part I: "Adjectives Are Always Dangerous"

137 he later admitted: "The Rev. William Wendt," St. Stephen and the Incarnation website, *http://saintstephensdc.org*.

137 with coarse features: Viorst, "How to Be a Good Guy Honky Priest on Fourteenth Street," *The Washingtonian*, July 1968, *http://saintstephensdc.org*.

137 with the city's poor: St. Stephen and the Incarnation website, *http://saintstephensdc.org*; Billington, "Wendts: A United Family," *The Washington Star*, April 29, 1975, D1–D2.

137 to desegregate bus lines: Ecclesiastical Court of the Diocese of Washington: The Board of Presenters v. The Rev. William A. Wendt, April 30, 1975–May 2, 1975, 365.

137 "Just rub my feet": Smith, *The Washington Post*, July 9, 2001, obituary; "Bill Wendt, After St. Stephen's," *http://saintstephensdc.org*.

138 "tears and laughter": Moore, "The Sirens, the Shots, the Explosions, the Shouting," Address at St. Stephen and the Incarnation, 1977.

138 "ordinations would be recognized": Ecclesiastical Court of the Diocese of Washington: The Board of Presenters v. The Rev. William A. Wendt, April 30, 1975–May 2, 1975, 370.

138 "or are deeply offended by it": Int. Alison Cheek, June 10, 2013.

139 "of our present dilemma": *Bread*, St. Stephen and the Incarnation newsletter, November 17, 1974, 3–4.

139 "give conscience to the highest authority": Ecclesiastical Court of the Diocese of Washington: The Board of Presenters v. The Rev. William A. Wendt, April 30, 1975–May 2, 1975, 381.

139 "bursts of spontaneous applause": Hyer, "Communion Is Celebrated by a Woman," *The Washington Post*, November 11, 1974, C1.

140 "means one vote no": Ibid.

140 "antedate the Dark Ages": Rowan, "In My View," *The Chicago Sun-Times,* May 20, 1975.

141 agents needed to hear them: Wallis, "A Holy Humanity," *Sojourners*, December 1985, 4.

141 "and the marginalized": Kennedy, "A Step Off America," *Sojourners*, December 1985, 21.

141 "Took [the mat] seriously": Ibid., 20.

141 "America should be listening to": Wallis, "A Holy Humanity," *Sojourners*, December 1985, 4.

141 "vaguely ahead of me": Robinson, "Air Crash Survivor: A Time for Tears," *The Washington Post*, June 7, 1975, pp. A1, A4.

142 "and saw the burns": Ibid., A4.

142 "so as to appear": Ecclesiastical Court of the Diocese of Washington: The Board of Presenters v. The Rev. William A. Wendt, April 30, 1975–May 2, 1975, 6.

142 "expect him to appear": Ibid., 7.

143 "was only an 'invitation' ": Ibid., 358.

143 "charges against him": Hyer, "Top Episcopalian Cited for Contempt," *The Washington Post*, May 3, 1975, A1.

143 "I'm not sure, sir," he said: Ecclesiastical Court of the Diocese of Washington: The Board of Presenters v. The Rev. William A. Wendt, April 30, 1975–May 2, 1975, 29.

144 "the life of the Church": Ibid., 30.

144 "express itself affirmatively": Ibid., 34.

144 ended his redirect: Ibid., 35.

144 "actions to that extent": Ibid., 42.

145 "of the second event": Ibid., 65.

145 "in the Philadelphia ordination": Ibid., 67.

145 had not been charged: Ibid.

145 "The entire file is noted": Ibid., 96.

145 "the household of God": Ibid., 112.

145 "give it a serious rethinking": Ibid., 112.

146 validity of the ordinations: Ibid., 122.

147 "I would resist that word": Ibid., 169–170.

147 "adjectives are always dangerous": Ibid., 183.

147 "admonitions as godly": Ibid.

147 "to be my penis": Int. Alison Cheek, June 21, 2013.

147 "preside at Eucharists": Ecclesiastical Court of the Diocese of Washington: The Board of Presenters v. The Rev. William A. Wendt, April 30, 1975–May 2, 1975, 197.

148 "accede to that request": Ibid., 199.

148 "nothing godly in that at all": Ibid., 204.

148 she "got radicalized": Int. Janet McCaa, June 22, 2013.

149 claimed such as feat: Ecclesiastical Court of the Diocese of Washington: The Board of Presenters v. The Rev. William A. Wendt, April 30, 1975–May 2, 1975, 276.

149 set in a courtroom scene: DeWitt to Corrigan, Ramos, and Welles, May 5, 1975, AWTS, Box 20, F11, Hiatt Papers.

150 "there are not many": Ecclesiastical Court of the Diocese of Washington: The Board of Presenters v. The Rev. William A. Wendt, April 30, 1975–May 2, 1975, 321.

150 "that blacks were fully human": Ibid., 322.

150 "intelligent human being should have": Ibid., 327.

150 "alright to do it?" Ibid., 327.

151 "applies to human beings": Ibid., 329.

152 "the whole Christian community": Ibid., 342–343.

Chapter 11: The Trials, Part II: But Conjunctions?

153 "of this Ecclesiastical Court": Ecclesiastical Court of the Diocese of Washington: The Board of Presenters v. The Rev. William A. Wendt, April 30, 1975–May 2, 1975, 358.

153 "and deep regret": Ibid., 359.

153 "has become necessary": Ibid., 360.

154 "is above the law": Ibid., 361.

154 "about many issues": Ibid., 379.

154 "who are in need": Ibid.

154 "early in August?" Ibid., 388.

154 "as they have done": Ibid.

154 "something that we can't": Ibid., 393.

155 "were terribly disturbed. . . .": Ibid., 430.

155 "question before this Court": Ibid., 456.

155 "act of three Bishops": Ibid., 447.

155 "matter of subjective view": Ibid., 449.

155 "my conscience made me do it": Ibid., 454.

155 "struck [him] as arrogant": Ibid., 449.

155 validating "mob rule": Ibid., 450.

155 "add[ed] to the trial": Ibid.

155 members of St. Stephen's: Ibid., 459.

155 "for the rest of the month": Ibid., 461.

156 a "question of validity": Ibid., 465.

156 "on the chain of command": Ibid., 468.

156 "by the accident of sex": Ecclesiastical Court of the Diocese of Washington, Decision, June 5, 1975, 7.

156 Janet McCaa said: Int. Janet McCaa, June 22, 2013.

157 by modern standards: Ecclesiastical Court of the Diocese of Washington, June 5, 1975, 14.

157 "based on race": Ibid.

157 "it to pass by": Ibid., 20.

157 proceedings in his article: Stringfellow, "On the Sentencing of Good Father Wendt," *The Witness*, March 1976, 6–7.

157 "contrary to God's word": In the Court of Appeals of the Diocese of Washington, Argued October 1, 1975, Decided on December 9, 1975, 6.

157 "contemptuous and demeaning": Ibid., "Judge Thorp, concurring," 1.

158 "the Lorde being my helper": Ibid., "Chief Judge Romig and Judge Beers, concurring," 3.

158 "disobeyed at his peril": Ibid., 4.

158 "ordered by others": Ibid., "Judge Bucklee, with Whom Judges Coleman and Dozier Join, Dissenting," 2.

158 "unity in the Church. . . .": Ibid., 1.

158 "tragically misinterpreted": Ibid., 10.

158 "life of the Church": Ibid., "Judge Coleman, with Whom Judges Bucklee and Dozier Join, Dissenting," 2.

158 it was then understood: Ibid., "Judge Dozier, with Whom Judges Bucklee and Coleman Join, Dissenting," 1.

159 "will be demeaned": Ibid., 2.

159 "that possibility into being": Ibid., 4.

159 "rare circumstances of this trial": Ibid., 5.

159 steps and passageways: Hyer, "Wendt Reprimanded for Defying Bishop," *The Washington Post*, B1, B2.

160 "be brought against me," Ibid.

160 "theater of the absurd": "We Have, After Due Consideration, Chosen Not to Make a Presentment . . . ," *Rauch*, May/June 1975, 14.

160 "rock the boat conservative": Sherman, "The Rev. Peter Beebe," *The Plain Dealer Magazine*, March 25, 1979, 31.

161 her tires were slashed: "N. Lorraine Beebe," The Michigan Women's Historical Center and Hall of Fame, online, *michiganwomen.org*.

161 "must be guarded carefully": "'Always Expect Miracle,' Says Beebe," *Oberlin News-Tribune*, April 24, 1.

161 "we need to stand up": Int. Barbara Drebing, August 5, 2013.

162 "which I am a member": Thompson, "Letter to Vestry," *WON: The Voice of Women's Ordination Now*, n.d., Issue 1, 2.

162 "authority entrusted to me. . . .": Burt to Beebe, December 3, 1974, Cheek private collection.

163 to obey him voluntarily: Burt to Cheek, November 19, 1974, Cheek private collection.

163 "of many fine parishioners": Heyward, *A Priest Forever*, 115.

163 last place she would celebrate: Ibid., 117.

163 "full personhood of women": Cheek to Burt, December 1, 1974, Cheek private collection.

164 "amoral stance is anomalous": qtd. in Holland, "Four at Beebe Trial Back Women Priests," *The Plain Dealer*, May 15, 1975, 6B.

164 "with openly and publicly": Heyward, *A Priest Forever*, 123.

164 "of my ministerial functions. . . .": Ibid., 124.

165 "the other side of the wall": Plagenz, "Beebe's Lawyer Didn't Give Up, April, 1976."

165 "to do it was now": Ibid

165 "find an attorney": Int. Peter Beebe, August 17, 2013.

165 "to minister in this Church": Ecclesiastical Court of the Diocese of Ohio, "The Standing Committee of the Diocese of Ohio v. the Reverend L. Peter Beebe," May 13–15, 1975, 2.

166 "it will be the latter": Heyward, *A Priest Forever*, 131.

166 "I had two children to take care of": Int. Peter Beebe, August 17, 2013.

166 "equitability within the canons": Ecclesiastical Court of the Diocese of Ohio, "The Standing Committee of the Diocese of Ohio v. the Reverend L. Peter Beebe," May 13–15, 1975, 6.

167 "Bishops and Standing Committees": Ibid.

167 "authorities of the Church": Ibid., 7.

167 into the licensing system: Ibid., 8.

167 Priests to Beebe's parish: Willoughby, "Ohio Priest Still Defiant," *The Washington Star*, June 23, 1975, A3.

168 as a priest associate: Lee Ann Hamilton, *The Plain Dealer*, July 14, 1975, A10.

168 "for truth and justice": Burt to Beebe, July 24, 1975, Cheek private collection.

169 as a priest in the diocese: Piccard to Burt, August 30, 1975, AWTS, Box 23, F17, Hiatt Papers.

169 inhibiting her from participating: Burt to Piccard, September 9, 1975, AWTS, Box 23, F17, Hiatt Papers.

169 women priests played the guitar: Holland, "Allowing Women Priests Endangers Church Grant," *The Plain Dealer*, September 15, 1975, 17A.

169 "the full personhood of women": Episcopal Digital Archives 75079, February 27, 1975.

170 "rules which now prevent it?": Wolfe to Dear Ladies, December 4, 1975, Cheek private collection.

170 Nancy Wittig: Bittner, Bozarth-Campbell, Hewitt, Hiatt, Moorefield, Piccard, Schiess, Swanson, and Wittig to Dear Friends, December 8, 1974, Cheek private collection.

171 "discussing the position": "Resolution of the Vestry," Christ Church, July 11, 1975, Cheek private collection.

171 "integrity and fair play" Burt to Cheek, July 24, 1975, Cheek private collection.

171 "and faithfully as possible": Cheek to Burt, July 30, 1975.

171 "the father buried . . . but NOW": Beebe, Christ Church newsletter, Midsummer 1975.

172 The Vestry majority resigns: Brittingham to Dear Friend in Christ, January 20, 1976, author collection.

172 "have exerted their control": "A Statement from the Episcopal Community in Support of the Priesthood of Women," Christ Church, January 1976, Cheek private collection.

172 " 'Invalidity!' and 'Collegiality!' ": Gilbert to Dear Friends, January 19, 1975.

172 "mild person like me": Ibid.

173 "what God is to us all": Atkins, "The Theological Case Against Women's Ordination," *The Ordination of Women: Pro and Con*, 25.

173 "Episcopal Church is organized": "World News Briefs," *The Episcopalian*, September 1974, 2.

173 who gave the admonishment: Court of Review of the Fifth Province of the Protestant Episcopal Church in the United States of America, The Standing Committee of the Diocese of Ohio v. The Reverend L. Peter Beebe, Argued February 5, 1976, Decided April 3, 1976, p. 5.

174 " 'duly licensed *and* ordained' ": Ibid.

174 a priest in his parish: Rea, "Beebe Case: Clue to the Future?" *The Witness*, September 1976.

174 "court said wasn't fair": Hyer, "Father Beebe's Retrial Stirs Episcopalians," *The Washington Post*, April 16, 1976, 9.

174 "They finally got me": Int. Peter Beebe, August 17, 2013.

Chapter 12: The Washington Four

175 "of her blue convertible": "Tally-Ho's for Home from Congo," *The Hartford Times*, July 11, 1962, 5.

175 "to think about marriage": Herzig, "A'ville Girl, Home from Congo, Is Ready for More Adventure," *Newsday*, July 12, 1962.

175 "in her schoolgirl French": "Tally-Ho's for Home from Congo," *The Hartford Times*, July 11, 1962, 5.

176 "just say something": Int. Alison Palmer, May 10, 2013.

177 "whole thing [was] a charade": Int. Alison Palmer, May 9, 2013.

177 "A Pint-Sized Crusader": McGrory, "A Pint-Sized Crusader," *The Washington Evening Star*, October 11, 1971.

177 "union 'shop steward' ": Palmer, "Palmer versus Church and State," unpublished memoir, AWTS, Series 6, Box 1, F1, p. 1 of Chapter 1, Palmer Papers.

178 "where it has a chance": Causey, "Priest Wins Battle with State Department," *The Washington Post*, February 16, 1976, p. B14.

178 "good cop/bad cop combination": Int. Lee McGee, June 13, 2013.

179 "to be blind back then": Ibid.

179 "the church then . . . ratifies that": Ibid.

179 remembered with a laugh: Ibid.

180 "He lived in his mind": Int. Betty Powell, October 19, 2013.

180 "Like a volcano": Ibid.

180 "Mother Church for me": Ibid.

180 understanding of divine guidance: Ibid.

180 for the family friend: Pennsylvania Academy of Fine Arts, *Andrew Wyeth Exhibit Catalog*, 1966.

180 "I've tried to become": Int. Betty Powell, October 19, 2013.

180 "I was supposed to take": Ibid.

181 "and the ugly": Ibid.

181 "raised tremendously, she said": Ibid.

181 "called to be a priest": Ibid.

181 friendly to women's ordination: Int. Lee McGee, June 13, 2013.

182 "supportive of each other": Ibid.

182 "sanctioning prejudice": Ibid.

182 "characteristic of the Gospel": Palmer to Creighton, January 12, 1975, AWTS, Box 23, F15, Hiatt Papers.

182 choose to reject them: Ibid.

183 "church will catch up": Ibid.

183 "unilaterally in the ordination of women": Creighton to Palmer, January 16, 1975, AWTS, Box 23, F15, Hiatt Papers.

183 experiences in her life: Palmer, "Palmer versus Church and State," unpublished memoir, p. 91, AWTS, Series 6, Box 1, F2, Palmer Papers.

183 "it was totally new": Ibid.

183 "natural and true": Ibid., 92.

184 "subject to financial blackmail": Ibid., 96.

184 Red Cross in Boston: Brelsford, "Diane Tickell: The Fullness of Priesthood," *Profiles in Change: Names, Notes, and Quotes for Alaskan Women*, 1983.

184 "a true minority was": Ibid., 179.

184 "really terrific, both": Ibid., 183.

184 "jail for the night": Ibid., 185.

185 "ordination with them": Ibid., 183.

185 "real leader in the Church": Int. Lee McGee, June 13, 2013.

185 Chinese earthquake victims: Tickell to Dear Sisters, July 1, 1976, AWTS, Box 25, F3, Hiatt Papers.

185 "to do something dangerous": Palmer, "Palmer versus Church and State," unpublished memoir, 97, AWTS, Series 6, Box 1, F2, Palmer Papers.

185 in Santa Barbara: Ibid.

186 "ordination by me": Lamond, "Let the Church Now Address Human Sexuality," *The Washington Star*, September 13, 1975.

186 "crippling the church": Hyer, "Ordination of 5 Women Set," *The Washington Post*, August 25, 1975, A1.

186 "excuses for delay": Palmer, "Palmer versus Church and State," unpublished memoir, p. 130, AWTS, Series 6, Box 1, F2, Palmer Papers.

186 "implications of it": Ibid., 153.

186 "suddenly walk in on us": 138.

186 "small army of staff members": Ibid.

187 "your Father in God": Ibid., 140.

187 possessed by demons: Ibid., no page number.

187 "Eucharist in the nude": Ibid., 33.

188 "we are in your hands": Int. Lee McGee, June 13, 2013.

188 "impediments to this ordination": Hyer, "4 Episcopal Women Get Priest Status," *The Washington Post*, September 8, 1975, A1–A2.

188 "offense of sex discrimination": Briggs, "4 Women Become Episcopal Priests," *NYT*, September 8, 1975.

188 received the "loudest": Willoughby, "Four Women Are Ordained as Episcopal Priests," *The Washington Star*, September 8, 1975.

188 "priesthood may be proclaimed": Cheek, "Charge Given by Alison Cheek at the Ordination of Eleanor Lee McGee, Alison Palmer, Betty Rosenberg, and Diane Tickell to the Priesthood of the Episcopal Church at the Church of St. Stephen and the Incarnation, Washington, D.C., September 7, 1975," Cheek private papers.

189 "infinity and eternity": Palmer, unpublished memoir, p. 149, AWTS, Box 6, F 2, Palmer Papers.

189 "my life, was present": Ibid., 144.

189 "to greet us, Palmer said": Ibid., 144.

189 "back across the country": Ibid., 151.

189 "open and read,": Palmer wrote: Ibid., 152.

189 "and nobody came?": Ibid., 153.

Chapter 13: Farewells: The General Convention of 1976

190 dough around on his finger: Bernstein, "You Can Find Fudge, Bread, and Coffins," *The Daily*, September 17, 1974.

190 "very well received": Ibid.

191 (the National Coalition and the EWC): Haldane, "On General Convention," *A-Cross*, 1976, 8–9.

191 "the vote in Minneapolis": Darling, "A Few Male Leaders Reflect," *Equally Applicable*, 1994, 24.

192 "of the General Convention": Bozarth, *Womanpriest*, 110.

192 "united about myself": Cheek, journal entry, September 11, 1976, Cheek private collection.

192 "would not take," Blau, "Episcopal Bishops Vote to Permit Women to Be Ordained as Priests" *NYT*, September 16, 1976, 20.

193 "inward in fear today": Ibid.

193 "issue of women's ordination": "Leader Protests to Rome," *Episcopalians United*, November 1, 1976, 1.

193 "fifty-eight domestic dioceses": MacKaye, "A Ho-Hum Even Unless . . . ," *The Witness*, August 1976, 4.

194 "when the bad news came": Bozarth, *Womanpriest*, 114.

194 "to be in the hundreds": *The Daily*, September 16, 1976.

194 "they may be excused": "There Were Some Light Moments, Too," *The Daily*, September 17, 1976, 3.

194 "At 5:50, debate ended": "Women to Be Priests," *The Daily*, September 17, 1976, 1.

194 "divisions we have": Ibid.

194 "a real love-feast": "Women to be Priests," *The Daily*, September 17, 1976, cover.

195 "nervous smiles and touches": Ibid.

195 "The outcome will be positive": Bozarth, *Womanpriest*, 115.

195 "section of the gallery": Ibid.

195 "thoroughly stunned": Ibid.

196 called to the priesthood: Bernstein, "Women Priests Are Still Pawns of Bishops," *The Daily*, September 21, 1976, 38.

196 "at the grassroots level": Bozarth, *Womanpriest*, 113.

196 "This is just the bare beginning": "Irregular Women Priests Call Action Bare Beginning," *The Daily*, September 17, 1976, 3.

196 "null and void": "Boycott of Women Priests Urged," *The Daily*, September 17, 1976, 1.

196 "valid or effective": Ibid.

196 "It was also an end": Bozarth, *Womanpriest*, 116.

197 "Resolution Passed by Bishops": Blau, "Ordination of Women as Priests Authorized by Episcopal Church," *NYT*, September 17, 1976, A1, D18.

197 "in its own priesthood": "Women as Priests," *The Christian Science Monitor*, September 21, 1976, 28.

197 "from death to resurrection": Raeside, "Episcopal Reconciliation in Minneapolis?" *Christianity and Crisis*, October 18, 1976, 232.

198 "Result: unity": Ibid.

198 "room arm in arm": Ibid.

198 "it could be repeated at home": Foley, "Bishops Okay Ways to Complete 15 Women's 'Irregular' Ordinations," *The Episcopalian*, November 1976, 12.

199 "of humiliating the women": Blau, "Episcopal Bishops Urge That 15 Women Priests Be Ordained Again," September 22, 1976, 19.

199 "get themselves ordained": Hyer, "For 15 Ordained Women, Issue Still Not Resolved," *The Washington Post*, September 18, 1976, A9.

199 "No Surrender, No Desertion, No Priestesses": Ibid.

200 "The Coalition . . . had gone home": Huyck, "To Celebrate the Whole Priesthood: The History of Women's Ordination in the Episcopal Church," June 1981, 237.

200 "pursuing ordination to the priesthood": Foley, "Bishops Okay Ways to Complete 15 Women's 'Irregular' Ordinations," *The Episcopalian*, November 1976, 24.

200 "communicants in the Episcopal Church": Ibid., 24.

201 "difference on both issues": Hiatt, "His Quiet, Tough Advice," *Sojourners*, December 1985, 25.

201 "Be fruitful and multiply": "Censured by the Club," *Time*, October 6, 1975, 97; Kingsolving, "Episcopal Common Sense and Sense of Humor," *The Daily Leader*, October 31, 1975, 4.

202 "other creatures with us": Heyward, *Flying Changes*, 17.

Bibliography

Archives and Collections

Carter Heyward Papers 1967–1998, *Archives of Women in Theological Scholarship,* The Burke Library at Union Theological Seminary, Columbia University Libraries, New York.

Suzanne Hiatt Papers 1963–1998, *Archives of Women in Theological Scholarship,* The Burke Library at Union Theological Seminary, Columbia University Libraries, New York.

Episcopal Digital Archives, The Archives of the Episcopal Church.

Episcopal Diocese of Rochester, Archives

Alison Palmer Papers 1937–2010, *Archives of Women in Theological Scholarship,* The Burke Library at Union Theological Seminary, Columbia University Libraries, New York.

Piccard Family Papers, Manuscript Division, Library of Congress.

Ann Robb Smith Papers, *Archives of Women in Theological Scholarship,* The Burke Library at Union Theological Seminary, Columbia University Libraries, New York.

Merrill Bittner, Private Collection.

Alison Cheek, Private Collection.

Carter Heyward, Private Collection.

Interviews

Carol Anderson, December 5, 2013

Peter Beebe, July 17, 2013

Merrill Bittner, May 25, 2013; September 11, 2013

Alla Bozarth, July 25, 2013

Alison Cheek, March 18, 2013; May 18, 2013; June 10, 2013; August 11, 2013; September 8, 2013; September 16, 2013; October 14, 2013

Linda Clark, November 20, 2012

Emily Hewitt, July 24, 2013

Carter Heyward, November 8, 2012; July 23, 2013

Jean Hiatt Kramer, September 4, 2012, June 2013

Lee McGee, June 13, 2013

Alison Palmer, May 9–13, 2013

Kathryn Piccard, August 30, 2013; October 10, 2013

Betty Powell, October 19, 2013

Betty Bone Schiess, July 16, 2013

Barbara Schlachter, October 24, 2012

Charles Willie, August 6, 2013

Nancy Wittig, August 2, 2013

Books and Periodicals

"Abuse of Power." *Philadelphia Daily News*, July 30, 1974. Cover.

"'Always Expect a Miracle,' Says Beebe." *Oberlin News-Tribune*, Thursday, April 24, 1975, 1, 7.

American Church Union, 1974. "Bill of Particulars," Box 1, Folder 10, Smith Papers.

Archives of Women in Theological Scholarship, The Burke Library at Union Theological Seminary, Columbia University Libraries, New York.

"A Statement from the Episcopal Community in Support of the Priesthood of Women." Christ Church, January 1976. Alison Cheek, private collection.

Atkins, Stanley, 1975. "The Theological Case Against Women's Ordination." In *The Ordination of Women: Pro and Con*, edited by Michael P. Hamilton and Nancy S. Montgomery, 18–28. New York: Morehouse-Barlow Co.

Becker, Donald E. "A Covenant Is Signed." *Episcopal News Service*, October 28, 1974.

———. "Swansons Move from West Missouri to Newark." *Episcopal News Service*, May 19, 1977.

Beebe, L. Peter. *Christ Church Newsletter*, Midsummer 1975, Vol. 6, No. 6. Oberlin, Ohio.

Benevolent Subversion: The Ordination of Women. Directed by Robert L. DeWitt, George West Barrett, RAPPORT (Organization) and Episcopal Women's Caucus. Laurel, MD: Episcopal Women's Caucus [distributor], 1993.

Bernstein, Paula. 1974. "At Episcopal Convention: You can Find Fudge, Bread and Coffins." *Daily News*, September 17.

———. 1976. "Women Priests are Still Pawns of Bishops." *Daily News*, Tuesday, September 21, 38.

Billington, Joy. 1975. "Wendts: A United Family." *The Washington Star*, Tuesday, April 29, D-1- D-2.

"Bishop Vogel Delays Mrs. Swanson's Ordination Completion." *Episcopal News Service*, January 6, 1977.

"Bishops to Meet in Mexico." October, 1974. *The Episcopalian: Pennsylvania Diocesan Edition.*

Blau, Eleanor. 1976. "Bishops Offer Alternative to 'Conditional Ordination.'" *The New York Times*, September 23, 28.

———. 1976. "Episcopal Bishops Urge that 15 Woman Priests be Ordained again." *The New York Times*, Wednesday, September 22, 19.

———. 1976. "Episcopal Bishops Vote to Permit Women to be Ordained as Priests." *The New York Times*, September 16, 20.

———. 1974. "House of Bishops Disputes Validity of Ordination of 11 Women as Priests," *The New York Times*, August 16, 34.

———. 1976. "Ordination of Women as Priests Authorized by Episcopal Church: House of Deputies Decides to Concur with Resolution Passed by Bishops." *The New York Times*, September 17, A1, D18.

———. 1974. "A Woman Priest Quits as Curate," *The New York Times*, November 3, 56.

Bone Schiess, Betty. 2003. *Why Me, Lord? One Woman's Ordination to the Priesthood with Commentary and Complaint*. Syracuse, NY: Syracuse University Press.

Borsch, Frederick Houk and Michael Marshall. 1976. *The Ordination of Women: An Exchange.* Anonymous Catacomb Cassettes.

Bowman, Susan B. 2011. *Lady Father*. Albion, Mich.: Aberdeen Bay.

Boyd, Malcolm. "Who's Afraid of Women Priests?" *Ms.*, December 1974, 47–49, 76.

Bozarth, Alla Renee. 2012. "Digging Down Into the Dusty Past." *Purgatory Papers*, 1–13.

Bozarth, Alla Renee. 1978, 1988. *Womanpriest: A Personal Odyssey*. Revised ed. San Diego, CA: LuraMedia.

Bozzuti-Jones, Mark F. 2003. *The Miter Fits just Fine! A Story about the Rt. Rev. Barbara Clementine Harris the First Woman Bishop in the Anglican Communion*. Cambridge, MA: Cowley Publications.

Braver, Barbara and Edmond L. Browning. 1986. "Women in the Episcopate?: Yellow Light Still Flashes." *Dps.*

Bread, St. Stephen and the Incarnation Newsletter, November 17, 1974.

Brelsford, Ginna. 1983. "Diane Tickell: The Fullness of Priesthood." *Profiles in Change: Names, Notes and Quotes for Alaskan Women.* Alaska Commission on the Status of Women.

Briggs, Kenneth. 1975. "4 Women Become Episcopal Priests." *The New York Times*, September 8.

Brooks, Cleanth. 1981. "God, Gallup, and the Episcopalians." *American Scholar* 50 (3): 313.

Burke, Daniel. "Last Episcopal Holdout Ordains Female Priest." *The Huffington Post*, October 20, 2010.

Burkhart, Kathryn W. 1973. "Bishop DeWitt Understands Why His Accusers Cry . . . 'Revolutionary!'" *Discover the Sunday Bulletin*, March 4, 4–18.

Burkhart, Kathryn W. 1975. "The Reverend Nancy Hatch Wittig: The Female Priest Who Left Her Church Rather Than Bow to Sexist Pressure," VIVA, May, Vol. 2, (8), 28.

Caldbeck, Elaine Sue. 1996. "Women's Ordination in the Episcopal Church: Diversity and Commonality among Episcopal Women Priests: Twenty Years at the Margins and Center."

Campbell, Crispin Y. 1975. "Controversial Priest Resigns." *The Free-Lance Star*, Wednesday, January 29, 23.

Cannon, Katie, G., Beverly W. Harrison, Carter Heyward, Ada Maria Isasi-Diaz, Bess B. Johnson, Mary D. Pellauer, and Nancy D. Richardson. 1985. *God's Fierce Whimsy: Christian Feminism and Theological Education.* New York: The Pilgrim Press.

Carter, Norene. 1979. "The Episcopalian Story." In *Women of Spirit: Female Leadership in the Jewish and Christian Traditions*, edited by Rosemary Radford Ruether and Eleanor McLaughlin, 356–372. New York: Simon and Schuster.

"A Case of Woman Trouble." *Time*, 1977, 110 (16): 86.

Casey, Rick. 1975. "Maine Bishop Wolf Rebukes Women Priests for 'Disobedience.'" *Portland Press Herald*, Thursday, July 24, 1, 6.

Causey, Mike. 1976. "Priest Wins Battle with State Department." *The Washington Post*, February 16, B14.

"Celebration of Defiance." *Time*, 1974, 104 (20): 170.

"Censured by the Club." *Time Magazine*, Monday, October 6, 1975, 97.

"Chronology," 1974. *The Episcopalian*, September, 6.

Conley, Walter J. "Change Comes to the Church." Box 20, Folder 6, Hiatt Papers. *Archives of Women in Theological Scholarship*, The Burke Library at Union Theological Seminary, Columbia University Libraries, New York.

Console, Dorothy. 1974. *The Episcopalian*, November, 17.

Convention Journal. 1976. "Special Meetings of the House of Bishops 1974," August 14 and 15.

Copage, Eric V. 2000. "C. Eric Lincoln, Race Scholar, is Dead at 75." *The New York Times*, May 17. Online.

Corrigan, Daniel, DeWitt, Robert, Welles, Edward. 1974. "An Open Letter." *Christianity and Crisis*, September 16, cover, 188.

Corrigan, Daniel. 1975. "Why I Ordained a Woman in Philadelphia." In *The Ordination of Women: Pro and Con*, edited by Michael P. Hamilton and Nancy S. Montgomery, 56–68. New York: Morehouse-Barlow Co.

Daly, Mary. 1973. *Beyond God the Father: Toward a Philosophy of Women's Liberation.* Boston, MA: Beacon Press.

———. 1968. *The Church and the Second Sex with a New Feminist Postchristian Introduction by the Author.* New York: Harper Colophon Books, Harper & Row, Publishers.

Darling, Pamela, W., ed. 1994. *Equally Applicable: Conscience and Women's Ordination in the Episcopal Church, USA, 1976–1994*. Stockton, CA: Episcopal Women's Caucus.

Darling, Pamela W. 1994. *New Wine: The Story of Women Transforming Leadership and Power in the Episcopal Church*. Cambridge, Mass.: Cowley Publications.

"Daughters of Prophecy: Episcopal Women Priests, 10th Anniversary, 1974–1984." 1984. *The Witness*.

Day, Chapin. 1974. "The Times They Are Changing: Women Priests Gain Favor," *The Philadelphia Inquirer*, October, 1A-2A.

———. 1974. "U.S. Bishops to Meet on Women Priests," *The Philadelphia Inquirer*, August, 1-A, 2-A.

DeVorkin, David H. 1989. *Race to the Stratosphere: Manned Scientific Ballooning in America*. New York: Springer-Verlag.

DeWitt, Robert L. "Introduction." *The Witness*, September, 1975, 2.

———. "Why the (Other) Bishops Balked." *The Witness*, 1984, 14–16.

"Disobedience on Trial." *Time,* 1975, 105 (19): 78.

"Dodging the Issue." *Time,* 1975, 105 (14): 78.

Donovan, Mary. 1988. *Women Priests in the Episcopal Church*. [S.l.]: Forward Movement Publications.

Donovan, Mary S. 1986. *A Different Call: Women's Ministries in the Episcopal Church, 1850–1920*. Wilton, CT: Morehouse-Barlow.

DuBois, Albert Julius, and Winthrop Brainerd. 1976. *The Ordination of Women, Why? Now?* [S.l.]: Episcopalians United.

Ecclesiastical Court of the Diocese of Ohio. 1975. "The Standing Committee of the Diocese of Ohio v. The Reverend L. Peter Beebe," May 13.

Ecclesiastical Court of the Diocese of Washington: The Board of Presenters v. The Rev. William A. Wendt, April 30, 1975–May 2, 1975.

"Editorial." *The Witness*, September, 1975, 2.

"Editorial." *The Witness*, special issue, 1984, 2–3.

Episcopal Church. General Convention. 1976. "The Daily of the General Convention of the Episcopal Church." *The Daily of the General Convention of the Episcopal Church*.

Episcopal Church. House of Bishops. 1972. *Report of Special Committee of the House of Bishops on the Ordination of Women, October 1972*. New Orleans, La.: The Committee.

Episcopal Church. Joint Commission on Ecumenical Relations. 1976. *Supplement to Section on Ecumenicity and Women's Ordination to the Priesthood* [S.l.: s.n.].

Episcopal Church, Barbara Clementine Harris, and Episcopal Church. Diocese of Massachusetts. 1989. *The Ordination and Consecration of the Reverend Barbara Clementine Harris as a Bishop in the Church of God and Bishop Suffragan of the Diocese of Massachusetts : [Held at] John B. Hynes Memorial Auditorium, Boston, Massachusetts, Saturday the Eleventh of February in the Year of our Lord Nineteen Hundred Eighty-Nine at 10:30 O'clock in the Morning*. S.l.: s.n.

Episcopal Digital Archives 96-9, October 29, 1971.

Episcopal Digital Archives 72161, November 3, 1972.

Episcopal Digital Archives 74200, July 31, 1974.

Episcopal Digital Archives 74215, August 15, 1974.

Episcopal Digital Archives 75079, February 27, 1975.

Episcopal Digital Archives 75140, April 11, 1975.

"Episcopal Outrage." *Time,* 1975, 105 (1): 81.

Episcopal Women's Caucus. 1974. "Theological Education Was Used": "Statement of Clarification and Concern from the Steering Committee of the Episcopal Women's Caucus," August 2. Box 1, Folder 11, Smith Papers. *Archives of Women in Theological Scholarship,* The Burke Library at Union Theological Seminary, Columbia University Libraries, New York.

"'Father, make Her a Priest'." *Time,* 1977, 109 (3): 67.

Flaherty, Neva. 1974. "She'll Become Priest Despite Church Rule . . . At Least for Awhile." *The Times-Union,* July 25, 15-A.

Foley, Judy Mathe. "Bishops Okay Ways to Complete 15 Women's 'Irregular' Ordinations." *The Episcopalian,* November 1976: 12.

"Ford at Immanuel." 1974. *The Episcopalian,* September, 2.

"Ford Lauds Sermon on Women's Status." 1974. *United Press International,* August 25.

"For Immediate Release," Statement of 10 of the 11 women priests, August 15, 1974. Alison Cheek, private collection.

Fresh Winds Blowing Highlights from the Ordination and Consecration of the Rev. Barbara Clementine Harris as Bishop Suffragan of the Diocese of Massachusetts, February 11, 1989. Directed by Barbara Clementine Harris, Episcopal Church. and Episcopal Church. Diocese of Massachusetts. Boston, Mass.: Offices of Communication, Diocese of Massachusetts and the Episcopal Church, 1989.

Gassett, William O. 1963. "Subject, Piccard Stratosphere Baloon [sic]," August 2, 4. Box 23, Folder 17, Hiatt Papers. *Archives of Women in Theological Scholarship,* The Burke Library at Union Theological Seminary, Columbia University Libraries, New York.

Go Stand in the Temple and Tell—the 25th Anniversary of the Episcopal Women's Caucus. Directed by Katie Sherrod. [S.l.]: The Caucus, 1997.

Gorrell, Donald K. 1978. *Ecclesiastical Equality for Women.* Boston: Intercollegiate Case Clearing House.

The Great American Disaster: A Brief Account of what Happened in the Episcopal Church (ECUSA) Over the "Women Priest" Issue. 1986. London: Irenaeus Publications.

Greene, Susan L. 1999. "Women's Mid-Life Career Change: The Case of Episcopal Women Priests."

Greenfield, Meg. "Women and the Image of God." *Newsweek,* September 1, 1975, 72.

Guilbert, Charles M. 1977. *Proposed the Book of Common Prayer and Administration of the Sacraments and Other Rites and Ceremonies of the Church Together with the Psalter Or Psalms of David According to the use of the Episcopal Church.* New York: The Church Hymnal Corporation and the Seabury Press.

Guthrie, Harvey H., Edward, G. Harris, and Hays H. Rockwell. 1974. "A Personal Report on the Meeting of the House of Bishops of the Episcopal Church in Chicago on August 14 and 15, 1974, and Some Reflections on Process and Theology." Alison Cheek Private Collection.

Guthrie, Harvey H. 1975. *The Ordination of Women, an Exchange: Yes.* Anonymous Catacomb Cassettes.

Guthrie, Polly. 1990. "The Politics of the First Ordinations of Women in the Episcopal Church."

Hacker, Kathy. "In Her Little Church, Dreams Get Lost in Survival." *The Philadelphia Inquirer,* Sunday, August 1, 1982, 24-A.

———. August 1, 1982. "The Price of Priesthood." *The Philadelphia Inquirer,* 24.

Haldane, Jean. Advent, 1976. "On General Convention." *A-Cross,* 8–9.

Hamilton, Lee Ann. 1975. *The Plain Dealer,* July 14, A10.

Hamilton, Michael, P. and Nancy S. Montgomery, eds. 1975. *The Ordination of Women Pro and Con.* New York: Morehouse-Barlow Co.

Harris, Barbara C. 1994. "Afterword." In *Other Sheep I Have: The Autobiography of Father Paul M. Washington*, 231–235. Philadelphia: Temple University Press.

Harris, Barbara C. "Pentecost Revisited." *The Witness*, special edition, 1984, 10.

Harris, Barbara C., Suzanne R. Hiatt, Rose Wu, and Mabel Katahweire. 2000. *Women's Ordination in the Episcopal Church: Twenty-Five Years Later*. Cambridge, Mass.: Episcopal Divinity School.

Harris, Edward G. Sermon. June 15, 1974. Box 1, Folder 8, Smith Papers. *Archives of Women in Theological Scholarship,* The Burke Library at Union Theological Seminary, Columbia University Libraries, New York.

Herdt, Gilbert and Theo Van De Meer. 2003. "Homophobia and Anti-Gay Violence: Contemporary Perspectives." *Culture, Health & Sexuality* 5 (2): 99–101.

Herzig, Doris. 1962. "A'ville Girl, Home from Congo, Is Ready for More Adventure." *Newsday*, July 12.

Hewitt, Emily. 2001. "St. Mary Mead." In *A Place in Our Hearts: Roland Park Country School*, edited by Betty Ann Schmick Howard, 146–149. Baltimore, MD: Roland Park Country School.

Hewitt, Emily C. and Suzanne R. Hiatt. 1973. *Women Priests: Yes or No?* New York: The Seabury Press.

Heyward, Carter. 1989. "Crossing the River." In *Speaking of Christ: A Lesbian Feminist Voice*, edited by Ellen C. Davis, 82–85. New York: The Pilgrim Press.

———. 2005. *Flying Changes: Horses as Spiritual Teachers*. Cleveland, OH: The Pilgrim Press.

———. 2002. *God in the Balance: Christian Spirituality in Times of Terror*. Cleveland, OH: The Pilgrim Press.

———. "In and through the Impasse." *Christianity and Crisis* 34 (15) (September 16, 1974): 188–194.

———. 2010. *Keep Your Courage: A Radical Christian Feminist Speaks*. New York: Seabury.

———. 1976. *A Priest Forever*. New York: Harper & Row, Publishers.

———. 1974. "Ordination to the Priesthood of Doug Clark," Box 1, Folder 5, Smith Papers. *Archives of Women in Theological Scholarship,* The Burke Library at Union Theological Seminary, Columbia University Libraries, New York.

———. 1999. *A Priest Forever: One Woman's Controversial Ordination in the Episcopal Church*. Cleveland, Ohio: Pilgrim Press.

———. 1982. *The Redemption of God: A Theology of Mutual Relation*. Washington, D.C.: University Press of America.

———. 1999. *Saving Jesus from those Who are Right: Rethinking what it Means to be Christian*. Minneapolis: Fortress Press.

Heyward, Carter, Dorothee Sölle, and Amanecida Collective. 1987. *Revolutionary Forgiveness: Feminist Reflections on Nicaragua*. Maryknoll, N.Y.: Orbis Books.

Heyward, Carter and Sue Phillips, eds. 1992. *No Easy Peace: Liberating Anglicanism*. Lanham, MD: University Press of America, Inc.

Hiatt, Suzanne R. 1953. "The Domestic Animal." Carter Heyward Private Collection.

———. December, 1985. "His Quiet, Tough Advice." *Sojourners: An Independent Christian Monthly*: 24–25.

———. Fall, 1983. "How we Brought the Good News from Graymoor to Minneapolis: An Episcopal Paradigm." *Journal of Ecumenical Studies* 20 (4): 576–584.

———. "July 29, 1974, Philadelphia: Kairos as Paradigm Shift." In *No Easy Peace: Liberating Anglicanism*, edited by Carter Heyward and Sue Phillips, 121–136. New York: University Press of America, 1992.

———. 1975. *Report from a Woman Priest*. Anonymous.

———. 1975. "Why I Believe I Am Called to the Priesthood." In *The Ordination of Women: Pro and Con*, edited by Michael P. Hamilton and Nancy S. Montgomery, 30–42. New York: Morehouse-Barlow Co.

Hill, Sheryl K. 2009. "'Until I have Won' Vestiges of Coverture and the Invisibility of Women in the Twentieth Century: A Biography of Jeannette Ridlon Piccard." Ohio University.

Hogan, Joseph L. 1974. "Women in the Church: Our Problem, Too!" *Courier-Journal*, September 11, 3.

Holland, Darrell. 1975. "Allowing Women Priests Endangers Church Grant." *The Plain Dealer*, September 15, 17A.

———. 1975. "Church laws vs. issues of human justice: Priest's Trial Throwback to Middle Ages." *The Voice of Women's Ordination Now*. Volume 1, 4, February, 1975, 12–14.

———. 1975. "Four at Beebe Trial Back Women Priests." *The Plain Dealer*, May 15, 6B.

"Home Provided Episcopal Bishop." *The Evening Bulletin*, August 30, 1947, 8.

Huyck, Heather Ann. 1981. "To Celebrate a Whole Priesthood: The History of Women's Ordination in the Episcopal Church." Ph.D., University of Minnesota.

Hyer, Marjorie. 1974. "Communion is Celebrated by a Woman." *The Washington Post*, November 11, C1.

———. 1975. "3 Episcopal Bishops Censured by Peers." *The Washington Post*, Wednesday, September 24, 23.

———. 1976. "Father Beebe's Retrial Stirs Episcopalians." *The Washington Post*, April 16, C9.

———. 1976. "For 15 Ordained Women, Issue Still Not Resolved." *The Washington Post*, September 18, A9.

———. 1975. "4 Episcopal Women Set to Get Priest Status." *The Washington Post*, September 8, A1–A2.

———. 1975. "Ordination of 5 Women Set." *The Washington Post*, August 25, A1.

———. 1975. "Top Episcopalian Cited for Contempt." *The Washington Post*, May 3, A1.

———. 1976. "Wendt Reprimanded for Defying Bishop," *The Washington Post*, January 11, B1, B2.

———. 1976. "Woman Priest Sues Bishop." *The Washington Post*, July 13, C8.

———. 1974. "Women's Ordination Voided." *The Washington Post*, August 16, A1–A3.

"In Chicago: The Bishops Hold and Emergency Meeting." *The Virginia Churchman*, September, 1974, Vol. 83, No. 4, 8–10.

"Informal Notes of Meeting," March 3, 1974, Box 45, Folder: Ordination of Women. Hiatt Papers. *Archives of Women in Theological Scholarship*, The Burke Library at Union Theological Seminary, Columbia University Libraries, New York.

James, Nancy C. "The Developing Schism within the Episcopal Church, 1960–2010 Social Justice, Ordination of Women, Charismatics, Homosexuality, Extra-Territorial Bishops, etc." Edwin Mellen Press.

Jean and Jeannette Piccard. 1937. "Some Problems Connected with a Stratosphere Ascension." FI</cja:Jid> *Journal of the Franklin Institute* 223 (4): 513–515.

Keaton, Elizabeth. *Twenty-Four Years Later*. Telling Secrets, online.

Karns, Dykstra. 1974. [*Cartoon for Sculpture of Non-Ordination of Women*].

"Katrina's Story." Katrina's Dream: Promoting the Full Inclusion of Women in Society. *www.katrinasdream.org*.

Keller, Rosemary Skinner, Rosemary Radford Ruether, and Marie Cantlon. 2006. *Encyclopedia of Women and Religion in North America*. Bloomington: Indiana University Press.

Kelly, Jason. May-June 2011. "Legacy Jeannette Piccard, SM'19 (1895–1981) A 'Pioneer of the Skies.'" *The University of Chicago Magazine*.

Kendall, Patricia A. and Episcopal Church. Diocese of Pennsylvania. Committee to Promote the Cause of and to Plan for the Ordination of Women to the Priesthood. 1976. *Women and the Priesthood: A Selected and Annotated Bibliography.* [Philadelphia].

Kennedy, R. Scott. "A Step Off America." *Sojourners*, December 1985, 20–21.

Kessler, Judy. 1974. "Nancy Wittig Will Fight to Remain a Priest." *People*, September 16, 23.

Kinsolving, Lester. 1975, "Episcopal Common Sense and Sense of Humor." *The Daily Leader*, October 31, 4.

Krumm, John M., Petty Bosmyer, and Robert E. Terwilliger. 1976. *Ordination of Women.* Anonymous.

Lamond, Thom. 1975. "Let the Church Now Address Human Sexuality." *The Washington Star*, September 13.

Larson, Roy. November, 1976. "By God, They Did It!" *The Witness*, 13–15.

"Leader Protests to Rome." *Episcopalians United*, November 1, 1976, 1.

Lipp, Murray. "We must Target the Origins of Homophobic Violence: Religion, Patriarchy and Heterosexism." *The Huffington Post*, May 23, 2013.

Longstreth, Morris. 1976. "Morris Longstreth's Personal Odyssey to Meet His Sister Priests." *De-Liberation* 2 (4): 8.

Lyles, J. C. 1987. "Episcopal 'Gentlemen's Club' Now Open?" *Christian Century* 104 (29): 909.

Lyles, Jean Caffey. 2000. "Dealing with Rebels." *Christian Century* 117 (22): 780.

MacKaye, William R. "General Convention: A Ho-Hum Event Unless . . ." *The Witness*, August, 1976, 4–8.

Macy, Gary. 2008. *The Hidden History of Women's Ordination: Female Clergy in the Medieval West.* Oxford; New York: Oxford University Press.

Marrett, Michael McFarlene. 1980. "The Historical Background and Spiritual Authority of the Lambeth Conferences and their Impact on the Protestant Episcopal Church in the United States of America, with Particular Emphasis on the Ordination of Women to the Priesthood."

Martin, Richard Cornish. *Commentary*, (January, 1973): 2.

McDaniel, Judith M. 2011. *Grace in Motion: The Intersection of Women's Ordination and Virginia Theological Seminary.* Brainerd, Minn.: RiverPlace Communication Arts.

McGrory, Mary. 1971. "A Pint-Sized Crusader." *The Washington Evening St*ar, October 11.

Medsger, Betty. September, 1975. "View from the Press Agent's Pew." *The Witness*: 22–23.

"Memories Are Not Enough." 1984. *The Witness*, special edition, p. 24.

Michal, Mary Louise. 1979. "Battle Barely Begun for Women Priests." *The Virginia Churchman*, December, 9.

The Michigan Women's Historical Center and Hall of Fame. "N. Lorraine Beebe." Online. michiganwomen.org.

Micks, Marianne H. and Charles P. Price, eds. 1976. *Toward a New Theology of Ordination: Essays on the Ordination of Women.* Somerville, MA: Greeno, Hadden & Company, Ltd.

Micks, Marianne H., Charles P. Price, and Reginald Horace Fuller. 1976. *Toward a New Theology of Ordination: Essays on the Ordination of Women.* Alexandria, Va.; Somerville, Mass.: Virginia Theological Seminary; Distributed by Greeno, Hadden & Co.

Miller, Claudius. "A Newsletter for the Diocese of Missouri," Association of Clergy, September 5, 1974.

Minnesota Coalition for Women's Ordination Now. n.d. *The Priesthood of Women: Questions and Answers.* St. Louis Park, MN.

Minnesota Committee for Women's Ordination Now. 1976. *Study Guide on Ordination of Women to the Priesthood*. Minneapolis: The Committee.

Moore, Paul, Jr. "Statement by the Rt. Rev. Paul Moore, Jr., Bishop of New York . . ." October 22, 1974. Box 1, Folder 2. Heyward Papers. *Archives of Women in Theological Scholarship,* The Burke Library at Union Theological Seminary, Columbia University Libraries, New York.

———. 1979. *Take a Bishop Like Me*. New York: Harper & Row.

Morgan, Mick. January 17, 1975. *WHAM Radio 1180: Editorial*, Merrill Bittner, personal collection.

Murray, Pauli. April 14, 1980. "Black, Feminist Theologies: Links, Parallels, and Tensions." *Christianity and Crisis* 40 (6): 86–95.

———. *Pauli Murray: The Autobiography of a Black Activist, Feminist, Lawyer, Priest, and Poet*. Knoxville: The University of Tennessee Press, 1987.

Myer, Connie. 1984. "What Progress for Women Clergy?" *The Witness*, special issue, 26.

Myers, C. Kilmer. 1977. Episcopal Digital Archives 77153, May 12.

———. 1972. *The Episcopalian*, February, 8–9.

National Committee of Episcopal Clergy and Laity for the Ordination of Women to the Priesthood (U.S.). 1976. *Women in Priesthood*. Washington, D.C.: Church House.

Nesbitt, Paula D. 1997. *Feminization of the Clergy in America: Occupational and Organizational Perspectives*. New York: Oxford University Press.

Niebuhr, Gustav. 1996. "Religion." *Working Woman* 21 (11): 71.

Norgren, William A. 1977. "Ecumenical Relations and Ordination of Women to the Priesthood in the Episcopal Church." *Mid-Stream: An Ecumenical Journal* 16: 374–392.

O'Connor, John. 1974. "11 Women Ordained as Priests." *Philadelphia Daily News*, July 30, 4.

Ogilby, Lyman. 1974. "Statement Presented by the Rt. Rev. Lyman Ogilby to the Special House of Bishops Meeting in Chicago." *Convention Journal*. 1976. "Special Meetings of the House of Bishops 1974," August 14 and 15, 2. Box 1, Folder 11, Smith Papers. *Archives of Women in Theological Scholarship,* The Burke Library at Union Theological Seminary, Columbia University Libraries, New York.

Oppenheimer, Mark. 2003. *Knocking on Heaven's Door: American Religion in the Age of Counterculture*. New Haven: Yale University Press.

Pace, Eric. 2000. "Bishop George W. Barrett, 92; Fostered Women's Ordination." *New York Times* 150 (51595): B15.

Palmer, Alison. "Palmer versus Church and State." Unpublished Memoir. Series 6, Box 1, Folder 1, Palmer Papers. *Archives of Women in Theological Scholarship,* The Burke Library at Union Theological Seminary, Columbia University Libraries, New York.

Panero, James. 2012. "Father Figure," March/April, *Dartmouth Alumni Magazine*. Online. *http://dartmouthalumnimagazine.com/father-figure/*

Petraske, Pat. 1973. "Jail Project Lessens Women's 'Punishments.'" *Courier-Journal*, Wednesday, December 19.

"Piccard Balloon Flights: From Gondola to Manned Spacecraft." Film, circa 1966. NASA. *http://www.youtube.com/watch?v=HuvAg4QJx5s*.

Piccard, Don, Jean Felix Piccard , and Jeannette Piccard. "Piccard Family Papers."

Piccard Flight Stratosphere Flight 1934: Jean Piccard, Jeannette Piccard, Pilots. Directed by Jean F. Piccard, Jeannette R. Piccard, Pathe News, Paramount News, and Metropolitan Films. 1989.

Piccard, Jeannette. 1934. "Mrs. Piccard Tells of Flight Thrills." *The New York Times*, October 24.

Piccard, Jeannette, Alison Cheek, and Carter Heyward, "News Release on Eucharist to be Celebrated by Newly Ordained Episcopal Women Priests," 4. Box 1, Folder 20. Smith Papers.

"Piccard, Jeannette (Mrs. Jean F. Piccard)." 1935. *American Women: The Official Who's Who among the Women of the Nation, 1935–1936.*

Piccard, Jeannette. 1979. *[on Women and the Bible].* Anonymous.

Piccard, Jeannette. 1975. *Fact Sheet Re: Ordination of Women.* Victoria, Texas: The Christian Challenge.

Piccard, Jeannette, "Should Women Be Admitted to the Priesthood?" *Library of Congress,* Box II:85, Folder 1, Piccard Family Papers.

Piccard, Jeannette. *Speeches and Writings: Jeannette Piccard Autobiographies:* undated, Piccard Family Papers.

Plagenz, George R. 1976. "Beebe's Lawyer Didn't Give Up." April. AWTS, Box 20, Folder 3, Hiatt Papers.

Plumer, Richard E. "Bishop Welles Gives His Views on Philadelphia." *Episcopal News Service,* December 5, 1974.

A Priest Indeed. Directed by Wendy S. Robins. [S.l.]: Produced for Episcopal Church Pub. Co. by Ideal Image, Inc., 1984.

Raeside, John. "Episcopal Reconciliation in Minneapolis?" *Christianity and Crisis.* October 18, 1976: 232–234.

Rea, John. 1976. "Beebe Case: Clue to the Future?" *The Witness.* September.

"Report to the Committee from the Standing Committee," November 8, 1974. Episcopal Diocese of Rochester Archives.

"The Reverend Betty Bone Schiess against The Diocese of Central New York of the Protestant Episcopal Church of the United States of America and the Right Reverend Ned Cole, Bishop." United States District Court, Northern District Court of New York. Alison Cheek, private collection.

The Rev. William A. Wendt. St. Stephen and the Incarnation website, *http://saintstephensdc.org.*

Rightor, Henry H. 1976. "The Existing Canonical Authority for Women's Ordination." In *Toward a New Theology of Ordination: Essays on the Ordination of Women,* edited by Marianne H. Micks and Charles P. Price, 101–110. Somerville, MA: Greeno, Hadden & Company, Ltd.

Robb-Dover, Kristina. 2005. "Psyched for Ministry." *Christian Century* 122 (24): 10–11.

Robinson, Timothy S. 1975. "Air Crash Survivor: A Time for Tears." *The Washington Post,* Saturday June 7, A1, A4.

Rowan, Carl. 1975. "In My View." *The Chicago Sun-Times,* May 20.

Sartori, Shirley. 1978. "Conflict and Institutional Change: The Ordination of Women in the Episcopal Church."

Schiess, Betty Bone. 2003. *Why Me, Lord?: One Woman's Ordination to the Priesthood with Commentary and Complaint.* New York: Syracuse University Press.

Schmick, Howard, Betty Ann, ed. 2001. *A Place in our Hearts: Roland Park Country School.* Baltimore, MD: Roland Park Country School.

Schmidt, Frederick W. 1996. *A Still Small Voice: Women, Ordination, and the Church.* Syracuse, N.Y.: Syracuse University Press.

Schoen, Louis S. *Women Priests: The Minnesota Perspective, A Report on Action at the 1975 Diocesan Convention.*

Scott, John M. 1987. "A Survey of Attitudes Toward Female Leadership in the Church of the Diocese of Pennsylvania." University Microfilms.

Service of Celebration & Thanksgiving on the Occasion of the 25th Anniversary of the Ordination of Women to the Priesthood in the Episcopal Church: On the Feasts of Saints Mary & Martha, July 29, 1999, 5:30 p.m., the George W. South Memorial Church of the Advocate, Philadelphia, Pennsylvania. 1999. Philadelphia: George W. South Memorial Church.

Shattuck, Gardiner H. 2001. *A Whole Priesthood: The Philadelphia Ordinations (1974) and the Continuing Dilemmas of Race in the Episcopal Church.* Cambridge, Mass.: Episcopal Divinity School.

Shatzman, Marci. 1974. "Ordination of 11 Women Set Despite Pressure." *The Evening Bulletin,* July 26, 6B.

Sherman, Mikie. 1979. "The Rev. Peter Beebe." *The Plain Dealer Magazine,* March 25, 31.

"Significant Happenings at the Diocese of West Missouri Annual Convention in Springfield on November 14–16, 1975, the Rt. Rev. Arthur Vogel Presiding." Box 23, Folder 13, Hiatt Papers. *Archives of Women in Theological Scholarship,* The Burke Library at Union Theological Seminary, Columbia University Libraries, New York.

Simpson, Mary Michael and Movement for the Ordination of Women. 1981. *Ordination of Women in the American Episcopal Church: The Present Situation.* London: Movement for the Ordination of Women.

Sims, Gayle R. 2003. "Right Reverend Robert DeWitt, 87, a Bishop and an Activist." *The Philadelphia Inquirer.* Wednesday, November 26, obit.

Smith, Ann Robb. 1974. "Notebook with Minutes of July 10 Meeting." Box 1, Folder 7, Smith Papers. *Archives of Women in Theological Scholarship,* The Burke Library at Union Theological Seminary, Columbia University Libraries, New York.

Smith, J. Y. 2001. "Rev. William Wendt Dies at 81; Founded Center for Grief, Loss." *The Washington Post,* July 9, B.06. *http://saintstephensdc.org.*

Spears, Robert R. Press Release, April 2, 1976.

Spears, Robert R. "To: The Standing Committee, Diocese of Rochester, From: The Bishop." July 30, 1974. Episcopal Diocese of Rochester Archives.

Steed, Mary Lou. 1986. "Church Schism and Secession: A Necessary Sequence?" *Review of Religious Research* 27 (4): 344.

Steed, Mary Lou. 1987. "Secession in the Schismatic Process: A Structural Analysis of the Episcopal Church."

Stickgold, Emma. "Robert DeWitt; Led Way for Female Reverends." *The Boston Globe,* December 2, 2003. Online.

Stringfellow, William. "The Bishops at O'Hare: Mischief and a Mighty Curse." *Christianity and Crisis* 34 (15) (September 16, 1974): 195–196.

Stringfellow, William. "The Church in Exile." *The Witness,* Vol. 58, No. 8, March 9, 1975, 6.

Stringfellow, William, "On the Sentencing of Good Father Wendt." *The Witness,* March, 1976, 6–7.

"Stunts Aloft." *Time* 24, no. 19 (November 5, 1934): 54.

Sumner, David E. 1987. *The Episcopal Church's History, 1945–1985.* Wilton, Conn.: Morehouse-Barlow Co.

"Swanson, Katrina Martha Van Alstyne Welles, 1935–2005, 1888–2008 (Inclusive), 1970–1990 (Bulk): A Finding Aid." Arthur and Elizabeth Schlesinger Library on the History of Women in America. Radcliffe Institute for Advanced Study Harvard University Library: OASIS.

"Switchboard," *The Episcopalian,* September, 1974.

Taft, Adon. 1976. "Women can be Priests, Church Says." *The Charlotte Observer,* September 17, 1A.

"Tally-Ho's for Home from Congo." *The Hartford Times,* July 11, 1962, 5.

Terwilliger, Robert Elwin. 1976. *Ordination of Women, no.* Anonymous Catacomb Cassettes.

Their Call Answered: Women in the Priesthood [Board of Clergy Deployment of the Episcopal Church] 1979. New York: The Board for Clergy Deployment.

"There Shall Be a General Convention of this Church." Louisville, 1973. Box 29, Hiatt Papers. *Archives of Women in Theological Scholarship,* The Burke Library at Union Theological Seminary, Columbia University Libraries, New York.

"There Were Some Light Moments, Too." *The Daily,* September 17, 1976, 3.

Thompson, Nona. n.d. "Letter to Vestry." *WON: The Voice of Women's Ordination Now,* Issue 1, 2. Oberlin, Ohio.

Trott, Frances, ed. 1973. *Our Call.* Wayne, NJ: Sheba Press.

———. ed. 1975. "We Have, After Due Consideration, Chosen Not to Make a Presentment . . . ," *Rauch: The Newsletter of the Episcopal Women's Caucus,* May/June, 14. Wayne, NJ.

"Until I have Won" Vestiges of Coverture and the Invisibility of Women in the Twentieth Century: A Biography of Jeannette Ridlon Piccard. Ohio University / OhioLINK.

van Beeck, Frans J. Summer 1974. "Invalid or Merely Irregular: Comments by a Reluctant Witness." *Journal of Ecumenical Studies* 11 (3): 381–399.

Van Beeck, Frans J. "Ordination of Women?—An Ecumenical Meditation and A Discussion." In *Toward a New Theology of Ordination: Essays on the Ordination of Women,* edited by Marianne H. Micks and Charles P. Price, 90–100. Somerville, MA: Greeno, Hadden & Company, Ltd, 1976.

Van Biema, David, Elisabeth Kauffman, Jeanne McDowell, Marguerite Michaels, Frank Sikora, and Deirdre Van Dyk. 2004. "Rising Above the Stained-Glass Ceiling." *Time* 163 (26): 58–61.

Vidulich, Dorothy. 1993. *Bishop a Woman, but She Still Wears a Miter.* Vol. 30 National Catholic Reporter Publishing Company.

Viorst, Judith. "How To Be a Good-Guy Honkie Priest on 14th Street." *The Washingtonian,* July, 1968. *http://saintstephensdc.org/wiki/index.php?title=The_Rev._William_A._Wendt&oldid=1161.*

Waggoner, Walter. 1981. "Rev. Jeannette Piccard Dies at 86; Scientist Entered Seminary in '70." *The New York Times,* May 19, C12.

Wallace, Andrew. 1974. "Episcopal Clergy Gets Warning." *The Philadelphia Inquirer,* Saturday, July 27, 1-B, 3-B.

———. 1974. "Women Priests: A Court Case?" *The Philadelphia Inquirer,* Friday, July 26, 1-A-2-A.

Wallis, Jim. "A Holy Humanity." *Sojourners,* December 1985: 4–6.

Wallis, Joy Carroll. 2004. *The Woman Behind the Collar: The Pioneering Journey of an Episcopal Priest.* New York: Crossroad Pub.

Washington, Paul M., and David McI Gracie. 1994. *"Other Sheep I Have": The Autobiography of Father Paul M. Washington.* Philadelphia: Temple University Press.

Welles, Edward Randolph. 1975. *The Happy Disciple: An Autobiography of Edward Randolph Welles II.* Manset, ME: Learning Incorporated.

"The Welles Express." September, 1974. *The Episcopalian,* 13.

Whisenand, Lucia. 1975. *The Voice of Women's Ordination Now,* February, 2.

"Why They Did What They Did," 1974. *The Episcopalian,* September, 8.

Willie, Charles. September 1974. *The Virginia Churchman* 83 (4): 9.

Willie, Charles V. 1984. "The Crisis that Blessed our Common Life." *The Witness,* 21.

Willie, Charles V. 1974. "The Everyday Work of Christian People: The Disobedience of Unjust Laws." June 9. Box 1, Folder 12, Smith Papers. *Archives of Women in Theological Scholarship,* The Burke Library at Union Theological Seminary, Columbia University Libraries, New York.

Willie, Charles. 1974. "The Priesthood of All Believers," Box 1, Folder 11, Smith Papers. *Archives of Women in Theological Scholarship,* The Burke Library at Union Theological Seminary, Columbia University Libraries, New York.

Willoughby, William. 1975. "Four Women Are Ordained as Episcopal Priests." *The Washington Star,* Monday, September 8.

———. 1975. "Ohio Priest Still Defiant." *The Washington Star,* June 23, A3.

Winiarski, Mark. 1975. "Celebration in Wisconsin." *National Catholic Reporter,* cover, 14.

Wittig, Nancy. "Obedience to God Comes Before Obedience to Man." Sermon preached on the Twelfth Sunday after Pentecost at St. Peter's Church, Morristown, New Jersey, August 25, 1974. Alison Cheek, private collection.

Wolf, William J. "Statement of Resignation," August 16, 1974. Box 1, Folder 11, Smith Papers. *Archives of Women in Theological Scholarship,* The Burke Library at Union Theological Seminary, Columbia University Libraries, New York.

"Women to Be Priests." *The Daily,* September 17, 1976, 1.

Women and Religion. Directed by Jeannette Piccard and Normandale Community College. 1978.

"Women as Priests." *The Christian Science Monitor,* Tuesday, September 21, 1976, 28.

"The Women Priests." 1974. *Time* 104 (9): 74.

"The Women's Rebellion." 1974. *Time* 104 (7): 64.

"World News Briefs," *The Episcopalian,* September 1974, 2.

"Wrist Slap for Wendt." 1975. *Time* 105 (25): 80.

Young, Frances M. 1979. *Thankfulness Unites: The History of the United Thank Offering.* Cincinnati, Ohio: Forward Movement Publications.

Index